An Introduction to the Philosophy of Animate Nature

By the Same Author

AN INTRODUCTION TO
THE SCIENCE OF METAPHYSICS

An Introduction to the Philosophy of Animate Nature

By HENRY J. KOREN, C.S.Sp., S.T.D.

B. HERDER BOOK CO.
15 & 17 South Broadway, St. Louis 2, Mo.
AND *33 Queen Square, London, W. C.*

Library of Congress Catalog Card Number: 55-11804

IMPRIMI POTEST

Francis H. McGlynn, C.S.Sp.
Provincial

IMPRIMATUR

✠ Joseph E. Ritter, S.T.D.
Archbishop of St. Louis

September 15, 1955

Reprinted 1957

Printed in the United States of America
by Vail-Ballou Press, Inc., Binghamton, New York

Preface

⁂ The purpose of this book is to serve as an introduction to the metaphysical study of life in undergraduate colleges where three or four credits can be devoted to this course and the study of philosophy is taken seriously. It presupposes that the student has made a study of general metaphysics or at least has been given a good introduction to the general problems of philosophy. Although acquaintance with experimental psychology is highly recommendable, and even necessary for a complete knowledge of living nature, the book does not presuppose that the student has studied either general or experimental psychology, for the simple reason that metaphysical studies are not based upon experimental science.

A fairly large number of references are given to Aristotle and Thomas Aquinas in the hope that the students will be induced to become personally acquainted with their works. Excellent translations of these works are available nowadays, so that ignorance of Greek and Latin no longer offers any difficulty in this respect. However, a word of warning concerning the reading of ancient philosophers may not be out of place—the student is bound to come across numerous passages containing utterly antiquated views in matter pertaining to what is now called experimental science. He should keep in mind that true philosophy is independent of experimental science, at least in its principles; hence no matter how queer and out-of-date ancient philosophical writings may be with respect to science, their philosophical principles may still be just as good as when they were written. Often the student himself will be able to separate philosophy from antiquated science; at other times, however, recourse has to be had to the guidance of one who is well-versed in both science and philosophy.

At the end of each chapter a summary has been added to make it easier for the student to obtain a comprehensive view of the matter. Perhaps it will not be superfluous to warn the student that his study is not to be limited to these summaries.

Certain sections and paragraphs are preceded by an asterisk (*) to mark passages which, at the discretion of the teacher, may be omitted if the allotted time does not permit a complete study of all that is offered. Nearly all "Historical Notes" are thus marked, because the author feels that it is impossible to do justice to the positions of others in the little space that can be provided for this purpose. Nevertheless, it may be useful to record these views if only to show that other positions have been taken with respect to the problems under investigation.

To help the student reviewing the subject matter, a number of questions have been added at the end of the book. The questions marked with an asterisk refer to passages bearing the same mark.

As an aid to further study and possible use for term papers, "Suggested Readings" are given at the end of each chapter. Most of these readings are meant for further study and do not simply repeat what has been studied in this textbook. Where appropriate, the last part of the "Suggested Readings" refers to experimental studies on the subject matter considered in the preceding chapter.

Henry J. Koren, C.S.Sp.

Duquesne University

Contents

SECTION FOUR

Intellectual Life

SECTION FIVE

The Origin of Life and Living Species

Introduction

Psychology or The Philosophy of Animate Nature?

*** 1. The most popular name of the course we are about to study is "psychology," which is derived from the Greek words *psychè* (soul) and *logos* (science) and thus may be transliterated as the science of the soul. It was introduced in the sixteenth century by the German philosopher Goclenius. Before him psychology used to be known as the treatise *de anima* or of "the soul."

The use of the term "psychology" for the study which we are going to undertake has certain disadvantages. Confusion may arise because the same term is used also to indicate one of the experimental sciences of living bodies. To distinguish the two, the qualifiers "philosophical" or "rational," and "experimental" or "scientific" are sometimes added to the term "psychology." However, even these qualifications are not without objections. The exclusive use of "scientific" for one kind of psychology is likely to suggest to many that the other kind of psychology is unscientific, i.e., primitive and antiquated, because they do not realize that the term "scientific" is used in the very restricted sense of "verifiable by sense experience." The use of "experimental" may give the impression that the other kind of psychology is not based upon experience, at least not upon accurate experience, and therefore not worth the effort of study. On the other hand, "rational" may be taken to imply that the other type of psychology is not in accordance with reason or at least not rationally interpreted, but a mere enumeration and classification of data. Lastly, the qualifier "philosophical" may give the impression that the psychology in question is the philosophical interpretation of the data supplied by the methods of experimental psychology.[1]

Moreover, the use of names such as psychology, theodicy, and cosmology may create the impression that each name indicates a distinct and autonomous science, whereas as a matter of fact these subjects are merely *parts* of one and the same speculative science called philosophy.

For these reasons we prefer to call our present study *The Philosophy of Animate Nature.*

The Philosophy of Animate Nature and the Sciences of Animate Nature

2. Apart from philosophy, two other sciences or groups of sciences are interested in animate nature, namely, biology and psychology. Care should be taken not to confuse these sciences with the philosophy of animate nature. In general, they may be said to be related to the philosophy of animate nature as physical science is related to the philosophy of inanimate nature. Physical sciences, such as chemistry and physics, study the nature of inanimate material things on the *sensory* level and tend to

[1] While we do not deny that occasionally so-called experimental psychology may discover data which will lead to a reconsideration of certain applications of philosophical principles, the philosophical study of living bodies as a whole does not take its starting point in the data supplied by experimental psychology. Cf. below, no. 4.

conclusions which, in principle, are verifiable by sense experience. The philosophy of inanimate nature considers the same material objects on the level of *being* and tends to conclusions whose verification is possible only by carefully checking the truth of the starting point and the correctness of the reasoning process which has led to the philosophical position.

In a similar way, biology, which is concerned with the manifestations of vegetative life, and psychology, which is interested in sensitive and intellectual life, tend to reach conclusions that are subject to experimental verification. Biology, for instance, is interested in the physical structure of living bodies, their functional reactions, chemical composition, etc. Psychology studies the conditions which affect the actions and behavior of animals, both rational and irrational, as animals, but does not pronounce judgment upon their metaphysical nature or mode of being. Philosophy of animate nature, on the other hand, is interested in discovering the metaphysical nature of animate bodies and wants to discover what *kind of beings* they are. It shows interest in the actions and behavior of animate bodies only insofar as they are indispensable steppingstones leading towards knowledge of the nature from which they spring. For the metaphysical nature of a thing is not immediately known to us; we can come to an understanding of it only by means of a careful study of its actions, in accordance with the metaphysical principle that everything acts according to its mode of being.[2]

3. Although it is theoretically true that the experimental *sciences* of life do not pronounce judgment upon the

[2] Cf. the author's *Introduction to the Science of Metaphysics* (St. Louis: B. Herder Book Co., 1955), chap. 13.

mode of being of their subject matter, in practice and as a matter of fact, the same cannot be said of the *scientists* who study life. Frequently, the biologist or the psychologist will exceed his area of specialization and indulge in, or tacitly assume the truth of philosophical considerations. For instance, he may project his findings against a philosophical background, as is exemplified by the term "split personality"; give a philosophical interpretation of his findings, as when he concludes that life is nothing but a mechanical process; or even be guided in his whole work by philosophical assumptions, as is the case with the behaviorists. No one can deny the scientist his human right to philosophize, but we may and must demand that he take cognizance of the fact that he is philosophizing and therefore should follow the methods of philosophy.

Like the scientist, the philosopher of life is exposed to the danger of overstepping the boundaries of his chosen field of study and offer solutions of problems that can be solved only by an experimental study of living bodies. As an historical example we may point to the philosophers of the sixteenth and seventeenth centuries who thought that they could explain instinctive activity in animals by pointing out that animals have a faculty called "instinct." Again, the human being who is a philosopher has a natural right to apply himself to the solution of the problems of experimental science, but he, too, should realize that with respect to these problems he must follow the methods of experimental science.

From the foregoing considerations, it should be clear that in the present treatise the student of the philosophy of animate nature should not expect any biological and psychological explanations of vital activities and behavior, and still less explanations of abnormal psychological conditions. Such matters rightfully belong to the study of experimental sciences of life. It should be clear also that neither biology and psychology nor the philosophy of animate nature alone are able to give complete knowledge of living bodies, but naturally complement each other.

Object, Starting Point and Method of the Philosophy of Animate Nature

4. *Object.* The *material* object, i.e., the general "subject matter" studied in the philosophy of animate nature, comprises all bodies which show themselves endowed with life. In using the term "life," we take it here in its commonly accepted meaning as applying to plants, animals, and men, without taking any philosophical position as to the nature of life and its distinction from other forms of existence. Thus the material object of the philosophy of animate nature is at least partly the same as that of quite a few other sciences, such as anatomy, physiology, and psychology. The philosophy of animate nature, however, differs from these sciences in its *formal* object, i.e., the aspect under which it considers living bodies, which is the metaphysical nature of life.

Starting Point. Like all sciences, philosophy must take its starting point in sense experience.[3] However, the sense experience which the philosophy of animate nature needs, as a rule is not the *complex experimental* data obtained in the laboratory, but the *primary experiential* data which can be supplied by a simple and careful observation of nature and is presupposed by experimental science.[4] We say "as a rule," because occasionally it may

[3] Cf. *op. cit.,* nos. 2 ff.

[4] These data are so elementary that they are presupposed by psy-

happen that laboratory experiments will reveal facts which demand a modification of the application of philosophical principles whose discovery was independent of these facts. As an example we may point to the philosophical explanation of the reproductive process. The assertion that the philosophy of animate nature is based upon "primary experiential data" should not be taken to mean that the philosopher can afford to be inexact in the choice of his starting point. On the contrary, he must make very certain that his starting point is unassailable and accurately determined, although he does not need a laboratory and scientific instruments to obtain his necessary data. In a sense this is even more necessary for the philosopher than for the student of experimental science, precisely because the philosopher has no possibility of verifying his conclusions by means of a return to sense experience.

Method. The method to be followed in the philosophy of living bodies is *inductive* in gathering the necessary data of experience, although usually this inductive process will be very simple. The induction is followed by a careful *analysis* of, and *reflection* upon the data, their implications and correlation to general metaphysical principles. Certain conclusions may be reached in this way, and these conclusions may be used as principles in *deductive* arguments to reach further conclusions. For instance, if experience shows that a quantitative element is always present in sensation, analysis and reflection may establish that this quantitative element belongs to the very nature

---

chology. For instance, visual and auditory experiments are not set up in the same way, because it is taken for granted that sight and hearing are functionally different.

of sensation, and from this the philosopher may conclude that sensation is of an organic nature, because quantity is a property of matter.

Moreover, it must be pointed out that very frequently our method will have to consist in first considering life as it is found in man and then in *arguing by analogy* from man's life to that of plants and animals. The reason is that man's life is known to us from immediate internal experience, while with respect to animals we can often proceed only by a kind of "dehumanization" of our own experience. For instance, from our own experience we know that man possesses something which we may call sense life. Although this sense life is profoundly affected by man's intellect, nevertheless the organic structure of many animals and their behavior unquestionably show striking similarities to man's sensitive organization and behavior; therefore, we conclude by analogy or a process of "dehumanization" that animals have sense life. Yet this sense life is profoundly altered by the absence of a true intellect.

Notwithstanding the fact that man is the primary source from which most of the necessary data for the philosophy of animate nature are obtained, it would seem preferable, at least in an introductory course, to proceed step by step, by considering first the life common to all organisms, then that which is found in all sensitive organisms, and finally the life proper to man. By following this procedure, we do not wish to suggest that, while plants have only one life, animals have two lives and man three. Man's life is one, but it manifests itself on three levels, and the first two of these may exist without the last. By treating these levels successively, we are able to emphasize the fact that man finds himself at the very apex of organic life. Moreover, it seems difficult to explain to those who do not have a clear notion of the lower vital activities, how these activities are affected by man's intellectual nature.

Definition of the Philosophy of Animate Nature

5. From the preceding considerations it follows that the philosophy of animate nature may be defined as the philosophic science of the nature of living bodies. It is called "philosophic," because it is concerned with the metaphysical nature of life and living bodies, and thus differs from biology and psychology, which study the nature of living bodies insofar as it is subject to verification by sense experience. It is called a "science," not in the arbitrarily restricted sense which limits science to the experimentally verifiable, but in the sense that it is systematic knowledge through causes.

This definition shows also the *place* of the philosophy of animate nature in the general division of science. It belongs to the group of sciences called "philosophy," in which it falls under the section "speculative," which we take to be identical with metaphysics. Speculative philosophy of metaphysics is divided into a number of parts, which are often indicated by special names—namely, the philosophy of being in general and finite being in general (ontology), the philosophy of the Infinite Being (theodicy), and the philosophy of finite material being or nature. In addition, there is a preliminary metaphysical investigation of being as it is in the cognitive faculties, which is called epistemology. The philosophy of nature is further subdivided into the philosophy of inanimate nature or cosmology, and the philosophy of animate nature, which is often called rational psychology.

Presuppositions of the Philosophy of Animate Nature

6. The present treatise presupposes that the epistemological position of moderate realism is accepted as valid and proven. We may summarize its position as follows:

There is a world which exists independently of the consideration of the human mind;

Man's cognitive faculties are essentially trustworthy, so that it is possible for man to have knowledge of the world as it is in itself.

Moreover, from ontology we accept as validly established several general principles, such as the principle of contradiction (it is impossible for a thing to be and not to be at the same time); the principle of sufficient reason (everything has a sufficient reason for its "to be"); the principle of causality (whatever comes to be has a cause); the axiom that action follows being, i.e., that everything acts in accordance with its nature; and the theory of act and potency, especially as revealed in the hylomorphic structure of material beings.

Because by their very nature general metaphysical principles are analogous, their use in this study will not consist in a univocal application to the subject matter under consideration.

Importance of the Philosophy of Animate Nature

7. It is hardly necessary to point out the importance of a philosophical study of animate nature. There are questions which cannot be answered by the experimental sciences of nature, precisely because these questions do not permit any verification by sense experience. For example, to the question, What is man? experimental

science can answer only in terms of structure, physical and chemical composition, functional reactions, relationship of actions, etc. The answer may be correct as far as it goes, but it does not go far enough. And if the scientist answers that his reply to this question is the only answer which *man* can reach, this assertion is not based upon his scientific data, but either upon the philosophical assumption that all knowledge must be subject to sense verification or upon the philosophical position of materialism.

Accordingly, the question, What is man? may be understood in a sense which lies beyond the confines of experimental science. It may be taken to mean, What ultimately is man? What kind of a being is man? But if any question concerning the ultimate nature of things deserves our interest, it surely is the question which is concerned with our very own nature. Man's desire to know may have no bounds, but his own self is in the very center of his intellectual curiosity. Therefore, even if the philosophy of animate nature did not have any practical consequences, it would still be the most deserving object of all study. As a matter of fact, however, this philosophy is of paramount importance, even from a practical point of view, because it considers such "vital" problems as the immortality of the human soul and the freedom of the will, which determine our entire outlook on life.

Division of this Study

8. The main division of this study flows naturally from the fact that three types of life are commonly accepted, namely, vegetative, sensitive, and rational life. The nature of each will have to be investigated in a different section. First, however, we shall have to consider that

which is common to living bodies in general. To these four sections a fifth will be added concerning the origin of life and the various species of living bodies.

- Animate Nature
  - Life in General—Section One (chaps. 1–3)
  - Kinds of Life
    - Vegetative—Section Two (chaps. 4–5)
    - Sensitive—Section Three (chaps. 6–9)
    - Rational—Section Four (chaps. 12–21)
  - Origin of Life and Species of Living Bodies —Section Five (chaps. 22–23)

SUGGESTED READINGS

9. Andrew G. van Melsen, *The Philosophy of Nature:* "Duquesne Studies, Philosophical Series," II (Pittsburgh: 2nd ed., 1954), chaps. I, III. The relationship of science and philosophy.

Alfred N. Whitehead, *Science and the Modern World* (New York: 1925), chap. V. The misuse of scientific method.

P. Henry van Laer, *Philosophico-Scientific Problems:* "Duquesne Studies, Philosophical Series," III (Pittsburgh: 1953), chap. III. The principle of verification.

George P. Klubertanz, *The Philosophy of Human Nature* (New York: 1953), chap. I and Appendix K. Science, metaphysics and the philosophy of human nature. For a critique of his position, see Oliver Martin, "The Philosophy of Human Nature," *The Review of Metaphysics,* 1954, pp. 452 ff.

Francis L. Harmon, *Principles of Psychology* (Milwaukee: 1953), Introduction.

Robert E. Brennan, *General Psychology* (New York: 1952), chaps. 1, 2.

——— *Thomistic Psychology* (New York: 1951), chap. 2.

Stefan Strasser, "Le point de départ en psychologie métaphysique," *Revue philosophique de Louvain,* 1950, pp. 220 ff.

SECTION I

Life in General

10. This section will comprise three chapters. In the first we shall study the characteristics which distinguish all living bodies from inanimate bodies. Because these characteristics require a principle of life called the soul, this principle will be studied in the second chapter. The third chapter will consider the operative principles or potencies by means of which the vital principle of the living body exercises its activity.

Schematic Division

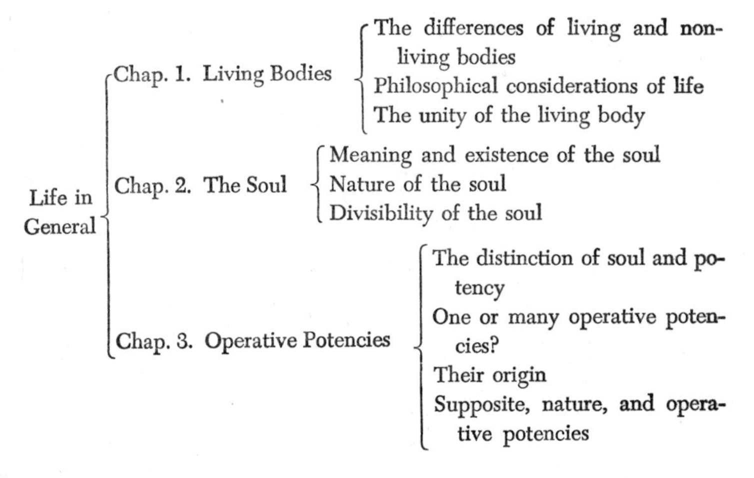

CHAPTER 1

Living Bodies

The Differences of Living and Nonliving Bodies

*** 11. *Life and Movement.* From daily experience everyone immediately knows that there is an intimate connection between life and movement. An object which shows no movement at all is not considered to be alive. On the other hand, not everything which moves is held to be living. A stone rolling down a hill moves, but we do not say that it lives; a dead body floating on the waves moves, but does not live; a river flowing towards the sea moves, but is not alive,[1] etc. If, however, an oppossum stops "playing possum" and begins again to move of itself or to move itself, we say: Oh, it was not dead but alive. Hence it is *self-movement* which characterizes life and is proper to living bodies.[2]

The examples show that the distinction between living and nonliving bodies is first derived from those things in which self-movement in the sense of *locomotion* can be observed. Further observation, however, makes it clear that

[1] At least not in the proper sense of the term. In a metaphorical sense one may speak of "living waters" in opposition to "dead water" (stagnant pools).

[2] Cf. Aristotle, *Physica*, bk. VIII, chap. 4 (255a 6); St. Thomas, *Summa theol.*, Ia, q. 18, a. 1.

mere self-locomotion is not the distinguishing characteristic of living bodies. For life is spoken of also in reference to things in which a change of place does not occur or at least is not the reason why they are called living; for instance, plants. Movement, therefore, should be taken in a wider sense so as to include any operation.[3] In this way *self*-movement comes to mean any activity whose principle and terminus are in the agent, and a living body will be any body which has within itself the principle of its own operation or activity.[4]

12. A more detailed observation of living bodies leads to the same conclusion. The main observable differences between living and nonliving bodies may be classified under two headings, namely, differences in structure and differences in activity.

Differences in Structure. Contrary to nonliving bodies the *physical* structure of living bodies is always *heterogeneous,* i.e., a living body has different parts adapted to different functions. For instance, in a cat we may distinguish the skeleton, muscles, digestive organs, etc. In higher forms of life each part or organ is built of cells, which are composed of a membrane, cytoplasm, and a nucleus. Some living bodies (protozoa) are unicellular, but most of them

[3] Movement, in the narrowest sense, means a change of place or position. In a wider sense, it means any transition from potency to act, whether instantaneous or successive, occurring in material things. Again, in a wider sense, it may mean any transition from potency to act, whether in a material or a spiritual being. In the widest possible sense, movement is used for any activity which is conceived as if it implied a transition from potency to act, even if in reality it does not involve such a transition. In this sense it extends even to the action of the Pure Act Himself.

[4] Cf. St. Thomas, *De veritate,* q. 4, a. 8.

are composed of enormous numbers of cells; for example, the human brain alone contains about nine billion cells. In unicellular bodies there is still the above-mentioned composition of membrane, cytoplasm and nucleus, each of which, in its turn, has its own component parts, such as chromatin, nuclear membrane, centrioles, etc. Some living bodies (slime molds) do not show the typical cell structure, but even in them a certain differential texture can be observed. Therefore, physically speaking, living bodies are heterogeneous.

Chemically, living bodies are always composed of many elements, most of which occur in the form of compounds. On the average, eighty percent of a living cell consists of water, and the remaining twenty percent is formed by proteins, fats, carbohydrates and salts. No living body consists of a single chemical compound; therefore, chemically speaking, a living body is not homogeneous but *heterogeneous*. Nonliving bodies, on the other hand, may be entirely homogeneous.

13. *Differences in Activity.* With respect to activity, living bodies are strikingly different from nonliving bodies. The activities common to all living bodies[5] are nutrition, growth, reproduction, and irritability.

a) *Nutrition.* Nutrition may be described as a process by which living matter changes nonliving matter into living matter. It is without parallel among nonliving bodies, at least if the term "nutrition" is taken in its proper sense. Metaphorically, we may speak of fire feeding on combustible matter; e.g., the fire of the candle feeds on the wax. But it is clear that there is no question here of

[5] There are other vital activities which are not common to all living bodies. They will be considered in the chapters concerned with cognitive and appetitive activities.

nutrition in the proper sense of the term. The fire is not a substance and therefore cannot change extraneous matter into its own substance, and the wax, obviously, is not feeding itself. A living body, on the other hand, is capable of intussusception, i.e., of taking extraneous matter and integrating it into its very substance by a process of assimilation. Assimilation is necessary in a living body, because it is continually losing energy and matter (by catabolism) and needs to replace them (by anabolism) if life is to continue. The whole complex process of changes involved in nutrition is called metabolism. *Its function is to make possible the continuation of life.*

b) *Growth.* Nonliving bodies increase in size by juxtaposition, i.e., by the addition of new layers of extraneous matter. Living bodies increase in size by growing, i.e., they *increase from within.* Multicellular organisms begin life as a single cell, which grows and after a time divides into two; these two again divide each one into two, and the process continues till the organism is fully formed and reaches the adult stage. Unicellular organisms also grow to full size, after which they divide into two separate individual organisms of approximately half the mass of the original cell. These two new unicellular organisms grow by assimilation to full size, after which they split, and the whole process begins all over again.

c) *Reproduction.* By reproduction is meant a process by which living bodies prepare, *as a part of their own substance,* living matter which is capable of being separated and developing into a new, distinct individual, usually of the same species as the original living body. No process like reproduction occurs in nonliving bodies.

d) *Irritability.* Another characteristic of living bodies is their irritability, i.e., the way they react to stimulation arising from changes in their surroundings. The stimula-

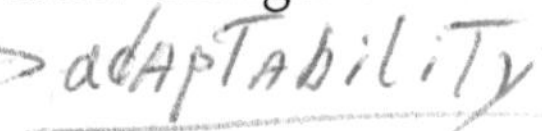

tion of a living body will give rise to a complex process of activity, the purpose of which is to *preserve and perfect the organism itself*. For example, if damage is inflicted, the organism does not take it passively, but immediately sets about repairing the damage as far as possible so as to insure the survival or well-being of the whole. Compare this to the passive way in which a rock undergoes damage.

14. From these observations we may draw the following conclusions:

1) The structure of the living body is *adapted to self-movement,* for it possesses different parts having different functions so that the whole can move itself by means of its parts.

2) The activity of the living body is self-movement, for it has its *principle and terminus in the living body itself*. That the principle of the movement is in the living body itself is clear, because all these activities are activities of the living body itself. That the terminus is in the living body itself should not be subject to doubt—in nutrition, the assimilated food becomes part of the organism; in growth, it is the organism itself which increases in size; in reproduction, it is the organism again which, either as a whole or in one of its parts, is prepared for the production of a new living body; in irritability, the reaction of the organism terminates in the preservation or perfection of the reacting organism itself.

Further Philosophical Considerations of Life

15. *Immanent Action.* An action of which both the principle and the terminus are in the agent is called an *immanent* action (from the Latin *immanens,* remaining

in), because it remains in the agent as a perfection of the agent.[6] To obtain a better understanding of immanent action, let us compare it with its opposite, transient action. *Transient* action means an action whose principle is in the agent and whose terminus is in a recipient distinct from the agent. Hence it is the recipient which is perfected by such an action. For instance, if a sculptor changes a shapeless block of marble into a beautiful statue, the principle of activity is in the sculptor (the agent), but the terminus of his activity is in the marble (the recipient), which is perfected by his operations. In vital activity, however, the agent and the recipient are one and the same; as a result, the perfection of the action remains in the agent. For this reason such activity is called the act of an agent. Transient action always consists in a transition from potency to act, because it is the perfection of a receiving subject by an outside agent. Immanent action, on the other hand, being the act of an agent, does not consist in such a transition, although as a matter of fact it does not occur without a transition from potency to act if the agent is in potency to vital activity.[7]

16. *Degrees of Immanence.* An action may be more or less immanent. It will be immanent *in the strict sense* if it perfects the power itself from which it emanates; and immanent *in a wider sense* if it remains in the same supposit or subject but not in the power or part itself from which it emanates. The functions of vegetative life are immanent only in a wider sense; for they remain in the living organism from which they emanate, but are com-

[6] Any action is an act or perfection.

[7] No finite being is its own action; therefore, no finite being has vital actions which do not imply a transition from potency to act.

municated from one part to the other. As a result, vegetative action may be called transient in the sense that it does not remain in the power from which it emanates, and also immanent in the sense that it remains at least in the supposit whose action it is. As we shall see later in Section Three, cognitive actions are immanent in the strict sense.

*With respect to the immanence of an action three grades are possible, as should be clear from the following consideration. In an agent we may distinguish the supposit, the remote principle of operation and the immediate principle of operation. To be immanent, an action must at least remain in the same supposit, although it may pass from one part or power to another. At a higher level of immanence, the action remains in the immediate principle of operation from which it emanates as its perfection, but this principle is not really identical with the essence of the supposit; hence the action is not immediately in the essence as its perfection. Finally, the immediate and the remote principle of operation are identical, so that the action is immediately in the essence itself (with which it is really identical). This last grade of immanence can be found only in the Infinite Being, because no finite being is its own principle of operation or its own action. The first grade of immanence is found in vegetative life, the second is proper to all finite cognitive life, as we shall see in subsequent chapters.

17. *Various Senses of the Term "Life."* Life is a term which expresses abstractly what "to live" expresses as a verb, just as "race" expresses abstractly the same as "to race" expresses as a verb. Contrary to race, however, life may refer not only to vital operations and activities, but

also to the substance from which such operations emanate. As a matter of fact, it is in the stricter sense of the term that life belongs to the living substance rather than to the operations of such a substance. For these operations are called "life" precisely because they manifest that the substantial nature from which they flow is a living substance. Accordingly, "living" is predicated primarily of living beings and only secondarily of the activities of living beings. Many authors indicate this distinction by saying that substantial life is the primary act of life, and vital operations are secondary acts of life.

Moreover, "to live" indicates the "to be" of a living body, for it means a mode of being that is proportioned to a nature adapted to self-movement. Thus "life" may indicate abstractly the "to be" of a being whose nature allows self-movement. In this case, our mind conceives "life" as if it were an essence, although "to be" is not an essence.[8]

18. *Analogy of Life.* From the metaphysical theory of analogy [9] and the preceding considerations it should be clear that life is an analogous concept, i.e., its meaning varies according to the subject of which it is predicated.

As predicated of "living waters" and things which are truly living, it is analogous by metaphorical analogy.

As predicated of living substances and vital operations, it is analogous because substance and operation do not belong to the same category. This analogy is that of attribution, because vital operations are called "life" insofar

[8] Cf. St. Thomas, *Contra gentes,* bk. I, chap. 98; *Summa theol.,* Ia, q. 18, a. 2.

[9] Cf. the author's *Introduction to the Science of Metaphysics,* nos. 34 ff.

as they are caused by, and therefore reveal that the substance from which they emanate is living.[10]

If the term "life" is restricted in its applications to living substances, it is still analogous because the mode of living is essentially different in the vegetative, the sensitive, and the intellectual order, as will become clear in the course of this study. Moreover, life may be predicated of God,[11] and any concept predicated of God and finite beings is analogous. However, life will be univocal if one considers exclusively the grade of life that is common to all living bodies, viz., vegetative life.[12]

Taken in the existential sense, as expressing the "to be" of a thing whose nature is adapted to self-movement, life will be analogous in the same way as being itself.

19. *Inadequate Self-Movement.* In every finite being, which is not its own action, movement or activity implies a transition from potency to act. Nothing, however, can be in potency and in act at the same time. Therefore self-movement of a finite being would seem to be a contradiction. For in a finite being self-movement im-

[10] Even if life is taken as predicated of vital operations only, it is still analogous, because some vital operations (the vegetative functions) belong to the category of action, while others (cognitive and appetitive functions) are qualities.

[11] Immanent action is the act of an agent and as such does not imply any imperfection; therefore, it may be predicated of God.

[12] Nevertheless, even in this case there is still the so-called "analogy of inequality" or of "generic predication," which means that the perfection expressed by the concept "vegetative life" is formally the same in all living bodies, but more perfectly realized in some than in others. Cf. St. Thomas, *De malo,* q.II, a.9, ad 16; Cajetan, *De nominum analogia,* chap. 1.

plies to move and to be moved; but to move is to be in act,[13] and to be moved implies to be in potency; hence *qua* moving the self-mover would have to be in act, and *qua* moved it would have to be in potency.

The answer to this difficulty lies in the distinction between adequate and inadequate self-movement. In *adequate* self-movement the finite being would have to be in act and in potency in the same respect, which is a contradiction. In *inadequate* self-movement, however, one part or power moves the other, so that the whole is in act with respect to one part or power and in potency with respect to another. In this way, the whole may be said to move itself by means of its parts, because the mover and the moved are truly parts of the same whole. For instance, an animal is able to move itself locally by means of its legs; the will moves the intellect to apply itself to serious study. Legs, will, and intellect are not independent subjects, but parts or powers of one and the same subject, which therefore in this sense moves itself.

The preceding considerations give us also the philosophical reason why a living body is an organic body, i.e., a body having different parts adapted to different functions, so that one part may move the other.

20. *Living Bodies Differ Essentially from Nonliving Bodies.* This assertion should be clear from the foregoing. The formal proof may be proposed as follows:

If the operations of living bodies are essentially different from those of nonliving bodies, living bodies are essentially different from nonliving bodies. But the operations

[13] An agent acts insofar as it is in act.

of living bodies are essentially different from those of nonliving bodies. Therefore, living bodies differ essentially from nonliving bodies.

The *major* follows from the metaphysical principle that action follows being. The *minor* has been proved above—living bodies move themselves, whereas nonliving bodies are moved by another; but active motion cannot be reduced to passive motion and therefore is essentially different from it.

Living bodies are not merely essentially different from nonliving bodies, but *essentially superior* to them. Living bodies are self-perfective by means of their immanent action, while nonliving bodies cannot do anything towards their own perfection, but need to be perfected passively through the transient action of other beings.

*21. *Grades of Life.* Considering the determining elements of movement we are able to establish that a threefold grade of physical life is possible. A being is called living insofar as it has self-movement. But in any movement three determining elements may be distinguished—namely, the *end* or purpose of the movement which moves the agent to act; the *form* or principle by virtue of which the agent acts; and the *execution* of the movement. If none of these three elements is determined from within, there is no self-movement, but merely passive motion. If only the execution of the movement is from within, but not the form nor the end, there is self-movement, but it is of the lowest grade. As we shall see, this is the case with plants. If there is also self-determination regarding the form or principle of movement, but no control over its purpose, there is a higher grade or self-movement. As we shall see in Section Three, this is the case with animals, in which sense-cognition becomes a principle of movement. Finally, a being may have also control over the end or purpose of its movement, and this will be the highest grade of physical life, i.e., of life communicated to a body. In Section Four we shall prove that man is endowed with this grade of life, because he is able to determine the end of his actions through intellect and will.[14]

22. *Solution of Some Difficulties.* A number of difficulties may be raised against the preceding considerations, the solution of which may serve to clarify the points at issue.

Is it not true that even nonliving bodies have within themselves a principle of movement and therefore may be said to move themselves? The answer is in the affirmative, but there is an important difference between the principle of movement in a living body and that in a nonliving body. The nonliving body has a purely *passive* principle of movement, while the living body possesses an *active* principle of movement. Moreover, even if the nonliving body, after being moved by another, actively moves, its movement is *transient,* whereas the movement of the living body is *immanent.*

*One could urge that at least certain nonliving bodies have also an active principle of movement and that this movement remains in the body itself, so that such bodies would have to be called living. For example, a rubber ball will resume its original shape as soon as external pressure is released. To this we may reply that a rubber ball has an active principle of movement, but not of self-movement. There can be question of self-movement

[14] Cf. St. Thomas, *Summa theol.,* Ia, q.18, a.3.

only if the ball *exercises control over its movement.* But the movement of the ball is wholly determined for it by its maker, and the ball itself exercises no control over its return to the original shape. Properly speaking, it is not the ball but the manufacturer of the ball who moves it back to its original shape,[15] because he has given the ball a quasi-natural shape. As long as this shape is not disturbed by extraneous causes, the ball does not act, but if the shape is interfered with, the ball acts to resume it as determined by its maker. It is true that this movement of the ball remains within the ball and therefore, in a sense, may be called immanent. But it is *not immanent in the technical sense* of the term, because it is wholly determined by the nature of the ball and not controlled by the ball itself. Moreover, it does not tend to a mobile equilibrium of forces, but to a stabile equilibrium, i.e., it tends to a state of immobility and not to a state which makes movement possible. A similar answer may be given to the objection that there is movement of subatomic particles within the atom and that therefore there is immanent movement in every atom.

Another difficulty could be raised from the fact that a living body is a finite being. Finite beings are in potency to action and therefore need to be moved to their action by an outside agent. Accordingly, no finite being moves itself. While there can be no quarrel with the antecedent of this objection, the conclusion goes too far. If an agent moves an object it is a mover, but it does not follow that

[15] The manufacturer does so *per se.* The releasing agent determines the movement *per accidens* and moves the ball insofar as it removes the obstacle preventing a return to the original quasi-natural shape. Cf. St. Thomas, *De veritate,* q. 24, a. 1 for a similar answer to a question based upon ancient physics.

this agent is also the first mover; for it itself may have been moved by another agent. In a similar way, if a mover moves itself, it does not follow that it is the first source of its movement, for it may have been *moved to move itself*. In such a case the self-mover does not have its self-movement of itself but of another. Only in the Pure Act could there be question of self-movement[16] which is wholly from within.[17]

Again, one could point out that a machine, such as a motorcar, has different parts exercising different functions and moves itself by means of these functions, as the very name "automobile" indicates. Therefore, either machines are living bodies or life has not been described accurately as self-movement. To this difficulty we may reply that there is no parity between a machine and a living body. A machine is an aggregate *without essential unity*, whereas a living body is an organic whole possessing essential unity. Both the machine and the living body may be called "organic," but their organization is essentially different, because the one is accidentally unified and the other essentially.[18] Moreover, the activity of the machine does not tend to perfect the machine itself, but tends to an *extrinsic purpose* assigned to it by its designer. It is not the principal cause of its activity, but a mere instrumental cause. But is it not possible that with the marvelous progress of modern technique man will succeed in producing a machine capable of servicing, repairing, and even reproducing itself? At least such a machine would not be essentially different from a living

[16] In the widest possible sense of the term. Cf. footnote 3.

[17] Cf. St. Thomas, *De malo*, q.3, a.2, ad 4.

[18] Cf. Alexis Carrel, *Man the Unknown* (New York: 1935), pp. 106 f.

body. To this we may reply that if such a "machine" would ever be produced, it would, indeed, not be essentially different from a living body, because such a "machine" would not be a machine but a living body. It would differ from other living bodies only *with respect to origin.* As to the possibility of such a "machine" ever being produced from inanimate matter, see below, Section Five.

However, there is one point in the preceding difficulty which could give rise to serious objection. Is a living body really only one being, or is it a colony of individuals leading their own separate lives? If a living body is not one being, there can be no question of one part moving another part of the same being, and therefore there would be no self-movement. Accordingly, it is important to investigate the unity possessed by a living body.

The Unity of the Living Body

23. *Meaning and Kinds of Unity.* By unity or oneness is meant that a being is not divided. In the case of a being which has no parts and therefore is not subject to any division, its unity will be *unity of simplicity;* otherwise the unity will be *unity of composition.* Unity of composition may be substantial or accidental. It is *substantial* if it consists in the union of "parts" or principles which together form one substance. Substantial unity of composition therefore refers to the unity of matter and form, the coprinciples of material substances, which exist by one "to be." Unity of composition is called *accidental* if there is question either of the *extrinsic* union of complete substances or of the *intrinsic* union of accidents to their subject of inhesion. Extrinsic unity may consist in the unity *of purpose* with respect to the activity of two or more complete substances, as happens in the play of a team,

or in unity *of juxtaposition,* as is exemplified by a house or a pile of bricks.[19]

24. *How to Discover the Unity of a Being.* Man does not have an immediate insight into the kind of unity of a being, but can arrive at knowledge of its unity by means of a study of its activity. For the activities of a being reveal its nature and therefore also its unity, as is clear from the principle that action follows being. Hence from the unity of activity we may argue to the unity of the agent. In the case of a composite being, it is the activity of the component parts which has to be investigated, for we want to discover what kind of union these component parts have with one another. The focal point of this investigation will have to be the *purpose* or final cause of the activity. The reason is that activity is unified either because of its origin from a single source (efficient cause) or because of its tendency to a common goal. But it is obvious that in the present question we cannot argue from the unity of activity insofar as it emanates from a single source, for it is precisely the sameness or unity of this source which is the object of our investigation.

With respect to purpose the activity of a composite whole offers the following possibilities:

a) Each part of the whole acts independently in such a way that *no common purpose* can be assigned to the actions.

b) Each part of the whole acts in dependence upon the other parts in such a way that there is a *common extrinsic purpose,* i.e., the purpose is not the good of the whole itself.

[19] The above-mentioned division of unity is not meant to be complete.

c) Each part of the whole acts in dependence upon the others in such a way that there is a *common intrinsic purpose*, i.e., the purpose of the activity is the good of the whole itself.

In the first case the unity of the whole is largely *fictitious*. There is hardly any real unity at all, except the unity of purely accidental local aggregation or congregation, such as in a multitude of human beings going their own ways across a common city square.

In the second case, the unity is more closely knit, because the activity of the component parts is directed towards the same purpose. Nevertheless, this unity is still of an *accidental* nature, because it is obtained under the influence of an outside agent who directs the activity of the parts towards his own purpose.[20] An example would be the activity of the various parts of a machine which is directed by its operator or designer.

In the third case, however, there will be *substantial* unity. The activity of the component parts is directed towards the whole itself. An independent agent will act for its own good, because any appetite is moved primarily by what is good for itself and not by what is good for another.[21] Therefore, if the different parts of a whole act primarily for the sake of the whole, they show that they are not independent agents, but controlled by the whole which directs their activity for its own good. In other words, the parts show by their actions that they belong

[20] Concerning the possibility of such an accidental unification preparing the way for substantial unity, see below, Section Five.

[21] Every agent acts for an end. This end is a good apprehended as desirable by the agent acting for the end or by the one who makes the agent act for the end. Cf. the author's *Introduction to the Science of Metaphysics*, no. 258.

to one and the same ultimate subject of activity, the same supposite or autonomous substance, so that the whole will be substantially unified.

25. *A Living Body is One Substance.* After these preliminaries, we assert that a living body is substantially unified or one substance. The proof is as follows:

If the component parts of a whole act primarily for the good of the whole, this whole is one substance. But the component parts of every living body act primarily for the good of the whole. Therefore, the living body is one substance.

The *major* premise is clear from the foregoing: in such a whole the activity of the parts is directed towards an intrinsic purpose and therefore requires an intrinsic principal of unification; hence the whole will be substantially unified.

The *minor* premise may be proved in this way: 1) Extraneous matter is taken in by certain parts of the living body, broken down, assimilated and distributed throughout the whole, in such a way that *the whole can continue to exist and function properly.* To give an example, if there is not sufficient food for the well-being of all parts, those parts which are more important for the whole are given a greater share so as to secure the survival of the whole.

2) A living body develops itself through epigenesis (successive production) from a single cell to adult size [22] in such a way that the activity of all parts is *subordinated to the production of a well-proportioned whole.* If, for instance, certain cells which would normally develop into a definite part of the embryo are removed, the activity of

[22] Unicellular organisms, however, often develop merely in size.

the remainder is modified in such a way that an integral whole results.

3) The activity of the living body is regulated in such a way that *the whole is preserved according to type.* Worn-out cells are replaced; within certain limits, damage is repaired; functions of severed parts are taken over by other parts if possible; even major parts often are regenerated completely. The most striking example is offered by the clavellina, a small invertebrate. When the frontal part is severed, the remainder gives up its organization and reforms in such a way that a complete but smaller clavellina results.

26. These and other activities of living bodies clearly show that it is the good of the whole which directs the parts in their operations. However, we do not mean to affirm that every body which at first sight appears to be one living body because of its coherence in space and time actually is only one body. In lower forms of life living organisms may cling together in such a way that occasionally it is difficult to determine whether together they form one organism or a mere aggregate of organisms. Moreover, even in higher forms of life living bodies may exist in close association but without substantial unity; e.g., if on the same trees apples and pears are grown, or if Siamese twins have certain parts in common but others of their own. The difficulty of recognizing individual substances as distinct in such cases does not weaken the evidence of distinction where it is clearly present.

It should be noted that in our proof we paid no attention to the vital activities which are specifically proper to animals and men, because at present we are concerned with the substantial unity of all living bodies, and only the vegetative functions are common to all living bodies. At a later stage we shall have to prove that specifically animal and human functions are performed by the same substantial being which exercises the functions of vegetative life.

27. *Evidence Against the Unity of the Living Body.* A number of facts may be adduced as evidence that living bodies are not one substance. They are the following:

a) Each cell of a multicellular organism is generated, grows, matures, and dies individually; therefore, each cell is an independent living body, and multicellular organisms are nothing but colonies of cells without a substantial unity of their own.

b) The spectrograph definitely shows that a living body contains a number of different chemical substances; therefore, a living body is not one substance.

c) In a living body chemical substances have the same characteristic activities as they have outside the living body; therefore, these substances either are not substances at all or are substances also when they are in the living body, so that this body is not one substance.

d) Any part of a living body can be severed and kept alive artificially; therefore, the parts of a living body have an independent life, so that the whole is not one substance.

While we do not intend to take exception to the facts adduced in the preceding arguments, we must deny that the conclusions follow. With respect to the vital activity of the individual living cell, it is true that this activity, considered separately from the whole of which the cell forms part, may seem to point to an independent life. However, if the activity of the cell is considered in the whole of which it forms part, it must be admitted that its activity is *subordinated to the good of the whole* and therefore lacks the independence which is proper to a substantial unit or supposit.

Regarding the presence of chemical substances in the living body, we must, first of all, point out the *ambiguous use of the term "substance."* In chemistry, substance means homogenous matter, whereas in philosophy a substance is a being having an autonomous existence, as opposed to accidents. Therefore, from the multiplicity of substances in the chemical sense one cannot draw any conclusion regarding its multiplicity in the philosophical sense. Secondly, experimental science cannot, and does not intend to answer the question whether a living body is one or many supposits, because such a question *does not fall within the scope of experimental science.* The only conclusion which may be drawn from the above-mentioned chemical evidence is that a living body is heterogeneous, but this conclusion can be reached also from primary experiential data.

Concerning the activity of chemical substances in the living body, it may be admitted that chemical elements and compounds retain most, if not all, of their characteristic actions when they are taken into the living body. But here, again, one should not overlook the fact that these characteristic activities are subordinated to the good of the whole and thus show that the *chemical substances do not act as independent beings.* Hence they are not substances in the philosophical sense of the term when they form a part of a living body. However, because their activities remain, philosophers often say that they are virtually present in the body.

The fact that a severed part of a living body can be kept alive separately merely shows that *after separation there is independent life.* To prove anything against the substantial unity of the living body, one would have to show that the parts live independently before they are severed from the whole.

Historical Notes

*28. *Plato* (427–347 B.C.), *Aristotle* (384–322 B.C.), *Thomas Aquinas* (1225–1274), and many others distinguish living from nonliving bodies by immanent action.

The ancient hylozoists (*Thales of Miletus*, 625–545 B.C.) and modern panpsychists (*Wundt*, 1832–1920) imply or state that all things are alive. Likewise, many materialists (*Haeckel*, 1834–1919) and pantheists (*Giordano Bruno*, 1548–1600) who conceive the universe as one living body.

The essential difference between living and nonliving bodies is denied by the mechanists. Some, such as *Huxley* (1825–1895), hold that the whole universe, including living bodies, is the result of the mutual interaction of the forces of molecules in the primitive nebulae of the universe. Others, such as *Lloyd Morgan* (1852–1936), maintain that life is an emergent (unpredictable) event of nature resulting from a particularly complex collocation of chemicals. Mechanists are unable to explain the intrinsic finality or immanence of activity which distinguishes the living from the nonliving body, and they do not account for the emergence of the more perfect (life) from the less perfect (inanimate matter). Concerning the possibility of life emerging from inanimate matter, see below, Section Five.

SUMMARY

29. Simple observation shows that it is self-movement which characterizes life. By self-movement is meant that

both the principle and the terminus of an act are in the agent. A more detailed observation of living bodies leads to the same conclusion. Living bodies are physically and chemically heterogeneous in structure and therefore adapted to self-movement; their characteristic activities of nutrition, growth, reproduction, and irritability have as their principle and terminus the living body itself.

Activity of which both the principle and the terminus are in the agent is called immanent action. Its opposite is transient action, of which the terminus is in a recipient distinct from the agent. Hence in immanent action the perfection of the action is in the agent, while in transient action this perfection is in the recipient. Immanent action, being the act of an agent, does not consist in a transition from potency to act, but transient action always consists in such a transition.

Life is predicated primarily of living substances and secondarily of their activity. As an abstract noun expressing what "to live" expresses as a verb, life is the same as the being of things that are adapted to self-movement. In its different predications life is an analogous concept.

In a finite being self-movement is always inadequate, because a finite being is in potency to action and therefore cannot move itself as a whole or adequately from potency to act.

Living bodies are essentially different from nonliving bodies, because their operations are essentially different from those of nonliving bodies. Living bodies perfect themselves through their actions, while nonliving bodies need to be perfected by others. Hence living bodies are essentially superior to nonliving bodies.

Living bodies are substantially unified, i.e., their various parts together form one substance, existing by one "to be." To discover the unity of a being we must study its activity, specifically the purpose of its activity. With respect to purpose, the activity of a composite whole may show no common purpose, a common extrinsic purpose or a common intrinsic purpose. In the first case there can be no other unity than that of local aggregation; in the second there will be the accidental unity of a machine; in the third case there will be substantial unity, because the component parts are controlled in their activity from within and thus show that they are intrinsically dependent upon the whole. Hence in this case the activities of the parts are really activities of the whole, which is the only ultimate subject of the actions, the only supposit. Living bodies belong to the third category of composite wholes, because the activities of their parts are primarily directed to the good of the whole and therefore demand that an intrinsic principle direct their activity to the whole.

SUGGESTED READINGS

30. *Aristotle, De anima,* bk. II, chap. 1 and *Physica,* bk. VIII, chap. 4.

Thomas Aquinas, *Summa theol.,* Ia, q. 18, a. 1; *De veritate,* q. 4, a. 8; *Contra gentes,* bk. I, chap. 97. The concept of life.

——— *Summa theol.,* Ia, q. 18, a. 2; *Contra gentes,* bk. I, chap. 98. Senses of the term 'life.'

——— *Summa theol.,* Ia, q. 18, a. 3; *Contra gentes,* bk. IV, chap. 11. Grades of life.

Hans Driesch, "The Breakdown of Materialism," *The Great Design* (New York: 1934), The insufficiency of mechanism.

LIVING BODIES

Michael Maher, "Life," *The Catholic Encyclopedia.*

Alexis Carrel, *Man the Unknown* (New York: 1935) chaps. III, IV. "The Unity of the Living Body."

George P. Klubertanz, *The Philosophy of Human Nature* (New York: 1953), chap. II. The unity of man.

W. B. Cannon, *The Wisdom of the Body* (New York: 1932). The activity of the body is for the good of the whole.

James Van Der Veldt, "Philosophical Life Theories," *Franciscan Studies,* vol. 24, 1943, pp. 113–142 and 277–305. A description of the various theories of life from the time of Descartes.

Robert E. Brennan, *General Psychology* (New York: 1952), chap. 3. The notion of organic life.

CHAPTER 2

The Soul

Existence of the Soul

*** 31. In the preceding chapter we have seen that some bodies are endowed with life while others are lifeless. So it is obvious that a body is not called living merely because it is a body, for otherwise all bodies would be living bodies.[1] A body is said to be living because its essence or nature is such that it is capable of immanent or vital actions. Hence every living body has within itself a principle which makes vital actions possible. This principle is traditionally called the *soul*.[2] We may describe it provisionally as the intrinsic principle which makes a body a living body and essentially distinct from nonliving bodies.

If the existence of the soul is so obvious, one could argue, why is it that not even with the most modern scientific equipment the slightest trace of a soul can be discovered? To say the least, its existence would seem to

[1] Cf. St. Thomas, *Summa theol.*, Ia, q.75, a.1.

[2] The student may be surprised to hear that all living bodies, including plants, have a soul, because he may associate having a soul with the immortality of the soul. The two questions are entirely distinct. Every living body has a soul, but only the human soul is immortal, as will become clear in the course of this study.

be scientifically unproved. In reply to this objection we must admit that the existence of the soul is unproved and even unprovable by the methods of *experimental* science, for the simple reason that the soul is not subject to sense experience. Its existence can be discovered only by the use of the methods proper to philosophy. However, this does not mean that the existence of the soul is not scientifically proved, unless the term "scientific" is arbitrarily restricted to "verifiable by sense experience."

But if the soul is not subject to experimental investigation, it seems useless to explain any biological processes, and is nothing but a relic of pre-scientific times. To this we may reply that although the nature of the soul cannot be investigated experimentally, this does not mean that it cannot be investigated scientifically by means of rational deductions from sense data which transcend experimental verification. The soul may be useless to explain biological processes, but it is not offered as such, but only as a *metaphysical explanation* of the nature of the living body on the level of being.

More positively, the claim could be made that the activity of a living body can be sufficiently explained by the organization of such a body, without the directing influence of a soul. Such a claim, however, conceives the soul as an extrinsic principle directing the activity of the body. In an organic body there is no need of extrinsic direction, because the activity is directed from within. In other words, the very notion of *an actual organic body includes the soul.*

But is it not true that no form of physical energy can be assigned to the soul as its cause? The efforts of vitalists, such as Stahl, Bichat, and Liebig to find any form of such physical energy have proved abortive. Again, therefore, it would seem that the existence of a soul is an antiquated theory. Our reply is that these vitalists failed in their efforts because they had the wrong idea of a soul. The soul alone is not the source of any physical energy. The soul is the *formal* cause of the composite of body and soul, and this composite is the source of the physical energy of the living body.

Nature of the Soul

32. *The Soul is Not an Accident.* Concerning the nature of the soul, it should be clear that the soul is not something accidental. It is the soul which makes the living body essentially different from a nonliving body. Now, an essential difference cannot be founded upon a mere accident, but must flow from the very substance of the being in question. Therefore, the soul is not something accidental, but belongs to the category of substance.

The Soul is a Substantial Principle of the Living Body. The category of substance embraces complete substances and substantial principles which by their union form one complete substance. The soul, however, is *not a complete substance.* If it were a complete substance, its union with the body could not result in one substance, but would be a mere accidental unit or aggregate. The reason is as follows: A complete substance cannot be at the same time a mere principle of substance; hence it cannot be united with another substantial principle to constitute together one substance, but only with another complete substance. But a complete substance has its own "to be." Therefore, the composite of two complete substances consists of components having their own "to be," so that it will be a mere aggregate. The living body, however, as we have seen above, is one substance. Therefore, the soul is not a complete substance but merely a substantial principle.

The Soul is the Substantial Form of the Living Body. Every corporeal substance is composed of two substantial principles, matter and form.[3] But it is clear that the soul is not the material principle of the living body, for matter is a potency and therefore a principle of limitation which does not confer any perfection, whereas the soul gives the composite the perfection of life. Hence the soul is not the material principle of the living body, but the formal principle or the substantial form.

Because the soul is the substantial form of the body, it is essentially *simple,* i.e., without composition of essential parts. For a substantial form is one of the ultimate component parts of a composite substance and therefore itself simple.

33. *The Soul is the Only Substantial Form of the Body.* The soul is related to the body as form is to matter or as act is to potency. Hence two substantial forms in the same body would mean that two acts of the same order at the same time actuate one potency, which is impossible. Once a potency is actuated it is no longer potency. Therefore, the soul is the only substantial form of the body.

From this thesis it follows that the different substances which compose the living body do not retain their own substantial form. However, as we have seen above in no. 27, at least most of their activities remain, and for this reason these substances are said to remain *virtually.*

[3] Cf. the author's *Introduction to the Science of Metaphysics,* chap. 5.

When we say that the soul is the substantial form of the *body,* this assertion should not be understood as if the soul informs matter which is previously rendered a body by a "form of corporeity." For the form of corporeity would be a substantial form and therefore would reduce the union of body and soul to an accidental union. Nevertheless, it is customary to say that the soul is the substantial form of the body and not of prime matter, because considered precisely as a principle of life the soul is the form of matter which is already rendered corporeal. In other words, as a substantial form, the soul makes matter a body, and as a soul, it makes this body a living body.

Solution of Some Difficulties. The unicity of the soul as the substantial form of the body could be attacked upon the following grounds:

a) When a living body dies it remains a body. Therefore, in addition to the soul, which makes it living, it has another form which makes it a body.

b) The transplantation of living arteries, skin, etc., from one body to another shows that these parts or their cells lead a life of their own and therefore must have their own principle of life or soul; hence the soul of the whole is not the only substantial form of the body.

c) In the case of Siamese twins it may happen that important parts of the body are possessed in common and function for both twins; yet each of the twins is considered to have his own soul. Therefore, the common organs must be informed by the souls of both.

With respect to the first argument, that a dead body still is a body, our answer is that at death the body seems to remain the same, but in reality *a new body is gener-*

ated. Because matter cannot exist without a substantial form, the corruption of the living body means the generation of a new body, which is composed of the same matter as the living body but has a different substantial form. Or rather, the dead body is an aggregate of many substances, composed of the matter of the previously living body and a number of substantial forms.

Regarding the transplantation of parts of a living body, this merely shows that there is an individual principle of life in these parts after their severance from the living body. To prove that the soul of the whole is not the only substantial form of these parts, one would have to demonstrate that these parts actually have their own principles of life *before* being severed from the original organism. For the philosophical explanation of transplantation, see no. 38.

The case of Siamese twins may be likened to grafts which lead their own life, but depend upon "common" organs for part of their functions.[4] The common parts would seem to be informed by the soul of one of the twins, although it may not be possible to determine which one.[5] The vital operations, however, of the common part can benefit both twins because of their extreme

[4] Contrary to grafts, however, Siamese twins, as all identical twins, start as one living organism.

[5] One might claim a special vital principle for the "common part." But according to the principle that entities must not be multiplied without necessity, this claim would have to be rejected, because the case can be explained without the admission of a third principle of life. Moreover, the ontogenetic evolution of the twins from one ovum by imperfect division into two and not into three parts would seem to militate against a third principle of life. In this respect such twins are different from the case of branches grafted upon an existing stem and root system, for in such a graft the stem and root system may retain its own vital principle.

similarity. With respect to the twin whose soul does not inform the common parts of the body, the operations of these parts which benefit both are not vital operations in the strict sense of the term, because they do not remain in the same supposite.

34. *The Soul is the Substantial Form of the Whole Body*. In calling the soul the substantial form of the whole body, we do not wish to claim that everything which is in the body is informed by the soul. Food, for instance, which is in the digestive system, but not yet assimilated, is not informed by the soul; likewise, waste products which are not yet eliminated. But everything which is really a part of the body is informed by the soul. For otherwise such a part would have its own substantial form, so that the soul would not be the only substantial form of the body.

Accordingly, the living cells of a body do not have their own substantial form, for they are parts of the living body. An exception must, perhaps, be made for abnormal growths, such as tumors and cancers, whose very activity suggests that they have escaped from the control of the vital principle of the whole and lead a life of their own to the detriment of the organism.

As the substantial form of the body, the soul is by its essence present *wholly and entirely in each part of the body*. Nevertheless, the soul is not able to exercise all its functions in each part, because these functions require specialized organs. Obviously we cannot see with our ears nor hear with our nose. Therefore, the soul is not present in each part of the body with the totality of its power.[6]

It is true, of course, that one cannot *imagine* how the

[6] Cf. St. Thomas, *Summa theol.*, Ia, q.76, a.8.

soul can be wholly in one part of the body and also wholly in another part. But this impossibility does not invalidate the thesis. A valid objection could be made if the soul were wholly present in each part in the way an extended body is present. For an extended body cannot be wholly here and wholly there. But the soul is *not an extended body;* but it is merely a substantial coprinciple which together with matter constitutes the body which has extension. Trying to imagine philosophical entities is positively dangerous, because our imagination can properly represent only extended objects and therefore fails with respect to the soul.

But if the whole soul is present in every part of the body, does it not follow, for instance, that each part of the body of a lion is a lion because it has the whole substantial form of the lion? The answer is in the negative. The conclusion would be correct if the soul were in each part as in an independent and separately existing entity. But the soul is in each part insofar as the part is an *integral part of the same whole.* Therefore, each part of the lion is "leonine" but not a lion.

Body and Soul Are Really Distinct, Enter into a Real Composition, and Do Not Need to be United by a Common Bond. These assertions are merely corollaries of the general theory of act and potency. The soul is related to the body as act is to potency; therefore, it is distinct from the body as act is from potency; enters into the same composition as act and potency; and needs no other bond than act and potency. But, as is evident from metaphysics,[7] act and potency are really distinct, enter into a

[7] Cf. the author's *Introduction to the Science of Metaphysics,* chap. 3.

real composition, and unite of themselves, so that there is no need of a common bond.

Definition of the Soul. The soul is traditionally defined as the first act of a natural organic body.[8] After the preceding considerations the understanding of this definition should not offer any serious difficulty. The soul is called an *act,* because it perfects the body, rendering it capable of immanent action. It is called the *first* act, which is the same as the substantial form, in opposition to vital actions, which are secondary acts. It is called the first act of a *body,* because it is through the soul that the body is alive. This body is qualified as *natural* in contrast to the mechanical body or machine. The term "*organic*" is added to indicate that the soul as a principle of life requires a variety of organs in the body so as to make self-movement possible. An organic body, taken as distinct from the soul, is the same as a body which is immediately potentially alive.[9]

Divisibility of Souls

35. *Living Bodies Can be Divided.* Experience clearly shows that living bodies can be divided in such a way that the parts stay alive. Cuttings, for instance, of plants

[8] Aristotle, *De anima,* bk. II, chap. 1 (412b 5). This definition is "a general formula applicable to all kinds of souls" (*ibid.*). When the term "soul" is taken in this general sense, i.e., as neither including nor excluding sense life and intellectual life, it is a univocal concept.

[9] In the same chapter (412a, 21, 29, 412b, 25) Aristotle adds to the definition of the soul "having life potentially in it" to indicate that the body, insofar as it is distinct from the soul, is potentially alive. However, there is no need to retain this addition, because it is contained in the term "organic." Cf. St. Thomas, *In II de anima,* lect. 1, no. 233.

do not die immediately, but continue to live for some time and in many cases are able to develop into complete plants. Lower types of animal life, such as flatworms, can be divided in such a way that each part remains alive or even develops into a complete individual flatworm. Even the embryos of higher types of animal life, in the early stages of embryonic development, are subject to division in such a way that both sections develop into complete animals. Finally, fully developed tissue of animals, severed from the whole, can be kept alive indefinitely, as was shown by the famous experiments of Dr. Alexis Carrel.

The divisibility of the living body gives rise to the question whether or not the soul itself is divided in the division of the body. At first sight, it would seem easiest to explain the above-enumerated facts by the division of the vital principle itself. Closer inspection, however, is necessary, for a division into parts is possible only in extended things. Therefore, we must first see whether or not the soul is extended.

36. *Is the Soul Extended?* Extension may affect a subject either directly or indirectly. Directly extended is that which is the subject itself of extension, namely the composite of matter and form. Indirectly extended is that which is affected by the extension of its subject; for instance, color is indirectly extended because its subject is an extended body. Now it should be clear that the soul is *not directly extended,* for the subject of extension is not the soul but the composite of matter and soul. Can the soul be indirectly extended? As we have seen the soul is the substantial form of the body. But a substantial form is prior in nature to all accidental forms, including exten-

sion. Therefore, it follows that the soul is *not indirectly extended,* because the matter informed by the soul is not extended prior to the reception of the accidental form "extension." [10]

The Soul Itself Is Indivisible. While the living body is divisible, the soul itself is not subject to division. Divisibility is based upon extension and may be direct or indirect according as an object is directly or indirectly extended. But, as we have just proved, the soul is neither directly nor indirectly extended. Therefore, it is neither directly nor indirectly divisible.

Moreover, as the substantial form of the whole, the soul is the principle of unity in the composite. But it would seem to be against the nature of the principle of unity or indivision to be itself subject to division.[11] Therefore, no soul can be divided.

On the other hand, it is not possible to deny the above-enumerated facts. If severed parts live it is obvious that they have a soul. So if this soul does not come from the division of the original soul into parts, we must provide another explanation for its origin.

37. *The Division of a Living Body May Actualize Potential Souls.* In one living body there is actually only one principle of life or soul. If, however, a part of the body is sufficiently organized for the preservation of life after being severed from the whole, such a part is potentially

[10] Cf. St. Thomas, in the texts referred to in no. 41.

[11] Moreover, the admission of divisibility of the soul would seem to put in jeopardy the spirituality of the human soul. If souls are divisible, the only reasonable explanation for the continued life of parts severed from the human body would seem to be the divisibility of the human soul. But a divisible soul cannot be of a spiritual nature.

alive by a life of its own. Prior to its separation from the body, such a part is actually informed by the soul of the whole, because it does not yet lead a life of its own, although it is capable of it. In other words, it has a soul in potency. The agent which severs the part from the whole reduces this potency to act, so that now the part actually has its own soul.

Accordingly, one organism has *actually only one soul, but potentially many*—as many as there are parts which can continue to live after being severed from the body. By the expression "actually one soul, but potentially many" is meant that the disposition of certain parts is such that mere severance from the main body will actuate independent principles of life in them, although before severance no independent principles of life exist in them, but only the soul of the whole.

If the disposition or organization of the severed part is sufficient for the continuation of the same kind of life as was possessed by the original organism, a soul of the same kind will be educed from the potency of matter. This is the case of plants and lower forms of animals which can be divided into two or more individual plants or animals. In higher types of life the division of a fully developed body does not result in two individuals of the same kind, because the higher type of life requires a great diversity of organization, which is lacking in these parts. Lower type of life have a relatively simple organization; therefore, even a part of the body may preserve a sufficient organization for the continuation of the same type of life. If the organization in the severed part is not sufficient for animal life but adequate for vegetative life, a vegetative principle of life will become the soul of this part. With respect to the division of embryos, often in the early stages any part may have a sufficient organization for the development of a complete animal; hence any such part will have its own principle of life in potency,[12] and this potency is actuated by the division of the part from the whole.

*38. *Transplantation of Parts of a Living Body.* The preceding considerations show also what happens in the case of the transplantation of parts from one body into another. Before its severance from the original organism, such a part is actually informed by the soul of the whole organism, but potentially it has a vital principle of its own. The act of severance from the original organism reduces this potency to act, so that the severed part has now its own soul. When the severed part is implanted in another body, there are three possibilities:

a) The transplanted part is not integrated into this body, but because of its close similarity to this body it is able to maintain life temporarily, e.g., long enough to permit the body to replace it gradually by its own cells. In this case, the transplanted part retains its own principle of life (or principles of life, if its cells lead separate lives) till it dies. This happens, for instance, in the case of skin grafts, except those between identical twins.

b) The transplanted part is so similar to the new body that it can be integrated into it, as happens in the case of skin grafts in identical twins. In this case the transplanted part does not retain its own vital principle, which is replaced by the actual soul of the new body.

c) The transplanted part is not integrated into the new body, but is so similar to it that it is able to survive indefinitely. In this case the part retains its own principle

[12] Concerning the human soul, however, cf. below, chap. 20.

of life, and the resulting whole is only accidentally unified. Probably the graft of branches of an apple tree upon a pear tree may be cited as an example.

Historical Notes

*39. The existence of the soul is denied by the mechanists who claim that life can be fully explained by physico-chemical processes; e.g., *Loeb* (1859–1924), *Le Dantec* (1869–1917), and *Rostand* (born 1894). All those who admit that life requires some other principle than mere physico-chemical energy are called vitalists. Some, such as *McDougall* (1871–1938), admit a special kind of vital energy (hormic activity, biotic energy, etc.); others, such as *Driesch* (1876–1941), an entelechy or formative agent of the organism and a psychoid or directive agent of activity. These theories do not explain the unity and immanence of life. The theory of life explained in the preceding pages is the Aristotelian-Thomistic theory of vitalism.

Concerning the nature of the soul, certain neo-vitalists, such as *Carrel* (1873–1944), seem to conceive the soul as a complete substance added to the organism as a directing principle, while for others, as *Broussais* (1772–1838), it appears to be something accidental. Among the ancient Greeks of the fifth century B.C. the soul was identified with one of the four elements, fire (*Democritus*), air (*Diogenes*), water (*Hippo*), or blood (*Critias*).[13] *Gassendi* (1592–1665) made the soul a subtle kind of a body.

Duns Scotus (*ca.* 1270–1308) admitted, in addition to the soul, the substantial form of corporeity. *Avicebron* or *Ibn Gebirol* (1020–1070) posited a substantial form

[13] Cf. Aristotle, *De anima,* bk. I, chap. 2.

for everyone of the generic and specific predicates. *Avicenna* or *Ibn Sina* (980–1037), *St. Albert the Great* (1193–1280), and several nineteenth century philosophers admit that chemical elements retain their substantial forms. More than one soul in every living body is admitted by those who affirm the existence of so-called cytodynamic principles in every living cell to explain its "independent life."

Regarding the extension and divisibility of the soul there is no agreement. Some ancient Greek philosophers as *Cleanthes* (310–232 B.C.) are said to have admitted even the divisibility of the human soul. *Scotus, Suarez* (1548–1617), and more recently *Nys* (1859–1926) held that all souls, except the human soul, are indirectly extended and divisible. *Cajetan* (1469–1534) and many others deny that any soul is even indirectly extended, but admit that the souls of plants and lower animals are indirectly divisible. *Plato, St. Augustine* (354–430), and more recently *Hugon* (1867–1929) and *Remer* (died 1910) deny that any soul is even indirectly divisible, but the last two admit that a soul which is actually one and potentially many may become actually many through the division of the body. It is not too clear whether or not *St. Thomas* rejected the indirect division of the souls of plants and lower types of animals.

SUMMARY

40. A body which is capable of vital actions must have a principle of life, for action follows being. This principle of life is called the soul.

The soul is not an accident, because living bodies are essentially different from nonliving bodies, and an essential difference cannot be based upon an accident.

Therefore, the soul belongs to the category of substance. However, the soul alone is not a complete substance, because otherwise the composite of body and soul could not be one substance. The soul is the substantial form of the living body, for it is the substantial principle which gives to the body the perfection of life. The soul is the only substantial form of the body, because otherwise the same potency would have to be actuated in the same order by two acts, which is impossible. Hence the forms of elements and compounds can be said to remain only virtually inasmuch as their activities remain. The soul is the substantial form of the whole body, for otherwise there would be more than one substantial form in the body. Accordingly, the cells of the body do not have their own vital principles. As a substantial form, the soul is essentially simple. Therefore, by its essence the soul is present in its entirety in the whole body and in every part of the body. But it is not present in each part with the totality of its powers, because the functioning of these powers may require special organs. Body and soul are really distinct, enter into a real composition, and do not need to be united by a common bond, because they are related to one another as potency to act.

The soul is traditionally defined as the first act of a natural organic body.

The soul is not directly extended, because it is not the subject of extension. It is not indirectly extended, because as a substantial form it is prior to the accident of extension. Consequently, the soul cannot be divided, whether directly or indirectly, because only that which is extended can be divided. However, the act of division of a living body may result in the actuation of a potential soul in the severed part if this part has a sufficient organization for the preservation of life. Therefore, we may say that a divisible living body has actually one soul but potentially many.

SUGGESTED READINGS

41. Aristotle, *De anima,* bk. II, chap. 1. The definition of the soul.

Thomas Aquinas, *In II De anima,* lect. 1–4; *De spiritualibus creaturis,* a. 4; *Summa theol.,* Ia, q. 75, aa. 1 and 5; q. 76, aa. 3, 4, 7, 8. The nature of the soul.

——— *In II De anima,* lect. 4 (no. 264 in Pirotta ed.); *Summa theol.,* Ia, q. 76, a. 8; *De spiritualibus creaturis,* a. 4; *In IV Sentent.,* d. 10, q. 3, a. 3, sol. 3 (no. 83 in Moos ed.). The divisibility of the soul.

R. P. Phillips, *Modern Thomistic Philosophy* (Westminster: 1950), vol. 2, chap. II of the philosophy of animate nature, pp. 185 ff. The divisibility of the soul.

Robert E. Brennan, *General Psychology* (New York: 1952), chaps. 4, 5. The theory of matter and form. The nature of organic life.

Franz Grégoire, "Note sur la Philosophie de l'Organisme," in *Revue philosophique de Louvain,* 1948, pp. 275 ff. Also available in booklet form. A study of the philosophical problems raised by biology.

CHAPTER 3

Operative Potencies

*** 42. In the preceding chapters we have seen that vital actions occur in those bodies which are called "living," and that a living body requires a vital principle or soul. We must now ask ourselves whether or not this vital principle is its own action. If the answer is in the negative, it will follow that the soul is in potency to vital action, and we shall have to investigate whether the soul is its own operative potency or operates through a potency or potencies which are really distinct from it. In the alternative we shall have to determine whether or not the soul has more than one operative potency, and if so, how these potencies are distinguished and diversified.

The Necessity of Admitting Operative Potency

The Soul Is Not Its Own Action. This assertion is clear from the fact that actions may come and go while the soul remains, for things which can be separated are really distinct.

*Moreover, if the soul were its own action, it would have to be its own "to be." For action is an act which is not ordered to any other act; hence if the soul were identical with its own action, it could not be in potency to "to be," but would have to be its own "to be." [1] Or to say it differently, action follows being; therefore that which is not its own "to be" is not its own "to act." But only God is His own "to be."

Accordingly, the soul must be conceived as in potency with respect to action. Thus the question arises whether the soul is in potency to action by its very essence or by something added to its essence; in other words, whether the soul is really distinct from its potency to act or its own operative potency.

The Soul Is Not Its Own Operative Potency. The real distinction between the soul and its capacity to act may be proved as follows:

*That which is not its own action cannot be its own operative potency, for a potency and its act must be in the same genus because they must be proportionate to each other. But the soul is a substantial form and therefore belongs to the genus of substance, whereas its action is not a substance but an accident. Therefore the soul's potency to act must also be an accident and, as such, really distinct from the soul, which is in the genus of substance.[2]

Moreover, by its very essence the soul is a substantial form and therefore in act as long as it exists. But if the operative potency of the soul were really the same as the soul, it, too, would always have to be in act. But experience shows that vital actions may be interrupted. Therefore, the soul is really distinct from its operative potency.[3]

*In calling the operative potencies accidents, we do not mean that they do not flow from the essence of the

[1] Cf. St. Thomas, *Summa theol.*, Ia, q. 54, a. 1.

[2] Cf. St. Thomas, *op. cit.*, q. 77, a. 1.

[3] Cf. St. Thomas, *ibid.*

soul, but only that they exist in the soul as in a subject which they perfect. In other words, they are so-called predicamental accidents, but predicable *properties.*

It should be noted that in asserting a real distinction between the soul and its operative potency we do not claim that the potency can exist separately. Real distinction does not mean the same as separability. A separable potency would not be an accident but a substance, because it would be capable of existing in itself. The operative potency should not be conceived as a being in its own right, but merely as a principle of activity in a substance.

43. *Solution of Some Difficulties.* Many modern writers consider operative potency, power, or faculty as just another medieval device to cover up ignorance of true science. One does not explain, they say, why a cat sees by saying that it has the power of sight. Hence such powers are to be rejected as useless relics of the past. To this we may reply that operative potencies are useless to explain why vital actions occur, but we must emphasize that they are not offered for this purpose. It is quite true that one does not explain why a cat sees by saying that it has the power of sight. But the reason why operative potency is admitted is the fact that vital actions occur *intermittently.*[4]

*A more serious objection lies in this that an operative potency itself is a perfection or act. For this would seem to imply that it will always have to be acting, which is against experience. The answer is that an operative potency may be called an act, but not an ultimate act, be-

[4] More than one operative potency will have to be admitted in the same subject if there is a plurality of specifically distinct actions.

cause it is ordered to a further act, namely, vital action. It may be said to be an act with respect to the soul since through it the soul is ordered to vital action. Nevertheless, *with respect to vital action, it is a potency,* to be perfected by the vital action. Therefore, it does not follow that the operative potency will always have to be acting.

*Nevertheless, this answer does not seem to be quite satisfactory, for one could argue: Potency and act must belong to the same genus; therefore, the soul and its operative potency must both be either accidents or substances, which is impossible. The solution of this argument demands that a distinction be made in the principle that potency and act must belong to the same genus. Potency and act must belong to the same genus if there is question of potency and act which are essentially ordered to each other. The soul, however, is *not essentially ordered to action,* but to the body as its substantial form, and to action only in a secondary way. Now it is the essential order which specifies the genus, and therefore the soul is the genus of substance. An operative potency, however, is essentially ordered to action and therefore belongs to the same general class as action, which is that of accident.[5]

*Again, one could urge that an operative potency which is really distinct from the substantial form is an accident and therefore can never cause a new substance, because cause and effect must be proportionate. But the reproductive potency causes the new living body, which is a substance. This objection stems from a misconception of the true nature of substance. Substance is not an inert substratum, but a *dynamic reality* acting through its op-

[5] Cf. A. Rozwadowski, "De distinctione potentiarum a substantia," *Gregorianum,* 1935, vol. 16, pp. 272 ff.

erative potency as a quasi-instrument. Acting on its own, the operative potency could never produce a new substance. But the operative potency acts by virtue of the substantial form, so that it really is the substance which is acting. Hence the action may terminate in a new substance without any violation of the principle that cause and effect must be proportionate. Note, however, that the operative potency is not an instrument in the strict sense of the term, for otherwise the substantial form would have to be immediately operative in its causal influence upon the potency. The operative potency has its quasi-instrumental nature from the very fact that it flows from the soul as its property.[6]

One or Many Operative Potencies?

44. Now that we have established the real distinction between the soul and its operative potency, we must face the question whether one operative potency is sufficient for all the vital activities of a living body or if a diversity of potencies is necessary. However, before this question can be answered, we must first determine the criterion by which operative potencies can be diversified and distinguished.

Operative Potencies Are Diversified by the Activity to Which They Are Directed. By the diversification of operative potencies we do not mean the distinction between potencies which results from the fact that they are found in distinct individuals or distinct species. Obviously, John's power of growth is individually distinct from that of Peter, and that of a lion is specifically distinct from

[6] Cf. St. Thomas, *In IV Sentent.*, d.12, q.1, a.2, sol. 2. (no. 76 in Moos ed.).

that of man because of the individual or specific distinction of the subjects to which they belong. Our concern is with the diversity of operative potencies *as potencies*, i.e., the diversity which flows from their own nature and not from that of their subject. The criterion for this diversity lies in the very activity to which the potency is directed. The proof is as follows:

By its very nature an operative potency is a potency directed to the production of an action. But a potency and its act must be proportionate to each other. Therefore, a diversity of vital activity presupposes a diversity of operative potencies.

*The objection may be raised that nothing is essentially determined by anything which is posterior to it. But action is posterior to operative potency; therefore, it does not determine the operative potency. To this we reply that action may be considered in the order of execution and in the order of intention. With respect to execution, action is posterior to the operative potency from which it emanates, but in the order of intention it is prior to the potency, for it is the end to which the potency is directed. It is in this order, which is the order of *final causality*, that action determines the operative potency.

Immediately, however, the question arises as to what diversifies vital activity. What makes vital actions diverse? [7]

Actions Are Diversified by the Nature of Their Objects. The reason is that any action is essentially directed to its object. Sight, for instance, is essentially directed to the colored, growth to quantity, etc. An action which would

[7] The thesis is valid not only for the vital actions of a living body, but for all actions of any finite substance.

not be directed to an object would be an action without a final cause. But according to the principle of finality, every agent acts for an end.[8] Therefore, actions are diversified by their objects, because the object is the end of the action.[9]

It is to be noted, however, that not every diversity of objects will result in a diversity of actions. Objects which are accidentally different, such as a white flower, a white man, and a white swan, do not result in a diversity of actions, because *as objects* of sight they are not formally different. For this reason the thesis states that a *diversity of nature* of the objects as objects diversifies actions. Or, as it is usually expressed, different formal objects diversify actions. With respect to that to which the act of sight is immediately directed, there is no difference beween a white flower, a white man, and a white swan. Sight is essentially directed to the colored and not to the material objects which are colored.

Now that we have found the criterion of the diversification of operative potencies, it will not be difficult to answer the first question—does the soul have one or many operative potencies? Obviously, our answer will have to remain somewhat vague, because we are speaking about the soul in general and not about the human or the animal soul. The reply is: There will be as many operative potencies as there are formally different objects to which the activity of the soul is directed. Later we shall examine how many operative potencies there are in each of the different grades of life. Nevertheless, it should al-

[8] Concerning this principle, cf. the author's *Introduction to the Science of Metaphysics,* chap. 14.

[9] In so-called passive operative potencies, such as sight, the object is also the principle which actuates the potency.

ready be clear that the objects, for instance, of nutrition and understanding are irreducible and therefore require distinct operative potencies. Hence we may say that the operative potencies of the soul are not one but many.

*Origin of the Operative Potencies

45. Regarding the origin of operative potencies[10] the following brief remarks may be made.

In the strict sense of the term the soul is not the efficient cause of its own operative potencies. For the soul is not immediately operative; hence to produce its own potencies it would need another potency and so on to infinity.

Operative potencies do not result from the actuation of receptive potencies in the soul by an extrinsic agent, as is the case with accidental modifications. Operative potencies are properties of the soul, and nothing can be said to be in potency with respect to that which of necessity flows from its very nature.

In the strict sense of the term the external agent which causes the soul is also the efficient cause of the soul's operative potencies. For in producing an effect the cause coproduces also the properties of this effect.

Nevertheless, in a sense the soul may be said to be "active" with respect to its operative potencies. For the soul itself is prior in nature to them and as such actually demands these potencies as its properties. In this sense, the operative potencies are said to emanate from the soul by natural resultance.[11]

The operative potencies emanate from the soul alone and not from the composite. Although most vital poten-

[10] The same remarks apply to all properties of any finite substance.

[11] Cf. St. Thomas, *Summa theol.,* Ia, q.77, a.7.

cies are organic, as we shall see in the course of this study, and therefore have the composite of body and soul as their subject, the soul alone is "active" in respect to them. For a thing is active insofar as it is in act. But the composite is in act through the soul.[12]

Supposite, Nature, Operative Potencies and Action

46. The distinction made between the body and the soul should not make us lose sight of the essential unity of the living body. While we make a real distinction between them, we do not wish to claim that they exist as complete and independent entities, but only that they are really distinct principles which by their union form one essentially unified living body.[13]

In a similar way, it must be stressed that the Aristotelian-Thomistic concept of the operative potencies does not consider them to be as independently existing psychological entities, but only as qualities, in the wide sense of the term, by virtue of which the soul is capable of acting intermittently and diversely.

The relationship of potencies, body, soul, supposite, and activity may be expressed as follows:

The individual substance which is the supposite is the only *principle which* acts. The supposite acts through its nature, which therefore is the *principle by means of which* all action occurs. The nature of a living material being is composed of body and soul; hence body and soul separately are partial or *incomplete principles* by means of

[12] Cf. St. Thomas, *Summa theol.*, Ia, q.77, a.6.

[13] For reasons which we shall study later, the human soul is capable of existing independently of the body, but not even the human soul, taken by itself, is a complete being.

which the supposite acts.[14] Because no finite being is immediately operative, its nature cannot be the direct principle of action, but merely is the *remote principle* by means of which the supposite acts. The *immediate principles* by means of which the supposite acts are its operative potencies. Strictly speaking, therefore, we should not say that our intellect understands or that our ear hears, but that we understand by means of our intellect and hear by means of our potency of hearing. It would be rather cumbersome, however, always to use this correct way of speaking, and therefore brevity is a valid excuse for the use of the shorter formula. Hence when in subsequent chapters we are going to deal with the various operative potencies of living bodies, care should be taken not to lose sight of the utter dependence of all operative potencies upon the supposite, which is the one and only independently existing and operating subject.

Historical Notes

*47. The real distinction of the soul from its operative potencies is rejected by the nominalists (*William of Ockam*, 1280–1348), *Descartes* (1595–1650), *de Condillac* (1715–1780), and the empiricists in general, who consider faculties as vain substitutes for scientific explanations. While it may be true that in the period of the decline of Scholasticism many philosophers spoke about operative potencies as explanations of vital activities, the same cannot be asserted of *Aristotle*[15] and *St. Thomas.*

[14] If any operation of a living body is intrinsically independent of matter, the soul alone will be the complete remote principle by means of which the supposite acts.

[15] Cf. W. D. Ross, *Aristotle* (London: 1953), chap. V, p. 133.

Since the revival of Thomistic philosophy the true character of operative potencies has once more been emphasized—their purpose is to explain why vital action occurs intermittently and is diversified. Many modern psychologists still shy away from the use of the term "faculty" because of its adverse historical connotations. In practice, however, they have returned to it, for they admit that the mind operates according to certain native patterns, each of which represents a general tendency to act in a particular way. Such "patterns" can be explained only if we admit the distinction of the soul from its operative potencies.

Duns Scotus distinguished the operative potencies from the soul by means of his formal distinction which is actual on the part of the soul.

SUMMARY

48. The soul is not its own action, as is clear from the fact that actions may come and go while the soul remains. *Moreover, to be its own action the soul would have to be its own "to be," because action is an ultimate act and not ordered to any further act. Therefore, the soul must be conceived as in potency with respect to action.

The operative potency of the soul is really distinct from it. For a potency and its act must be proportionate to each other; but the soul is in the genus of substance while action is an accident; therefore, the soul's potency to act must be an accident and as such really distinct from the soul.

More than one operative potency must be admitted if in the soul there is a diversity of irreducible activity, for potency and act must be proportionate to each other. Hence operative potencies are diversified by the actions to which they are directed. The actions themselves are diversified by the nature of the objects to which they are directed. Every action is directed to an object, because every agent acts for an end. If actions, therefore, are directed to objects of an irreducibly different nature, they are irreducibly or essentially different.

*Operative potencies are properties of the soul and therefore efficiently coproduced by the agent which causes the soul. The soul itself, however, may be said to be "active" with respect to its operative potencies insofar as being prior in nature to them it actually demands these potencies as its properties.

The real distinction between body and soul does not mean that body and soul exist as autonomous and complete beings, for body and soul are essentially unified. Likewise, the real distinction between the soul and its operative potencies should not make us lose sight of the fact that these potencies are not independent entities acting in their own right, but merely principles by means of which the supposite acts. Strictly speaking, only the supposite or complete individual substance is that which acts; the nature is the remote principle by means of which the supposite acts; and operative potencies are the proximate principles by means of which the supposite acts.

SUGGESTED READINGS

49. Aristotle, *De anima,* bk. I, chap. 5.

Thomas Aquinas, *Summa theol.,* Ia, q. 77, a. 1; *De anima,* a. 12, 13. Distinction of soul from its operative potencies.

——— *Summa theol.,* Ia, q. 77, a. 2, 3; *In II De anima,* lect. 6. Plurality and diversification of potencies.

——— *Summa theol.,* Ia, q. 77, a. 4; *In I Sentent.,* d. 3, q. 4, a. 2. Emanation of operative potencies from soul.

Henri Renard, *The Philosophy of Man* (Milwaukee: 1948), chap. III, pp. 53–62.

C. Spearman, *Psychology Down the Ages* (New York: 1937), I, chap. XI. A vindication of the faculties.

Mortimer Adler, *What Man Has Made of Man* (New York: 1936), pp. 79 ff. The erroneous concept of faculty and modern psychology.

SECTION II

Vegetative Life

50. In this section we shall consider the philosophical problems of life as it manifests itself on the vegetative level. Vegetative life is found not only in plants, but also in animals and men. Hence many of our considerations will apply also to men and animals insofar as they have vegetative life.

At the beginning of our study of vegetative life we cannot define plants as "organisms endowed with vegetative life only," because it remains to be seen whether or not plants have also sentient and even rational life. We shall have to be satisfied with the vague description of plants as such things as trees, grasses, shrubs, etc., or organisms which in general have a constructive metabolism.

It should be understood, too, that it is not our task to determine such questions as whether, for example, the yellow fever virus is a living body or merely a chemical substance, or whether a euglena is a plant or an animal. Such questions are not concerned with the nature of vegetative life, but with the exact boundaries between the living and the lifeless or between plants and animals.

The section is divided into two chapters. In the first, we shall study the nature of vegetative operative potencies; in the second, the nature of the purely vegetative soul. This order is chosen, because it is through its activity that the nature of a being reveals itself to the mind.

Schematic Division

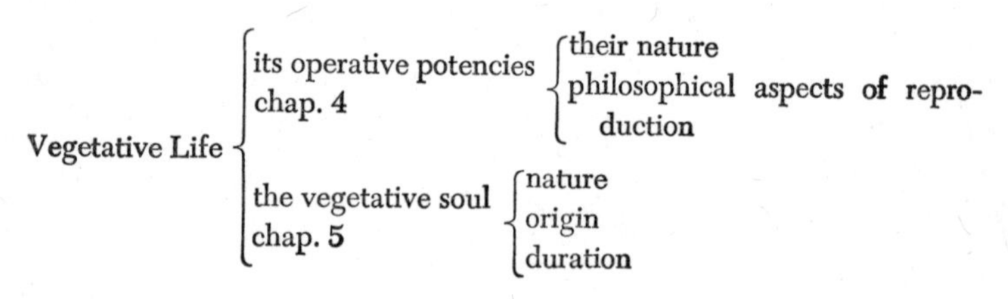

CHAPTER 4

The Operative Potencies of Vegetative Life

Existence and Nature of Operative Potencies of Vegetative Life

*** 51. *Existence of Distinct Vegetative Potencies.* Regarding the *existence* of operative potency on the level of vegetative life, there should not be any special difficulty after the considerations offered in the preceding chapters. The native physico-chemical forces active in a plant are subordinated to the good of the whole in such a way that the whole is self-perfective. But, as we have seen in no. 42, the soul is not immediately operative; therefore, it does not immediately influence these forces, but subordinates them by means of its operative potency. The three ways in which the physico-chemical forces are subordinated to the good of the whole are called nutrition, growth, and reproduction, as should be clear from Chapter One.

Nutrition, growth, and reproduction require *distinct* operative potencies, because they are directed to distinct objects. Nutrition is directed to the conversion of non-living matter into living matter; growth to the quantity and fully developed structure which are due to the nature of the plant in question; and reproduction to the generation of new individual living substances.

Plants Do Not Have Operative Potencies Implying Awareness. It would be irrational to admit potencies implying awareness in plants if they do not show any signs of awareness, for one does not admit anything for which there is no evidence. But in plants there are no signs of activity involving awareness. Therefore, we cannot admit that plants have any potencies implying awareness, such as sensation and intellection.

The *minor* premise of this argument is attacked by opponents who point to so-called tropisms in plants, i.e., to the way they respond to physical stimuli. For instance, the leaves of a plant show heliotropism, for they turn towards the sun; the roots are geotropic, for no matter how the seed is put into the soil, the roots grow down and not up; the "mimosa pudica" shows itself "sensitive" to touch. These facts would settle the argument in favor of sensation if they could be explained *only* as responses following upon the *awareness* of the physical stimulus by which they are provoked. But if these facts can be explained equally well *without* awareness, as purely physical and mechanical responses to physical stimuli, this explanation has to be preferred, because it would be unreasonable to assume the working of a higher cause for effects which can be explained equally well by a lower cause. Now it seems that the various forms of tropism occurring in plants can be explained at least equally well without the plant's awareness of physical stimuli.[1] We say

[1] For an explanation see Thomas V. Moore in the book quoted in no. 56.

"at least, equally well," for, as a matter of fact, plant tropisms lack something of the typical response following upon the awareness of a stimulus in animals. In a plant the responses to a stimulus are typically *invariable*, whereas responses which follow upon awareness are characterized by a definite lack of uniformity. Sunlight, for instance, will always cause a plant to turn its leaves to the sun, but when a dog sees his master, the reaction may vary between an exuberant greeting and complete indifference.

Moreover, in animals and men there are highly complex organs for the perception of stimuli, while in plants there is no trace of any sense organs. Hence it does not seem very likely that they could be capable of performing the complex operation of sensation with the relatively simple organic structure which is at their disposal.

52. *The Organic Nature of the Vegetative Potencies.* By an organic potency is meant an operative potency which is intrinsically dependent upon an organ in the very exercise of its activity. Dependence upon an organ may be either intrinsic or extrinsic. In the case of *intrinsic* dependence, the operative potency together with the organ constitutes the complete immediate principle or *cause* of activity. In *extrinsic* dependence the operative potency alone is the immediate principle of activity, but cannot exercise its function unless first an organic *condition* is fulfilled. At first sight the difference between intrinsic and extrinsic dependence may appear rather trivial, because in both cases the organ is necessary. Nevertheless, from a philosophical point of view the distinction is of great importance. In intrinsic dependence upon an organ, the organ itself is the coprinciple of activity, and the op-

erative potency and the organ are one principle of operation. In extrinsic dependence, the organ is merely a necessary condition. Let us illustrate the difference with a comparison. I am seated in a rowboat which is heavily loaded, and because of the low tide sinks deep into the mud near the shore. My efforts to move the boat are in vain. A friend sees my plight and comes to my rescue. Together we pull the oars and succeed in moving the boat. In moving the boat, I am intrinsically dependent upon my friend—we are coprinciples of the boat's motion. If no friend turns up, but I wait till the tide comes in before pulling the oars, I alone am the principle of the motion of the boat, but the incoming tide is a necessary condition. Like most comparisons, this one is not quite exact, for when my friend and I move the boat, there are two subjects and two *acts* of pulling, although there is only one *effect.* In intrinsic dependence upon an organ, there is only one subject and only one principle of activity, which is formed of the potency and the organ. The potency is, as it were, the form, and the organ is, as it were, the matter of this principle of activity.[2]

Whether an operative potency is intrinsically or extrinsically dependent upon an organ may be discovered by paying attention to the *object* of its activity, for, as we have seen in no. 44, the nature of the object specifies the operative potency. So if this object is something material as such, matter must enter into the very nature of the operating principle. In other words, in such a case, the complete operating principle of the vital action is the organ as "informed" by the potency.

After these preliminaries we are in a position to prove the organic nature of the vegetative potencies. This *proof* is as follows:

[2] Cf. St. Thomas, *In II De anima,* lect. 24 (no. 555 in Pirotta ed.).

An operative potency whose object is something material as such is organic. But the operative potencies of vegetative life have as their object something material as such. Therefore, they are organic.

The *major* premise is evident from the preceding considerations. Regarding the *minor,* nutrition, growth, and reproduction are concerned with the living body as a body; therefore, their object is something material as material.

After these few brief remarks about the operative potencies of vegetative life in general, we must now devote our attention to them in particular. The first two, however, do not offer any special philosophical problems. In nutrition, any matter which is assimilated by the living body loses its own substantial form, which is replaced by the substantial form of the living body. In regard to growth, the individual substance of the living body remains essentially the same inasmuch as the substantial form of the individual remains the same. Reproduction, however, offers certain philosophical problems and therefore deserves to be studied more extensively.

Philosophical Aspects of Reproduction

53. *Biological Data.* Many of the facts needed for a correct philosophical view of what happens in reproduction have become known only through modern biology. This is not surprising because reproductive cells are exceedingly small and therefore observable only by means of the microscope and other modern techniques. The following paragraphs summarize the pertinent data which must be known for a correct philosophical idea of reproduction.

Reproduction may be *gametic* or *agametic* according as it takes place with or without special reproductive cells.

Types of agametic reproduction are the cell divisions called mitosis and amitosis; gemmation or budding, in which cells accumulate around a part of the organism; and sporogenesis, in which new individual living bodies arise from spores, i.e., nucleated masses of protoplasm. In gametic reproduction gametes or germ cells develop in one or different individuals. Usually a union of different types of cells is necessary—a sperm unites with an ovum to form a unicellular organism which develops into an adult individual.

Contrary to what most of the ancients held the reproductive cells are alive before they separate from the parent organism; both types of cells, the male sperm as well as the female ovum, are active in the process of reproduction; the fecundated ovum begins at once to exercise the vital activities of nutrition and growth; and in certain cases both types of reproductive cells may begin to develop even without being united to the other type of reproductive cell.[3]

Philosophical Aspects. With respect to reproduction by *cell division,* we may refer to no. 37—before the division, the soul is actually one but potentially many, and the act of division makes the souls actually many.[4] In *gemmation* and *sporogenesis* the soul of the original organism is the soul of the cells forming the bud or spore till the bud or spore begins to lead an independent life. At the moment when independent life begins, the bud or spore is

[3] This may happen either naturally, as in the case of drones, or artificially, as in the case of frog's eggs, which may begin to develop when subjected to mechanical shock.

[4] If in the generation of man there is a rational soul from the first moment of fecundation, the explanation would have to be different with respect to man. Concerning this question, see below, chap. 20.

actuated by a new soul, which is educed from the potency of matter.

In *gametic reproduction,* the germ cells are informed by the soul of the parent organism to which they belong as long as they form part of this organism. When they are separated from it, the germ cells need a new vital principle or soul, for they continue to live. Even in the case of animals and men, this soul must be considered to be of a purely vegetative nature, because the only type of life manifested by the cell is vegetative. The soul of the reproductive cell is of a *transitory* nature, for its function is to keep the cell alive and capable of acting when it is united with the other type of germ cell. It is, moreover, of an *instrumental* nature, because it serves the parent organism in the production of a new individual of the same species as the parent. Because of its instrumental nature, it is possible for the vegetative soul to produce an organism endowed with a higher kind of life than the germ cell itself has; for an instrument shares in the causality of the principal cause. At the moment of fecundation the transitory and instrumental souls of the germ cells are replaced by the vital principle of the zygote, which develops into the new individual. This soul of the zygote comes from the potency of matter, at least in the case of plants and animals.[5] Thus we see that in this process of reproduction there is a succession of souls leading to the soul of the embryo.

Note. The problems of spontaneous generation and evolution, which are often considered together with the process of reproduction, will be studied at the end of this treatise in Section Five.

[5] Whether in man the fecundated ovum has a rational soul from the first moment of fecundation, see below, chap. 20.

Historical Notes

*54. The existence of operative potencies of vegetative life is denied by the materialists (*Haeckel*) who explain the activity of plants in a purely mechanical or chemical way; also by *Descartes* and *Tongiorgi* (1820–1865), who conceive plants as complex machines whose activity is directed from without.

Suarez denies that nutrition and growth require distinct operative potencies. *Aristotle* ascribed nutrition and reproduction to the same faculty.

Empedocles (*ca.* 490–435 B.C.), *Plato, Leibnitz* (1646–1716) and the hylozoists admit sense life in plants. In more recent times, *Wagner* (born 1869) has attributed to plants sensation, memory, and even a kind of unconscious reasoning. The modern tendency, however, is rather in the opposite direction and aims at explaining animal reactions attributed to awareness in a purely mechanical way.

Regarding reproduction, *Aristotle* and *St. Thomas* thought that the reproductive elements were nonliving; that only the male element is active; and that the fecundated "ovum" does not begin to live until some time after fecundation. Hence they endowed the reproductive elements with a nonliving substantial form, which at the moment of fecundation was replaced by the substantial form of the composite. As soon as the composite was sufficiently disposed for life, its substantial form was replaced by a vital principle of vegetative life. In the case of animals, this vegetative soul was replaced by a sensitive soul as soon as the organism was sufficiently disposed for sense life. With respect to man, the sensitive soul in its turn was replaced by a rational soul. Although this explanation of reproduction is antiquated, at least in part,[6] its main principle remains untouched by our better knowledge of the pertinent facts—in reproduction by means of germ cells there is a succession of substantial forms.

SUMMARY

55. The physico-chemical forces of a plant act in subordination to the good of the whole; hence we must admit operative potencies of vegetative life, for the soul does not act immediately but by means of operative potencies. These potencies are nutrition, growth, and reproduction, which are really distinct because they are directed towards specifically distinct and irreducible objects.

Plants cannot be said to have any powers of sensation or intellection, because they show no evidence of sensation or intellection and have no organs analogous to the sense organs of animals. Their tropisms are not a proof of sense life, because they can be explained, it seems, on a purely physical basis and do not show the characteristic lack of uniformity displayed in responses following upon awareness.

The operative potencies of vegetative life are organic, i.e., intrinsically dependent upon matter, because their object is the body as a material thing.

In gametic reproduction, the soul of the parent organism is the vital principle of the germ cells as long as these cells form part of the parent organism. As soon as they are separated from it, the germ cells obtain their own vital principle, which is always purely vegetative. This vital principle is of a transitory and instrumental nature, because its function is to keep the cells alive and

[6] Regarding the question whether in the human embryo there is a succession of souls, see chap. 20.

capable of acting till they are united with each other, and to serve the parent organism in reproducing itself. When the male and female cells unite, the composite is actuated by a vital principle of its own.

SUGGESTED READINGS

56. Aristotle, *De anima,* bk. II, chap. 2, 4.

Thomas Aquinas, *Summa theol.,* Ia, q. 78, a. 2; *De anima,* a. 13. The vegetative potencies.

——— *De potentia,* q. 3, a. 9, ad 9. "Reproduction."

W. D. Ross, *Aristotle* (London: 1953), chap. III, p. 102; chap. IV, pp. 118 ff.; chap. V, p. 135. Growth, nutrition and reproduction.

Thomas V. Moore, *Dynamic Psychology* (Philadelphia: 1926), pp. 79 ff. Tropisms.

W. Gordon Whaley e.a., *Principles of Biology* (New York: 1954), pp. 98 ff., 258 ff., 283 ff. Reproductive processes.

CHAPTER 5

The Vegetative Soul

*** In this chapter we shall consider briefly the nature of the purely vegetative soul, its origin and duration.

The Nature of the Vegetative Soul

57. The nature of the vegetative soul is not directly open for inspection by the intellect, but can be determined from its operations in accordance with the metaphysical principle that action follows being.

The Vegetative Soul Is Material. By calling the plant soul material we do not intend to say that it is composed of matter, but only that it is intrinsically dependent upon matter for its very existence. The proof is as follows:

If the operations of a plant are intrinsically dependent upon matter, the vegetative soul is material. But a plant depends in all its operations upon matter. Therefore, the vegetative soul is material. The *major* premise follows from the principle that action is in accordance with being; the *minor* was proved in the preceding chapter.

The Vegetative Soul Is Not Subsistent. Subsistent is that which can exist by itself or autonomously. But the vegetative soul can exist only in dependence upon the body of the plant; hence it is not subsistent. It is the composite of body and soul of a plant which subsists or exists as a substance; the component parts of this composite whole are merely coprinciples of this substance.

The Origin of the Vegetative Soul

58. Because the purely vegetative soul is intrinsically dependent upon matter, its origin has to be explained in the same way as that of other material substantial forms. The Thomistic position [1] in this question may be summed up as follows:

Coming-to-be must be proportionate to "to be." But, strictly speaking, the "to be" of a material substance belongs to the composite and not to the component parts which cannot exist separately. The substantial form is not called a being as if it exists in its own right, but only because through it the composite is. Hence no material substantial form may be spoken of as coming to be in the proper sense of the term. However, such a form may be said to come to be *indirectly*, i.e., insofar as it is part of the composite whole which comes to be. The composite comes to be when it is actuated by a new form. This new form is "*educed from the potency of matter,*" which means that it is not added to matter from without, but is a mere actuation of the potency of matter. Matter is in potency to all substantial forms, but this potency needs to be actuated by an external agent.[2] This actuation takes place when the agent introduces in the body material conditions which render matter indisposed for its present form but dispose it for a new form.

[1] Concerning the origin of the material substantial form, see P. Hoenen, *De origine formae materialis* (Rome: 1951).

[2] What is in potency to an act cannot give itself this act, but needs to be actuated by an agent, i.e., a being in act.

Accordingly, a plant soul is educed from the potency of matter as soon as matter is sufficiently organized for vegetative life. In the case of multiplication of plants by mere division, the dividing agent causes the transition from potency to act in the severed part. In the cause of multiplication of living bodies by the union of reproductive cells, the parent organisms whose activity leads to this union may be considered to be the external agents disposing matter for actuation by a new soul. In the case of fertilization of a reproductive cell by mechanical or chemical means, the sources of these forces are the agents disposing matter for actuation by a new soul.

The Duration of the Vegetative Soul

59. From the preceding considerations, it will be easy to derive the answer to the question how long the vegetative soul continues to exist and how it ceases to be. Because the vegetative soul depends upon the body for its very existence, it *will cease to be when the plant ceases to be as a plant,* i.e., at the moment of death of the plant.

Death means the corruption of a living whole, and corruption is the decomposition of a composite whole into its parts. Hence only that which is composed can be *directly* subject to death. However, we may speak about the death of a plant soul in the same way as we may speak about its coming-to-be. Just as this soul is said to come to be indirectly insofar as it is a part of the whole which comes to be, so also may it be said to die *indirectly* insofar as it forms part of a whole which dies.

At the death of the plant its vital principle ceases to actuate the body of the plant, and another substantial form (or forms) is educed from the potency of matter. The vegetative soul is said to be "reduced to the potency of matter." This expression means that the soul is not annihilated,[3] and that the material principle of the plant can again be informed by a vegetative soul if the proper dispositions are given to matter.

Historical Notes

*60. The materiality of the plant soul was denied by those who conceived every soul as a spirit, a doctrine usually attributed to the so-called "School of Montpellier."

Plato and *Avicenna* maintained that souls and other substantial forms come from without.

The root of both positions lies in the misconception that a material substantial form is not a mere principle of being but a being in its own right.

SUMMARY

61. The soul of a plant is material in the sense that it is intrinsically dependent upon matter for its very existence. Hence it is not a subsistent form. It does not come into existence directly, but only indirectly insofar as it is a part of the plant which comes to be. The plant soul is not introduced into the plant from without, but educed from the potency of matter. Because the plant soul depends upon the body for its very existence, it will cease to be when the plant dies. However, it is not annihilated, but merely reduced to potency.

[3] The death of a plant does not mean its "reduction" to nonbeing in the absolute sense, but merely its decomposition. Hence the soul of a plant is not annihilated, because the plant itself is not annihilated.

SUGGESTED READINGS

62. Aristotle, *Metaphysica,* bk. VII, chaps. 7, 8.

Thomas Aquinas, *Summa theol.,* Ia, q. 45, a. 8; q. 65, a. 4; *De potentia,* q. 3, a. 8; *Contra gentes,* bk. II, chap. 86. The origin of the material form.

——— *Quodlibet.* IX, a. 11. The origin of the vegetative soul.

——— *Ibid.; De anima,* a. 14. Direct and indirect corruption.

Raymond J. Anable, *Philosophical Psychology* (New York: 1949), chap. four. The nature of the plant soul.

SECTION III

Sense Life

63. From the preceding chapters we know that plants have a vital principle or soul, for they exercise the vital functions of nutrition, growth, and reproduction. Because it is manifest that animals and men have the same functions, it follows that they, too, have a vital principle or soul. At present, however, we wish to investigate whether or not animals and men have other vital functions of a different nature, which would require a different kind of soul. Experience shows that they have sensation and appetite; hence we shall have to study the nature of these operations in order to arrive at knowledge of the nature of their soul. However, in view of the fact that, apart from sensation, there is also another type of cognition called intellection, the study of sensation will be preceded by that of cognition in general. The same will be done with respect to sense appetite, because, apart from the appetite based upon sensation, there is also an appetite that is consequent upon understanding.

SENSE LIFE

Schematic Division

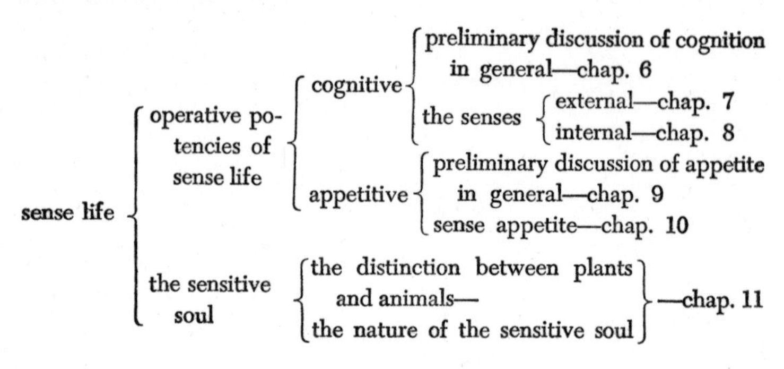

CHAPTER 6

Cognition in General

The Nature of Cognition

*** 64. *Union of Subject and Object.* The meaning of the term "cognition" is clear to everyone, at least in a confused way, from personal experience. It is the task of the metaphysical science of life to determine its nature more accurately by an analysis of our own personal acts of knowing. This experience shows that knowing always implies that in some way or other the knowing subject is united with the object of his knowledge. When I see a building its color somehow is in me; when I hear a symphony orchestra playing its sound is in me; when I think about the atomic bomb it is in me; etc. Without some kind of *union* knowledge obviously is unthinkable.

However, in order that a cognitive union may take place it is necessary for the object to possess some determinations or forms, for a thing which is altogether indeterminate cannot be known.[1] Thus the cognition of an object will always be cognition of its determinations or forms, so that the knowing subject must somehow be *united with the form* or forms of the object. We say

[1] At least not in itself. It may be known insofar as it implies a relationship to something determined.

"somehow." Not every kind of union is sufficient. For instance, if a lump of modeling clay is given the shape or form of a rabbit, there is a union of the clay with the form of the rabbit, but no one will claim that the clay knows the rabbit. The clay has the form of the rabbit *as its own form*. In cognition, on the other hand, the form of the object becomes the form of the knower in such a way that the knower does not have to give up his own form, but in addition to his own form acquires the form of the object. The form of the object is in the knower *as the form of the object*. When, for instance, I look at a ring, the form of the ring is united with me, not as my own form, but as the form of the ring. I retain my identity, but in addition to being, say, this man Peter, I become a ring because I have acquired the form of a ring. It was in this sense that Aristotle said that the soul in a way becomes all things—physically the knower remains what he is, but cognitively he becomes whatever is the object of his knowledge.[2]

The Knower and the Object Known Retain Their Identity. It is to be noted that cognition is not the only way in which a subject can become united with something else. Even on the inanimate level we find that objects can become united with something else. A lump of clay may be shaped into a statue and thus receive an accidental form which previously it did not have; a body may undergo a substantial change and thus obtain a new substantial form. In both cases, the acquisition of the new form is achieved at the cost of a loss of identity of the *subject*. For in acquiring the new form the subject has to

[2] *De anima*, bk. III, chap. 8 (431b 21). Cf. St. Thomas, *Summa theol.*, Ia, q.14, a.1.

give up its own form, and to this extent it *loses its identity.*

On the vegetative level also, there is a tendency to become united with other things. In the process of nutrition extraneous substances become united with the organism. Again, however, the union is brought about at the cost of a loss of identity, though this time it is the *object* which loses its identity. The vegetative subject succeeds in uniting with the object upon which it feeds, but does so at the expense of the object, which is forced to give up its own form and thus *loses its identity.* Accordingly, unitive processes below the cognitive order do not achieve a union without destroying either one or the other of the uniting elements.

In the cognitive order, however, a union between a subject and an object is achieved in such a way that *both retain their form and their identity.* In knowing, man remains man, but in addition he becomes the object of his act of knowing; the object does not cease to exist, but is given an additional mode of existence in the knowing subject.

Twofold Existence of Knower and Object Known. Both the knower and the object known have a double "to be." The knowing *subject* continues to be in the physical order as this man Peter or that dog Fido, but in addition to his physical mode of being he acquires a new mode of being in the cognitive or intentional [3] order as this ring, that tree, or whatever else may be the object of his knowledge, for he has obtained the form of this object.

The *object* known, likewise, has a twofold "to be." It

[3] Intentional here does not mean "deliberate"; it refers to the order in which a subject is not entirely "fixed," but capable of "stretching out towards" (*intendo*) other things, i.e., the cognitive order.

exists in the physical order as this ring or that tree, just as it did before being known. In addition, it exists cognitively or intentionally in the knowing subject as the object known. The physical "to be's" of the knower and the object remain as distinct as they were before the act of cognition, but the cognitive "to be" of the object is identical with the cognitive "to be" of the knower; for the knower as a knower has become the object known.

At first sight, it may seem contradictory that a subject be identical with an object from which it is distinct; yet this would have to be asserted in the case of a subject knowing something other than itself. There would be contradiction, indeed, if we asserted that the knower and the object were simultaneously physically identical and physically distinct. But our contention is that the knower and the object may be *physically distinct* while they are *cognitively identical,* and this does not imply any contradiction.

65. *The Foundation of Cognition.* From the preceding considerations the difference between a knowing and a nonknowing being should be manifest—the knowing being is not limited to being itself but capable of being other than itself, while the nonknowing being is limited to being itself. What is the reason why certain beings are capable of being other than themselves? Above, we have seen that in knowing the knower has in addition to his own form the form of the thing known, i.e., the knower has the form of the other as the form of the other. Hence our question may be formulated in this way: what makes some beings capable of having the form of the other as the form of the other?

It should be clear that this capacity means an *absence*

of limitation with respect to form. From general metaphysical principles[4] it is known that the principle of limitation is potency and that the principle of limitation with respect to form is the potency called matter. Therefore, it follows that freedom from matter, or *immateriality, is the foundation of cognition* or the reason why a knower can have the form of another in addition to his own.

Matter as matter is potency and can receive only as potency, so that any form received by matter as such, or materially, actuates it in the sense that it makes it matter actually having this form and no other. When modeling clay is given the form of a rabbit it cannot at the same time have any other form. Anything which receives in a purely material way, as a passive potency, is limited to one form at a time. A knower, however, has, in addition to his own form, the form of another. Therefore, the knower does not receive the form of the other insofar as he is in potency with respect to this form, for to receive a form potentially is to receive it materially. The knower receives the form of the object insofar as he is in act, as actually having a form. In other words, cognition is not the act of a being in potency but the *act of a being in act.* Cognition, therefore, is an *immanent* action.

*It is to be noted that although cognition does not *consist in* a transition from potency to act, nevertheless an act of cognition may *require* a transition from potency to act. If a knowing subject is not its own action, but acts by means of operative potencies, it is in potency to cognition before actually knowing. But a finite being is not its own action, and therefore in such a being an act

[4] Cf. the author's *Introduction to the Science of Metaphysics,* chap. 3.

of cognition does not occur without a transition of its cognitive potency from potency to act.

When we say that *immateriality* is the foundation of cognition, the term "immateriality" should not be misunderstood. Immateriality may mean *absolute,* both intrinsic and extrinsic, independence of matter. In this sense, it is synonymous with the purely spiritual and applies only to God and other pure spirits (if there are any created pure spirits). Immateriality may also mean the *intrinsic* independence of matter which is proper to the human intellect, as we shall see in Chapter Twelve. In this sense there is still question of spirituality in a strict sense, for there is essential independence of matter. But immateriality may mean also that a subject which is intrinsically dependent upon matter for its existence and operation is *not* so *totally immersed* in matter that it is limited to a purely passive reception of forms. In this sense, immateriality may be found even in organic powers. At least this degree of independence of matter is required in a cognitive subject.

66. *Corollaries.* Because cognition is based upon immateriality or independence of matter and this independence admits *degrees,* it follows that the perfection of cognition will be in inverse ratio to the degree of materiality of a knowing subject. The more a subject depends upon matter, the less perfect its cognition will be. Thus, for instance, sense cognition is less perfect than intellectual cognition, because the senses are much more intimately dependent upon matter than the intellect.

*A cognitive union is the *most intimate of all unions.* In any physical union the parts together constitute a whole which is neither one nor the other of the components but their composite. But in a cognitive union the knower becomes the object known—cognitively he is identical with the object.

Cognition does not consist in a *purely passive* reception of forms, for to receive passively is to receive materially. For if the acquisition of knowledge were a purely passive process, it could be soaked up by students as water is soaked up by the soil. Nevertheless, cognitive potencies are called passive, because any potency which does not change its object but is changed by it is called *passive*. An *active* potency is a potency which changes its object, as is done, for instance, by the nutritive potency.

Because in cognition the subject becomes the object, and because cognition is based upon immateriality, it should be clear that the subject as knowing and the object as known must be *proportionate to each other in immateriality*. They could not become "one" if their mode of being were not proportionate. As a matter of fact, as we shall see later, the senses, which depend intrinsically upon matter, have as their object forms as concreted and individualized in matter, while the intellect, which is intrinsically independent of matter but takes its object from the senses, has as its object material forms as abstracted from their concretization and individualization in matter.

The Process of Cognition

67. *Impressed Species.* Cognition is an action by which the knower actually comes to be and is the object known. From general metaphysical principles it is evident that a finite being is first potentially that which it comes to be actually. Hence the question arises *how the knower will be the object potentially* before being the object actually.

It will not be sufficient to answer that by its very nature a cognitive potency is potentially the object to be known by its act. Such an answer fails to explain why the knower begins to know here and now and not before, although he possessed his cognitive potency all the time, nor why he knows this particular object and no other. A cognitive potency is potential with respect to many objects, but an act of cognition is always concerned with a definite object. Hence there must be something which determines the cognitive potency in such a way that it will elicit here and now an act of cognition of this object and no other.

Speaking a priori, there are several ways in which this determination may exist in the cognitive subject. It may be either from within or from without. It will be *from within,* if the cognitive subject is identical with the object to be known. If the determination comes *from without,* the object will determine the cognitive potency either *immediately,* by itself, or through an *intermediary.* This intermediary determinant of the cognitive potency is technically called the *impressed species of the object*—a "species," because it is a form which determines and specifies the cognitive potency; "impressed," because it comes to the cognitive potency from without and is passively received by it; "of the object," because it acts as a representative of the object.

In which of these three ways is the cognitive potency determined to its act of knowing the object? The answer is that *an impressed species of the object is necessary to determine a cognitive potency to the act of knowing any finite object other than itself.* The proof of this assertion is as follows:

The cognitive potency needs to be determined to a definite object before it elicits its act of cognition. But there are three ways in which this determination may be in the cognitive potency—namely, by identity with the object, by immediate determination by the form of the object, and by means of an impressed species. Of these three, *identity* has to be excluded, except in the case of self-knowledge, because a being which knows by means of a cognitive potency is finite, and therefore not identical in its being with anything other than itself. *Immediate determination* by the form of the object has to be excluded, because any finite form is limited to being the form of this object and cannot be the form of anything else.[5] Therefore, there remains only determination by means of an *impressed species.*

Nature of the Impressed Species. Concerning the nature of the impressed species, the following are to be noted.

The impressed species *actuates* the cognitive potency and thus renders it fully capable of eliciting its act. In doing so, it also *specifies* that the act will be an act of knowing this particular object and no other. Considered entitatively, i.e., as a pure actuation and determination of the cognitive potency, the impressed species is something physical or subjective and does not belong to the cognitive or intentional order in the strict sense of the term. It is an accidental modification of the cognitive potency with which it enters into composition. However, the impressed species also *presents the object* whose spe-

[5] We say any *finite* form, because for a form which is absolutely infinite it would not be impossible to actuate and determine the knower immediately. According to theologians, this is what happens in the beatific vision.

cies it is to the cognitive potency and thus enables this potency to become the object to be known. Taken in this way, the impressed species belongs to the cognitive order in the strict sense of the term.

The mere reception of an impressed species is not yet cognition. For this reception is purely *passive* on the part of the receiving potency, while cognition is action.

The *physical* change which occurs in cognitive sense organs is not the impressed species of sense cognition. Such physical changes may be prerequisite, but they belong to the material order.

The impressed species is not that which is known, but *that by means of which* the object is known. It is prior in nature to the act of cognition and therefore not directly present to our awareness in cognitive acts. Its existence becomes known only through a process of reasoning.

*The impressed species is needed for cognition not only by reason of the subject but also by reason of the object. It is needed *by reason of the subject,* because the cognitive potency needs to be actuated and specified to a definite object. It is needed *by reason of the object,* because cognition requires an object which is proportionate in immateriality to the cognitive potency. Hence the object must present itself to the cognitive potency in an immaterial way. But no material object, taken as it is physically, is immaterial; whence the necessity for it to be made immaterial in the knower by means of an impressed species. This immateriality, however, of the impressed species does not flow from the external object but from the cognitive subject in which the species is received, for whatever is received is received according to the mode of being of the receiver.

68. *Expressed Species.* In the preceding part of this chapter we have seen that usually an impressed species is necessary to actuate and determine the cognitive potency to its operation and make it *potentially* the object to be known. The impressed species plays a role in constituting the immediate principle of the cognitive act. When this principle elicits its act, the knower *actually* becomes the object. In other words, the act of cognition has as its terminus the object known. Thus the question arises as to *how it is possible for the object to be the terminus of the cognitive act.* No special difficulty will be involved if the object is immediately present to the cognitive potency and proportionate to it in immateriality, because in that case the act can terminate in the object itself. If, however, the object known is not immediately present or not proportionate to the cognitive potency in immateriality, it will not be possible for it to be the terminus of the cognitive act. We are thinking here, for example, about the acts of imagination and intellect. The object remembered is not actually present and acting upon the knower; hence it cannot terminate the act of remembering. The act of understanding is concerned with an abstract essence, such as "plant" or "animal." The object of this act does not exist in the immaterial and universal way in which it is known, but only in concrete and individual realizations; yet my act of understanding requires a terminus corresponding exactly to that which is known. Thus there appears a necessity for a suitable terminus in which the object can be known. This terminus is usually called the *expressed species* of the cognitive act and may be described as an image of the object known which is produced by the act of cognition as the

terminus in which the object is known. Thus the knower is actually the object known in the expressed species.

Nature of the Expressed Species. Concerning the nature of the expressed species, the following are to be noted.

Cognition is not for the sake of producing an expressed species, for it does not cease with the production of the species. But the expressed species is *for the sake of cognition,* as a means to reach the object when the object itself cannot be reached immediately.

**Physically* or entitatively, the expressed species is an accidental modification of the subject and related to it as act is to potency; *cognitively* or intentionally, the expressed species is united with the actuated potency as act with act, and makes the knower actually other than himself.

An expressed species is *not always necessary* for cognition, but only when the object itself cannot terminate the act of cognition. The need for an expressed species is generally recognized in the case of the imagination and the intellect. Their expressed species are called respectively the *phantasm* and the (formal) *concept* or mental word. Whether or not there is an expressed species in external sense cognition is a hotly disputed question, which shall be considered in Chapter Seven.

*The expressed species is *really distinct* from the impressed species. The impressed species is concerned with the principle or cause of cognition, while the expressed species is produced by the act of cognition; hence the two species are related as cause and effect and therefore really distinct.

Definition of Cognition

69. From the preceding considerations it should be clear that cognition is an immanent action. A *transient,* predicamental, or physical action is the production of an effect or terminus outside the producing subject, or at least outside the producing potency, and therefore always tends to perfect the recipient. An *immanent,* transcendental or metaphysical action, on the other hand, does not consist in the production of an effect or terminus; it does not tend to perfect a recipient but the agent himself. As we have seen above, cognition is not for the sake of producing a terminus and does not cease with the production of the terminus even when such a terminus is necessary. Therefore, cognition is not transient but immanent in the strict sense of the term, i.e., it remains in the operative potency as the perfection of this potency. By means of this immanent action the subject has the form of the object immaterially. Hence we may define cognition as an *immanent action by which the form of an object is had immaterially.*

*This definition or rather description of cognition is realized in the various types of cognition according to the proper mode of each type, and therefore analogous in this sense. Even with respect to the same type of cognition the description applies analogously if this cognition is found in those beings which are different in their immateriality; e.g., God and man.

Historical Notes

*70. Idealists, such as *Kant* (1724–1804) and *Hegel* (1770–1831), maintain that cognition is wholly intrinsic and does not arise from anything outside the cognitive power. Hence there is no necessity of an impressed species.

The materialists deny the immanent and vital nature of cognition. They assert that the object is physically present in the knower, somewhat like an image is in the photographic plate, and that this physical presence is sufficient to explain knowledge.

The necessity of an impressed species in man's knowledge of finite objects is admitted by nearly all scholastic philosophers. They also unanimously admit an expressed species in the imagination and the intellect, but are divided about its necessity in the external senses (cf. chap. 7).

SUMMARY

71. Cognition implies a union of knower and object to be known. In some way the determinations or forms of the object are united with the knowing subject. Thus the knower has the form of the object known. However, he does not have this form as his own form, but as the form of the object. Retaining his identity, he becomes the object. Accordingly, the knower has a twofold "to be"—he exists physically as this man or that animal, and cognitively as the object known. The object, too, has a twofold "to be"—it exists physically, outside the knower, as this tree or that ring, and cognitively in the knowing subject as the object known. The cognitive "to be" of the knower and the cognitive "to be" of the object are identical.

The foundation of cognition lies in immateriality. Cognition means that a being is not limited with respect to form. But the principle of limitation with respect to form is matter. Therefore, it is absence of matter or immateriality which enables a being to have more than one form. By immateriality or absence of matter we do not mean here absolute and essential independence of matter, but merely that a cognitive being must have at least a certain emergence above the totally passive reception of forms which characterizes matter as matter. Accordingly, cognition does not consist in a passive reception of the form of the object or a transition from potency to act, although in a finite being it does not occur without such a transition.

A cognitive potency is potential with respect to many objects, but its acts are acts of knowing definite objects; hence the potency will have to be determined to the object which it will actually know. Except in the case of self-knowledge this determination will come from without. Since the form of a finite object is limited to being the form of this object and no other, it cannot immediately be the form determining the knower, but has to determine the knower by means of an intermediary, called an impressed species. This impressed species actuates the cognitive potency, specifies the act of knowing as knowledge of this definite object and no other, and presents this object to the knower, thus enabling him to become the object.

*The impressed species is needed not only by reason of the subject which needs to be actuated and determined, but also by reason of the object if the object is not as immaterial as the cognitive potency; for object and potency must be proportionate to each other in immateriality because the knower has to become the object.

The act of cognition has as its terminus the object known. If the object is not immediately present to the cognitive potency or not proportionate to it in immateriality, it cannot itself act as such a terminus. Hence in such a case there is need for something corresponding exactly to the object as it is known to terminate the cognitive act. This is produced by the act of cognition and so it is called the expressed species. It may be described as an image of the object produced by the knower as the terminus in which the object is known. Note, however, that the expressed species is merely a means in which the object is reached and not the object itself which is known. Cognition is not for the sake of producing an expressed species, but the expressed species is for the sake of cognition.

Cognition may be described as an immanent action by which the form of an object is possessed immaterially.

SUGGESTED READINGS

72. Aristotle, *De anima,* bk. II, chap. 12 and bk. III, chap. 4.

Thomas Aquinas, *In II De anima,* lect. 24, nos. 551–557; *De veritate,* q. 2, a. 2; *Summa theol.*, Ia, q. 14, a. 1. The nature and foundation of cognition.

——— *Summa theol.*, Ia, q. 84, a. 2. "Grades of Immateriality."

——— *In III De anima,* lect. 7, nos. 675–676 and lect. 8, no. 718; *Summa theol.*, Ia, q. 84, a. 1; *Quodlibet.* V, a. 9, ad 2. The necessity of species.

——— *Summa theol.*, Ia, q. 79, a. 2. Senses of being passive.

Jacques Maritain, *The Degrees of Knowledge* (New York: 1938), pp. 134–143.

Etienne Gilson, *The Spirit of Mediaeval Philosophy* (New York: 1936), chap. 12.

George P. Klubertanz, *The Philosophy of Human Nature* (New York: 1953), chap. 4.

CHAPTER 7

External Sense Cognition

*** In this chapter we shall first briefly describe the different external senses and then consider the various philosophical problems of cognition by means of external senses.

Description of the External Senses

73. By senses in general are meant those cognitive potencies by means of which a subject knows concrete and individual qualities of material objects. A sense which is able to reach an object not apprehended by another sense of the same subject, is called an *external* sense, not so much because it has a receptory organ close to the external surface of the body as because it directly reaches the external world. If a sense reaches its object through the external senses, it is called an *internal* sense.

Traditionally, five external senses are enumerated, namely, sight, hearing, taste, smell, and touch. The traditional internal senses are the common or central sense, imagination, memory, and instinct or the estimative sense.

Sight. The organ of sight is the eye or, more specifically, the rods and cones of the retina. Its object is color, which is light as reflected or refracted by a surface.[1] The main characteristics of color are its quality (hue or shade) and intensity or brightness, i.e., its approach to whiteness. From the viewpoint of sensation, there are eight principal colors, namely, black, white, red, orange, yellow, green, blue, and violet.[2] Between these eight colors, there are many intermediate colors; e.g., there are literally hundreds of shades of grey and thousands of shades of green. Because color is actually found only in extended objects, extension itself can be seen insofar as it is affected by color.

Hearing. The organ of hearing is the ear or, more specifically, Corti's organ in the inner ear. Its object is sound. Sound is experienced when a vibrating surface communicates its motion to a medium in contact with the ear. Its characteristics are pitch, i.e., the number of vibrations per second, which makes a sound "high" or "low"; intensity or volume, which ranges from barely "audible" to "earsplitting"; and timbre or tone quality, which is the tempering of a fundamental tone by a number of harmonious overtones. A tone, in opposition to noise, is a sound with a regular pitch which is in harmony with other sounds.

Taste. Its organs are the tongue and certain parts of the palate and throat or, more specifically, the taste buds on these parts of the body. Its object is flavor, of which there are four kinds, namely, sour, sweet, salty, and bitter. Flavor is experienced when certain soluble substances are brought

[1] Light as light is not the object of sight, because under certain objective physical conditions light is not visible.

[2] We say "from the viewpoint of sensation," because physically white is not a principal color, and black is no color at all.

into contact with the taste buds. Well-known phenomena of taste are its adaptation or weakening of the sensation resulting from protracted exposure to the same flavor; its contrast effects, by which, for example, plain fresh water tastes sweet after a taste of salt; and its close association with the sense of smell, by which, for example, we are able to "taste" the difference between an onion and an apple.

Smell. The organ of smell is the nose or rather the olfactory bulbs in the mucous membrane of the nose. Its object is odor. The sensation of odor is aroused when the organ of smell is struck by particles of "odorous" substances suspended in air or gas. The sense of smell is subject to adaptation.

Touch. Touch is a generic name for several more or less distinct species of senses involving contact between the body and an object. We may distinguish the sensations of warmth, cold, pressure, and pain. With the exception of pain these sensations seem to have their own organs. *Pressure* is sensed by the hair follicles and Meissner corpuscles, which report differences of pressure relative to the internal pressure of the body. Sensations of roughness, smoothness, softness, and hardness are reduced to sensations of pressure. Likewise, so-called kinesthetic sensation, by which we are aware of the position and motion of our body, is reducible to the sense of pressure, for position and motion imply pressure of parts of the body upon one another. *Temperature* is sensed relatively to the temperature of the part of the body in which the sense organ is located. Relative cold seems to be sensed by the Krause bulbs, and relative warmth by the end organs of Ruffini. The sensation of *pain* does not seem to require any special organ, but results from a "painful" stimulation of free nerve endings.

Distinction of the External Senses

74. Do the sensations of color, sound, flavor, etc., require different cognitive potencies or are they merely different functions of one and the same potency? In other words, are the external senses really distinct or not? The principle from which the answer to this question may be derived was given above, in no. 44—there are as many distinct cognitive potencies as there are formally distinct objects or aspects under which the object is attained by the knower. Now it should be clear that the objects of the senses enumerated above are formally distinct. The sensation of color is not reducible to that of sound or of any other sense object; nor that of flavor to pressure, etc. Therefore, the external senses are *really distinct.* Note, however, that touch is not a species of sense but a genus containing a number of specifically different senses.

Philosophically speaking, it makes very little difference whether there are five or five hundred distinct senses. What really matters is the nature of sensation, which we will discuss in no. 77.

In stating that the above mentioned senses exist, we do not mean to assert that all of them are found in every type of organism endowed with sense life, but merely that these senses exist at least in some sensing organism. It may be left to the experimental sciences of life to determine which senses are possessed by the various kinds of animals.

Objects of the External Senses

75. By the object in general of a sense is meant that which in any way can be apprehended by a sense. It is called a *sensible*. The object of an external sense is called an *external* sensible. External sensibles are divided into *essential (per se)* and *accidental* sensibles, according as they are sensible in themselves or not. For instance, Peter's color and size are essential sensibles, but Peter himself is an accidental sensible. Essential sensible are either common or proper.

By a *proper* sensible is meant an essential sensible which directly refers to only one sense; e.g., color is the proper sensible of sight. This proper sensible is often called the secondary sense quality. It is the proper sensible which specifies the sense potency.

A *common* sensible is an essential sense object which can be sensed by more than one sense; e.g., size can be sensed by both sight and touch. Common sensibles are often called primary sense qualities. Although common sensibles are sensed in themselves, they are not sensed immediately, but by means of a proper sensible. For example, Peter's size is seen by means of its color, and may be felt by means of its pressure and temperature, which are proper sensibles of the senses of sight and touch. Motion, rest, number, size, and shape are common sensibles.

The *accidental* sensible of an external sense is not in itself an object of this sense, but apprehended by another cognitive potency as accompanying that which the external sense grasps. For instance, the bodily substance of an orange is an accidental sense object of the sense of sight, because the intellect apprehends it as the subject of the orange-colored sphere. Likewise, by sight alone I cannot perceive the delicious flavor of the orange, but when I see the visible element of an orange, my imagination and memory are capable of adding the flavor to my actual sensation, and in this sense flavor may be said to be an accidental object of the sense of sight.

The Organic Nature of the Senses

76. From experience we know that sensation is always concerned with concrete and individual things. In some way concrete and individual matter acts upon the animal body, and this action results in a sensation. Hence there is no doubt that sensation is dependent upon the body, i.e., upon an organ. However, as we have seen in no. 52, dependence upon an organ may be either intrinsic or extrinsic. If an organic condition, i.e., the organ as acted upon by the object, is merely a prerequisite for the act of sensation, the sensitive potency cannot be called organic. In this case the sense potency belongs to the soul alone and not to the composite of body and soul, and the immediate principle of sensation is not the organ as quasi-informed by the potency [3] but the potency alone. If, on the other hand, the sense potency depends intrinsically upon the organ, the organ as quasi-informed by the potency is the immediate principle of sensation, so that the sense potency is not a potency of the soul alone but of the composite of body and soul. Such a potency, therefore, will be an organic potency in the strict sense of the term.

Are the external senses merely extrinsically dependent upon their organs or are they organic potencies in the

[3] Cf. no. 52.

strict sense of the term? Our answer is that they are *organic*, and the proof is as follows:

If sensation is organic the senses are organic. But sensation is organic. Therefore, the senses are organic.

The *major* premise is clear from the principle that potencies are specified by their act. Regarding the *minor*, sensation will be organic if its object implies something which is essentially *material*. But the object of sensation is always something material as acting upon an organ. The object of sight, for example, is matter as acting upon the eye; that of hearing is matter as acting upon the ear; that of smell is matter as acting upon the nose. Hence matter enters into the very nature of sensation. Moreover, the sense object always includes a *quantitative* aspect, whether it be number or extension in space or time, and this quantitative aspect modifies the sensation. For instance, the sensation of color differs according to size; that of sound according to rhythm, tempo, etc.; that of taste according to the volume of the flavored object. But quantity is a property of matter, and therefore matter enters into the very nature of sensation.

**Location of Sensation.* The sense organs are connected with certain areas of the brain which control these organs by means of the nervous system. This has led a number of psychologists to the conclusion that these sensory areas of the brain are the place where sensation takes place. As evidence they point to the fact that the destruction of a sensory area in the brain entails the loss of the corresponding sense, even if the surface organ of the sense is not damaged. However, their conclusion would seem to go too far, for the evidence merely implies that the brain plays a necessary and perhaps even essential role in sensation, but not that sensation takes place in the brain *alone.* If the role played by the brain is really essential, we are quite willing to concede that the nervous system and the brain are part of the whole organ needed for sensation. However, from a philosophical viewpoint, this whole question is of little importance.

Impressed Species and the Terminus of Sensation

77. *Impressed Species.* As was mentioned above, in no. 66, all cognitive potencies are passive in the sense that they need to be acted upon before being fully ready to elicit an act of cognition. They do not change their object but are changed by it. In the case of sensitive potencies, which act through an organ, the organ itself first undergoes a material change; e.g., when I touch a piece of iron the iron presses against my hand;[4] hot water physically heats my skin; etc. This material change does not belong to the cognitive order in the strict sense, although it is a condition for sensation. But, in addition to the material change the object produces in the sense organ, it also changes the sensitive potency immaterially by impressing its species on it.

Concerning the nature of this impressed species of the senses or the sensible species, the following are to be noted. The sensible species received in the sensitive potency is an *immaterial* representation of the object. For whatever is received is received according to the mode of being of the receiver; but a cognitive potency is im-

[4] The hand also presses against the iron in accordance with the principle of action and reaction. In this respect there is no difference between the interaction of an object and a sense organ and that of two purely material objects, because materially they are subject to the same laws.

material; therefore, the species or form received in it is immaterial, or *without matter.* On the other hand, sense cognition does not reach the object as entirely free from the limitation of individual matter, as universal, but embraces it in its concrete individuality. Sight, for instance, does not sense whiteness, but this or that particular white (thing). Therefore, the sensible species must retain those characteristics which distinguish and determine the individual concretely. These characteristics, which St. Thomas calls the "*conditions of matter,*" are the particular shape, size, weight, color, etc., of the object. When I sense a skyscraper, the form of the skyscraper is in my senses without the matter it has in its physical existence, but it is not in my senses without the concrete individual conditions which make it a skyscraper of this particular shape, size, and color. Accordingly, the sense object is received in the senses without matter, because cognition is based upon immateriality, but with the conditions of matter, because sensation is cognition of individual things in their concreteness.

The Terminus of Sensation. Above, in no. 68, we have seen that an expressed species is sometimes necessary to terminate the act of cognition. Hence the question arises whether there is any expressed species in sensation, or the object itself is the terminus of sensation.

Regarding this question, St. Thomas and most of his followers agree that there is *no expressed species in sensation.* For the purpose of such a species is to terminate the act of cognition when the object itself cannot do so either because it is not present or because it is not proportionate to the cognitive potency in immateriality. But the object of sensation is actually present to the sensing subject and proportionate to it in immateriality. Hence it would be useless to admit an expressed species of sensation. Therefore, we must admit that sensation terminates in the sense object itself.

*Another question, however, is whether sensation terminates in the sense object as it exists *physically* and is physically present to the knower. Although this view is defended by certain Thomists, it does not seem to be true. For taken as it is actually present physically, the sense object does not belong to the cognitive order; it is not proportionate to the cognitive potency in immateriality; hence it cannot be the terminus of a cognitive or immaterial union. We must therefore say that the terminus of sensation is the sense object taken as it is *actually present cognitively*. The reason is that sensation is limited to objects which are here and now acting upon the senses, and thus sensation is cognition of an object which is *actually* present; and this presence must be in the *cognitive* order, because it is in this order that subject and object are united, and it is only in this order that the object is proportionate in immateriality to the sensing subject. But the sense object is present cognitively through its sensible species; therefore, sense cognition terminates in the object *as present through its sensible species*. Accordingly, the sensible species not merely prepares the act of cognition by actuating the sense potency, but also plays a role in the act of sensation itself, as the terminus in which the sensing subject knows the sensible object.

Sensation and Perception

78. Although the terms "sensation" and "perception" are very often used synonymously, *sensation*, in the strict sense of the term—and this is the sense in which the

term has been used here—means the sole act of a sense without that which is added to sensation by memory, intellect, and other senses. *Perception,* on the other hand, includes everything which is added to a sensation. For instance, if at 2:00 A.M. I am rudely awakened by some awful noise coming from the roof near my window, and my roommate sleepily asks: "What is it?" I may answer: "Two cats," or, "A screeching noise." The first answer indicates my perception, the second my sensation.

**The Perception of Motion.* The senses of touch and sight reveal the changes in position of external objects with respect to our body, but without a term of comparison they do not reveal whether our body or the external objects are moving. This can easily be observed when one is seated in a train and looks at another train which seems to be moving slowly over an adjacent track. If the wheels of the train do not fall within the field of vision, it will be impossible to determine by sight alone which of the two trains is moving. Likewise, when one is seated in an open car, the sole sense of pressure of the wind does not reveal whether the car is moving or a strong breeze blowing.

Motion which we ourselves execute can be perceived by the senses of touch and sight. But motion which is common to our body and all its surroundings, such as the rotation of the earth, cannot be perceived by any external sense. Its existence can become known only through a process of reasoning.

From experience we know that objects which seem to be moving when we are being transported, e.g., in a train, are only apparently moving.

Historical Notes

*79. The organic nature of the external senses is denied by the materialists, who try to explain sensation as a purely mechanical process without any vital principle. Likewise, by *Plato* and *Descartes,* who did not admit the substantial union of body and soul and therefore claimed that sensation was an act of the soul alone.

An expressed species of sensation is defended by *Suarez,* who did not admit that the sensible species is a formal representation of the object; also by the interpretationists (*Card. Mercier,* 1851–1926), who deny the objectivity of secondary sense qualities.

Among Thomists, *Cajetan* (1468–1534), *Boyer* (born 1884), *Renard* (born 1894), and others hold that the sense object as intentionally present is the terminus of sensation, while *Gredt* (1863–1940), *Gény* (1871–1925), *Remer,* and before them perhaps *John of St. Thomas* (1589–1644) defend the view that the sense object is reached as physically present.

SUMMARY

80. A sense in general is a cognitive potency by means of which a subject knows the concrete and individual qualities of material objects. A sense is external if it directly reaches the world outside the sense; it is internal if it takes its object from another sense. The external senses are sight, hearing, taste, smell, and touch, but touch is a generic name for the senses of pressure, heat, cold, and pain. These external senses are really distinct potencies, for their formal objects are different.

Sense objects or sensibles are divided into essential and accidental sensibles according as they are sensible in themselves or not. A proper sensible is an essential sensible which directly refers to only one sense. A common sensible is an essential sense object which can be sensed by more than one sense. Common sensibles are motion, rest, number, size, and shape. A sense object is called accidental when it is apprehended by another cognitive potency as accompanying that which a sense senses; e.g., the taste of an orange is an accidental object of sight.

The external senses are organic potencies, because they depend intrinsically upon an organ. Their object is always something material as acting upon an organ and always includes a quantitive and therefore material aspect. Accordingly, the external senses are not potencies of the soul alone, but of the composite of body and soul.

The external senses are passive in the sense that they need to be acted upon before being fully ready to elicit their act of sensation. By means of the material change operated by the sense object in the sense organ, the object impresses its species upon the sense potency. This impressed species is an immaterial representation of the sense object. Nevertheless it is not wholly free from matter, because it represents the object with the conditions of matter, i.e., with its concrete and individual determinations.

There is no expressed species in sensation. Expressed species is necessary to terminate the act of cognition if the object itself cannot do so. But in sensation the object is capable of terminating the act of cognition, because it is present to the sensing subject and proportionate to it in immateriality, at least if the object is taken as present through its sensible species.

Sensation in the strict sense refers to the sole act of a

sense without that which is added to it from past experience, other senses or the intellect. Perception, on the other hand, includes everything which is added to sensation from other cognitive sources.

SUGGESTED READINGS

81. Aristotle, *De anima,* bk. II, chap. 5 to bk. III, chap. 2; *De sensu.*

Thomas Aquinas, *Summa theol.,* Ia, q. 78, a. 3; *De anima,* a. 13; *In II De anima,* lect. 14; *In De sensu et sensato commentarium.* The external senses.

——— *Summa theol.,* Ia–IIae, q. 22, a. 2; *In II De anima,* lect. 11, no. 366. Passive nature of senses.

——— *Summa theol.,* Ia, q. 54, a. 5; *In II De anima,* lect. 24. The subject of sensation.

——— *In II De anima,* lect. 5, nos. 281 ff. and lect. 24. Immateriality of sensation.

——— *Summa theol.,* Ia, q. 17, a. 2; q. 78, a. 3; *In II De anima,* lect. 13. Kinds of sense objects.

——— *De veritate,* q. 2, a. 6; *Quodlibet,* V, a. 9, ad 2. The terminus of sensation.

George P. Klubertanz, *The Philosophy of Human Nature,* chap. 6. External sensation.

Henri Renard, *The Philosophy of Man,* chap. 6. The external senses.

Robert E. Brennan, *General Psychology,* chap. 9. Sensation in general, chaps. 10–13. The external senses.

Thomas V. Moore, *Cognitive Psychology* (New York: 1939), Part Three, chap. 1. Stimulus and sensation.

Francis L. Harmon, *Principles of Psychology* (Milwaukee: 1953), chaps. 6–10. Perception and the external senses.

CHAPTER 8

Internal Sense Cognition

The Existence of Internal Sense Cognition

*** 82. Our own internal experience shows immediately that sense cognition is not limited to the mere sensation of colors, sounds, odors, etc. For instance, I do not merely see a color and hear a sound, but am also sensitively aware of the fact that I see a color and hear a sound; I am able to distinguish sensitively between them; I can combine the various sensations of the external senses into an integrated whole; I remember past sense experiences as past. Such cognitive actions are still on the sense level, as is evident from the fact that they may occur even before an infant is capable of making use of his intellect. Moreover, animals show by their behavior that they, too, are capable of such cognitive activity. For example, a cat will combine a squeak and a grey shape with the delicious (at least, for the cat!) flavor of a mouse; a deer will turn its ears towards sound and thus show that it distinguishes sound from color; a dog will wag his tail when he recognizes a distant shape as that of his master.

Hence it should be clear that there are acts of sense cognition which are not reducible to the actions of the external senses. These acts are attributed to the so-called internal senses—*internal,* because they have no organ on the surface of the body, but more especially because they do not take their object immediately from the external world but from the external senses which experience this world. They may be defined in general as cognitive sense potencies which act in dependence upon the action of the external senses.

Usually, four internal senses are enumerated. They are the central or common sense, imagination, the memorative, and the estimative sense. In claiming that these senses exist, we do not intend to affirm that they are found in every sentient body, but merely that they exist at least in some sentient organisms.

The Central Sense

83. The central sense, which is also called the common, synthetic or unifying sense, is an internal sensitive potency by means of which a knowing subject perceives the actual sensations of the external senses, distinguishes between them and combines them. The existence of such a sense, as distinct from the external senses is proved from the following:

An external sense *cannot sense that it is sensing,* for sensation is neither the proper nor a common sensible of the external senses. Sight as sight, for example, is not visible and therefore cannot be sensed by the sense of sight. Nevertheless, I am sensitively aware of the fact that I am sensing. Moreover, to sense that it is sensing, the external sense would have to reflect upon itself. But the external senses are organic potencies and act through their organs, which are extended and therefore unable to reflect upon themselves.

An external sense *cannot distinguish* between its own object and that of another external sense. It is true that an external sense can distinguish various objects referring to its own mode of sensitiveness; e.g., sight is able to distinguish between green and red. But sight cannot distinguish color from sound, nor can smell distinguish odor from pressure. Nevertheless, it is a datum of experience that man and at least the higher types of animals are capable of distinguishing between various sensations and their objects; e.g., between flavor and odor. With respect to man, this is manifest from our own experience; regarding animals, it may be inferred from their behavior, for they turn their ears towards sound, and their eyes towards visible objects. Therefore, both man and at least the higher types of animals have a cognitive potency by means of which they can distinguish between the sensations of the external senses.

By the same argument we may conclude that the external senses are *unable to combine their sensations.* Each of them is capable only of knowing its proper object, while combining sensations requires knowledge of all the sensations and therefore presupposes a potency which knows all external sensations. Without the action of the central sense, the sensing subject could not unify its sensations and would know merely a number of unrelated sensations of color, sound, etc.

From these considerations it follows that, apart from the external senses, we must admit the existence of a sense cognitive potency which senses the sensations of the external senses, distinguishes between them and combines them. This sense we have called the central sense.

The central sense is an *organic* potency, because its object is the concrete and individual sensations which here and now affect the sensing subject. Accordingly, the central sense has an organ. The exact location of this organ is not known, although it is usually placed in the brain.

It is to be noted that the proper object of the central sense is not the *common sensibles,*[1] although this is sometimes asserted. Common sensibles can be known by the external senses through their proper sensible; e.g., shape can be seen through color. The proper object of the central sense is the sensations of the external senses.

*The central sense is also the cognitive potency by means of which the sensing subject knows concretely that he is *actually awake and sensing* and not merely sleeping and dreaming. For this reason, Aristotle described sleep as the inhibition of the functioning of the central sense.[2]

*The *impressed species* which actuates the central sense is produced by the actual sensation of the external senses. The action of the central sense does not produce an *expressed species,* but terminates in the external sensations as here and now acting upon the central sense. The reason is the same as the one given in no. 77—the external sensation is actually cognitively present to the central sense through its impressed species.

*The objection may be raised that the sensations of the external senses are *sensations of one and the same subject;* therefore, this subject is able to distinguish one sensation from another, so that there is no need to admit a special central sense. However, this argument fails to consider

[1] For this reason it would seem preferable not to call the central sense the "common sense." Moreover, the term "common sense" could give rise to the notion that the central sense is to be identified with the general intellectual insight. St. Thomas speaks of the "common sense" as "the common root and principle of the external senses." Cf. *Summa theol.,* Ia, q.78, a.4, ad 1.

[2] *De somno,* chap. 2; 455a 25.

that no finite being is immediately operative, as was shown in no. 42; therefore, if the sensing subject distinguishes between different sensations it does so by means of an operative potency, which is called the central sense.

Imagination

84. By imagination is meant an internal sensitive potency by means of which subjects are capable of retaining the species of objects apprehended by the external senses and the central sense when these objects are no longer actually affecting the sense organs. Because imagination can retain these species, it can also reproduce them and combine them into more complex images.

The *existence* of such an internal sense in man is evident from our own internal experience. At least the more perfect types of animals show by their behavior that they have the same retentive power. Animal training, for example, is based upon the fact that animals are capable of learning, i.e., of retaining their sense experience. Moreover, animals are subject to dreams, as is evidenced by motor reactions during their sleep; [3] and they go in search of prey, by which they show that somehow they know what they are looking for.

The imagination is *really distinct from the external senses,* because an external sense cannot retain the impression of the sense object when this object is no longer acting upon the organ; for instance, I cannot see a motorcar which actually has turned the corner.

[3] For instance, a dog may suddenly during his sleep start growling or even barking. The explanation seems to be that he had the sensation of an exciting object (a cat), even though no such object was actually present.

The imagination is also *really distinct from the central sense.* The central sense depends directly upon the sensations of the external senses and operates only when the external senses are sensing an object. The imagination, on the contrary, can operate and produce images of sense objects even when these objects are no longer actually stimulating the sense organs. Thus the proper object of the central sense is the actual sensation of the external senses, while that of the imagination abstracts from the actual presence of the sense objects. But, as we have seen in no. 44, a difference in proper object means a real distinction of cognitive potencies.

The imagination is an *organic* potency, for its object is the concrete and individual sense object as it has acted upon the external senses. The organ of the imagination is usually placed in the brain, although its exact location is not known.

*The imagination is actuated by *impressed species* received from the central sense. In some way, the imagination is able to retain this species.[4] When actuated by this species, the imagination produces as the term of its action an *expressed species,* called a phantasm. Such an expressed species must be admitted, because the act of imagining requires a term corresponding exactly to that which is imagined. But the object imagined may be absent or even nonexistent; e.g., a gremlin or a fairy. Yet the act of imagining has to terminate in something pres-

[4] How exactly is not known. Some say that the psychical disposition resulting from the actuation of the imagination remains present in the manner of a habit; others that the organic modification upon which the impressed species is based remains present in the organ as a habit; others, again, that both the psychical disposition and the organic modification remain habitually.

ent and corresponding exactly to it. Accordingly, the imagination has to produce in itself an image of the object imagined, and this image is the expressed species of the imagination or the *phantasm.* Note, however, that phantasms are not retained when the imagination ceases to act; for a phantasm is the terminus of the act of imagining and therefore ceases when this act ceases. Whenever the imagination is actuated again by the retained impressed species, the corresponding phantasm is produced.

*The *reproduction of phantasms* may have various causes. We may distinguish the following:

a) *Physiological stimulation.* Pressure and other action upon the brain, the organ of the imagination, may cause a stimulation similar to that caused by the external sensation which first gave rise to the phantasm.

b) *Association of images.* The laws of association of images have been accurately determined by the so-called school of associationism (Stuart Mill, Spencer), but their main elements were known to Aristotle and St. Thomas.[5] They are the laws of contiguity, of contrast, and of similarity. If objects are perceived as contiguous in space or time, the imagination tends to reproduce them together; e.g., a visit to your alma mater will bring back to your imagination events that happened there when you were a student. The perception of certain objects tends to lead to the reproduction of phantasms of their opposites; e.g., the sensation of white will easily give rise to the concomitant phantasm of black. Present objects will bring back the phantasms of similar objects experienced in the past; e.g., a heavy pipe smoker will cause the reproduction of the phantasm of a smokestack.

c) *The action of the will or another internal sense.* Man

[5] Cf. *In De memoria et reminiscentia,* lect. 5, nos. 363 ff.

is able to order his imagination to produce certain phantasms or to combine them with others. Examples are the make-believe games of children; imaginary beings such as fairies and gremlins; the more serious activity of the imagination resulting in great works of art and new inventions. The ability of the imagination to produce and combine phantasms under the guidance of intellect and will is so-called creative imagination. In animals "instinct" may lead to the combination of phantasms. For instance, a dog which has been whipped several times, may shrink away from the instrument of punishment, because he combines the phantasm of the whip with that of pain and therefore of harmfulness.

Estimative Sense

85. By the estimative potency, which is often called "instinct,"[6] an animal is capable of perceiving concretely certain aspects of sense objects, such as their beneficial or harmful character, which are not experienced by any of the other senses. The perception of such a beneficial or noxious character is followed by a movement of the sense appetite and action to avoid the harmful or attain the beneficial. Thus the estimative potency is primarily directed towards action and may be called a practical sense.

The *existence* of the estimative potency is evident from experience. Without any previous experience of birds of prey chickens know them to be harmful, as is manifested by their behavior when a hawk comes into sight; without any previous experience birds know when and where to build their nests; without previous experience, animals

[6] Instinct, however, is really more inclusive than estimative potency. In instinct not only the cognitive factor indicated by the term "estimative potency" plays a role, but also emotive and motor factors.

usually know what kind of food is good or harmful. In general, we may say that animal activity which follows an unlearned pattern that is uniform for the whole species is guided by the estimative potency.

It is to be noted that such activity is not directed by the pleasant or unpleasant *sensation* caused by the object which gives rise to the activity. On the contrary, often the activity is continued even though it is unpleasant; for instance, when animals defend their young against a stronger enemy. Nor can instinctive activity be explained as a *mere chain of reflexes* to stimuli.[7] For animals show that their instinctive actions are within the range of their consciousness by adapting them to the particular set of circumstances seized by their senses as affecting them here and now; hence their instinctive actions are not entirely automatic and stereotyped. Accordingly we must conclude that instinctive activity is directed by the concrete apprehension of what is beneficial or harmful, and that this apprehension need not be based upon previous sensations of the harmful or beneficial nature of the object. For this reason St. Thomas says that the estimative sense perceives "insensate intentions," i.e., objects of knowledge not yet sensed by any other sense.

The estimative potency is *really distinct from the other senses.* Its object is that which is not yet sensed by any of the other senses, such as the useful or harmful character of sense objects. But a distinction in object points to a distinction in cognitive potencies. Of course, once the beneficial or noxious nature of an object has been experienced as such by the other senses, the animal may be able to reproduce the phantasm of this experience.

The *organic* nature of the estimative potency should be

[7] A reflex is a stereotyped and automatic muscular or glandular response to a stimulus.

clear from the fact that its object is the concrete and individual sense object as beneficial or harmful here and now to the sensing subject. The organ of the estimative potency is usually considered to lie somewhere in the brain.

*The question may be raised as to how the estimative potency obtains the *impressed species* by means of which it knows the usefulness or danger of an object. The easiest answer would be to say that these species are innate and not derived from experience. However, such an answer would amount to appealing to God, as the author of nature, as the only explanation, and such an appeal must not be made unless no other explanation is possible. Accordingly, it would seem to be more consonant with reason to admit that the impressed species of the estimative potency comes from the sense objects themselves, though not immediately,[8] but as apprehended by the other senses.[9] Of course, we do not mean that the other senses, say, of a lamb, perceive the beneficial or harmful character of a wolf, but when the wolf is perceived, the lamb concretely apprehends in this perception the element of danger which escapes other senses. Thus the estimative potency remotely resembles and works much like the intellect, which also is able to apprehend in the object perceived by the senses certain characteristics that escape the senses.[10]

[8] It would not seem possible for an external object to act directly upon a sense which has no external organ.

[9] Specifically, the central sense in the case of present objects, and the imagination in the case of absent objects.

[10] Cf. St. Thomas, *Summa theol.*, Ia, q.78, a.4, ad 4. There would seem to be no need for a special expressed species of the estimative sense, because the act of this sense can terminate in the object as present through the central sense or the imagination.

The *estimative potency of man* is called the cogitative power, the discursive power, or the particular intellect. By man here is meant man insofar as he is a being guided by reason. The very names given to man's estimative potency indicate that in him this power approaches reason more closely than in animals. In animals the estimative potency is fixed in its estimations and leads to an almost wholly fixed and determined set of actions aiming either at the preservation of the animal or its species. This determination of the estimative sense of animals is necessary because they have no higher power by means of which they can guide themselves.[11] In man, on the other hand, an estimative potency that is altogether fixed in its estimations of concrete good and evil would militate against his reason, because it would make it impossible for reason to exercise control over any activity based upon sense life. Hence man's estimative potency has to be profoundly different from that of mere animals. It cannot be more than a mere instrument of reason. As such, its function will be to apply on the concrete and individual level what the (practical) intellect judges on the universal level,[12] viz., to arrive at concrete estimations about a sense object which correspond to universal judgments of the intellect. These concrete estimations of the useful or harmful character of a sense object cannot be dispensed with, because the sense appetite has to be moved to action by a sense object estimated to be good or evil here and now.

Memorative Potency

86. By the memorative potency is meant an internal sense cognitive potency by means of which an animal is

[11] Cf. chap. 15.

[12] Cf. St. Thomas, *De veritate,* q. 10, a. 5.

capable of retaining the perceptions of the estimative sense which cannot be retained by the imagination. Thus the memorative potency is to the estimative sense as imagination is to the external senses and the central sense. Among the aspects of perception which the imagination cannot retain is the concrete pastness of a sense experience. This pastness is retained by the memorative potency, which thus enables its subject to recognize the past as concretely past.

The *existence* of the memorative potency in mere animals is manifest from experience. A dog, for instance, will show by his behavior that he remembers the usefulness of obeying his master—a fact which plays an important role in animal training; he will recognize his master's voice, home, his young, etc., and thus show that he is aware of having perceived them before. The existence of a memorative potency in man is too obvious for comment.

The memorative potency is *really distinct from the other senses,* because its object is different from that of the other senses. Specifically, it is distinct from imagination which can retain only that which has been perceived by the external senses and the central sense; and from the estimative sense, which cannot recognize its perception.

The *organic* nature of the memorative potency is clear from the fact that it is limited to the recollection of concrete material perceptions. The organ of this potency is usually considered to be located in the brain.

*The memorative potency obtains its *impressed species* from the estimative sense, in a similar way as the imagination obtains its species from the central sense. There would seem to be no need for a special *expressed species* of the memorative potency, because the act of this sense can terminate in the sense object as present through the central sense or as retained in the imagination.

The *memorative potency of man* is ennobled by its subjection to the intellect. The purely animal memorative potency is a power of simple recall of the past. In man this power may be used to search deliberately for a "forgotten" image, and in such a case it is called *reminiscence.* For instance, if I do not remember where I left the car keys, I will try to remember when I last used them, what I did immediately after returning, etc., thus retracing my steps in order to recall the place where I left the keys. This process is somewhat similar to the way in which we try to reason from one thing to another, and shows the superiority of a sense power guided by reason to the same power as left to its own resources.

Note that the term "*memory*" as used in ordinary language covers more than we have ascribed to the memorative potency. Memory is used also to indicate the power of retaining past sense experience which we have called *imagination*. Moreover, memory may refer also to the intellectual power of retaining ideas, and in this sense it is the same as the intellect itself, as we shall see in Chapter Thirteen.

Interdependence of the Senses

87. From the foregoing considerations it should be clear that the various senses are not juxtaposited without any connection, but are interdependent. Only the external senses deal directly with the outer object. The central sense takes its object from the external senses; the imagination depends for its object on the central sense; the estimative sense receives it from the central sense or the imagination; and the memorative potency depends for its

object upon the estimative sense. Without the central sense the animal could not find any connections between its sensations and would not even know that it is sensing; without imagination the animal would not be able to make any progress in sense life, but would have to make a fresh start with every new act of sensing; without the estimative sense it could not profit from its sensations to avoid evil and to seek the good; without the memorative power it could not learn to profit from past useful or harmful experiences. Thus we see that the various sense powers are ordered to secure for the animal the attainment of the maximum of perfection possible in a purely sensitive being. In man, however, the sense potencies are further ennobled by serving as instruments in the preparation of intellectual activities, as we shall see in Chapter 13.

Historical Notes

*88. The organic nature of the internal senses in man was denied by *Descartes,* who held that all cognitive powers belong to the soul alone and therefore are inorganic. In animals he did not admit any sensation at all, and explained all their actions in a purely mechanical way.

The behaviorists (*Watson,* born 1878) try to explain all animal (and human) activity as reflexes to purely physical stimuli.

Among other philosophers, there is fairly general agreement about the existence of internal sensitivity, but considerable disagreement about secondary questions of internal sense cognition. *Mercier* and perhaps *Aristotle* [13] himself do not consider the central sense as a really dis-

[13] Cf. W. D. Ross, *Aristotle* (London: 1953), chap. V, pp. 139 ff.

tinct sense; *Moore* (born 1877) combines the central sense with the estimative and calls the combination the synthetic sense; *Suarez* considers the four internal senses as four different functions of one and the same cognitive potency; *Avicenna* divides the imagination into a power of forming images and a power of combining and dividing images.

While there is general agreement about the existence of expressed species in the imagination, opinions vary with respect to the necessity of such a species in the estimative, the memorative, and the central sense. *Renard* seems to admit an expressed species in each; *John of St. Thomas, Gredt,* and *Brennan* (born 1897) admit one in the estimative power and the memorative sense; *Klubertanz* (born 1912) seems inclined to deny the expressed species in all three and admit it only in the imagination.

SUMMARY

89. By internal senses are meant sense cognitive potencies which do not take their object directly from the external world but from the external senses through the central senses. Usually four such senses are distinguished, namely, the central sense, imagination, the estimative, and the memorative sense.

The central sense is an internal sense which enables its subject to perceive the sensations of the external senses, distinguish between them and combine them. Its existence and distinction from the external senses is proved from the fact that the external senses cannot sense that they are sensing, distinguish their object from that of the other senses or combine their sensations. The central sense is organic because its object is the concrete and individual sensations of the external senses taken concretely and individually. It is actuated by an impressed species received from the external senses.

The imagination is an internal sense by means of which the sensing subject is capable of retaining the species of the objects apprehended by the external senses and the central sense, when these objects are no longer acting upon the sense organs. It is distinct from the external senses and the central sense, which can operate only in the presence of an object actually stimulating their organs. The imagination is organic, for its object is the concrete and individual object in its concreteness. It is actuated by a species received from the external senses and the central sense. The act of imagining produces an expressed species or phantasm, because the object imagined may be absent or even nonexistent. The phantasms are not retained but reproduced whenever the imagination is again actuated by the retained impressed species. *The reproduction of phantasms may be caused by physiological stimulation; by association of images according to the laws of contrast, of contiguity and of similarity; or by the action of the will and instinct.

The estimative potency is an internal sense by means of which its subject is capable of perceiving concretely certain aspects of sense objects which are not perceived by the other senses; e.g., the concrete good and evil of a sense object with respect to the sensing subject. The estimative power is distinct from the other senses, because its object is different, viz., the unsensed aspects of a sense object. The estimative potency is organic, for it is concerned with the concretely and individually useful, harmful, etc. as such. In man, the estimative potency is called the cogitative or discursive power or the particular intellect, because its functions are modified by the fact that man's intellect can guide man in determining the good or evil nature of an object. In man, as guided by reason, the cogitative power is an instrument of reason and applies on the concrete level the judgments made by the intellect on the universal level.

The memorative potency is an internal sense by means of which its subject is capable of retaining the perceptions of the estimative potency, especially the concrete pastness of a sense experience. Thus it is by means of the memorative sense that an experience is recognized as having been perceived in the past. The distinction of the memorative sense from the other senses follows from the difference of its object from that of the other senses. Its organic nature is evident from the fact that it is concerned with the concrete and individual as such. In man this potency can be used under the influence of reason to search deliberately for a "forgotten" image, in which case it is called reminiscence.

The various senses are not merely juxtaposited without any connection, but are interdependent. They are ordered to secure for the sensing subject the maximum possibility of a perfect sense-guided life.

SUGGESTED READINGS

90. Aristotle, *De anima,* bk. III, chaps. 2 ff.; *De memoria et reminiscentia.*

Thomas Aquinas, *Summa theol.,* Ia, q. 78, a. 4; *De anima,* a. 13.

Robert E. Brennan, *Thomistic Psychology,* chap. 5, pp. 121–146.

Henri Renard, *The Philosophy of Man,* pp. 104–115.

George P. Klubertanz, *The Philosophy of Human Nature,* chap. 7; *The Discursive Power* (St. Louis: 1952), chap. 9.

Julien Peghaire, "A Forgotten Sense, the Cogitative," in *The Modern Schoolman,* 1943, pp. 123–140 and 210–229.

Thomas V. Moore, *Cognitive Psychology* (New York: 1939), pp. 237 ff. (the synthetic sense); pp. 405 ff. (memory).

——— *The Driving Forces of Human Nature* (New York: 1948), pp. 231 ff. Human instinctive activity.

Robert E. Brennan, *General Psychology*, chaps. 14–17.

Hubert Gruender, *Experimental Psychology* (Milwaukee: 1935), chaps. 12, 13. Instinct.

CHAPTER 9

Appetite in General

Natural and Elicited Appetite

*** 91. Appetite is the traditional name for what modern psychology calls the force of conation, or orexis. Its action is appetency, but often the term "appetite" itself is used instead of appetency. In its broadest sense appetite means any tendency of a thing to an end. Taken in this sense the term includes chemical affinity and other physical tendencies, as well as emotions and acts of will. By a *natural* appetite we mean any inclination which is consequent [1] upon the very nature of a thing and not based upon an act of cognition. Such an appetite is innate, uniform, and wholly determined by the nature itself of its subject. It is not influenced by the knowledge its subject may have of the existence of the inclination. For instance, if his parachute fails to open the unlucky airman may know that he is rapidly "tending" towards the earth, but this knowledge exercises no influence upon the action of his "appetite." A natural appetite exists in anything that acts; for every agent acts for an end, and therefore naturally tends to this end or has an appetite

[1] A natural appetite is consequent upon a nature in a purely logical sense and not as if it really "followed" this nature.

for it. Such an "appetite," however, is not an action of a distinct operative potency, but merely the order of a thing to its end. In this sense we may say that hydrogen has a natural "appetite" for oxygen, because it "tends" to unite with it; or that a body has a natural "appetite" for another body by which it is attracted.[2]

In opposition to natural "appetite" we distinguish the so-called *elicited* appetite, i.e., an inclination called forth (elicited) by an act of cognition. According to the nature of the cognition by which it is called forth the elicited appetite is further divided into *sense appetite* and intellectual appetite or *will.* Thus sense appetite will be the tendency towards a good which flows from the apprehension of this good by the senses, and intellectual appetite will be a tendency towards a good which is consequent upon the apprehension of this good by the intellect. Note, however, that the good to which an appetite tends may be not only something positive but also the absence of an evil, because the absence of an evil is something good.

Elicited Appetite

92. Concerning elicited appetite in general, we assert that it exists, i.e., that cognition is followed by appetite; that it is really distinct from the nature of its subject, or a real operative potency; and that it is really distinct from the cognitive potency from which it flows.

Appetite Follows Cognition. The truth of this statement is known from *experience.* As a matter of fact, advertising is based upon it—knowledge of saleable goods is given,

[2] We use "appetite" between quotation marks, because it is only in a metaphorical sense that the term is used for an inclination which is wholly independent from consciousness.

because such knowledge awakens a desire for their possession. Animals, too, show by their behavior that appetite follows cognition, for at least part of their actions is motivated by their perceptions. A cat, for instance, will move to the mouse which it perceives.

It is possible to prove also *a priori* that appetite follows cognition. By an act of cognition a form is possessed by the knower. But any form is followed by an inclination, because any form is a nature and has an end to which it orders the subject having the form. Moreover, if cognition were not followed by appetite, knowledge would be utterly sterile. The knowing subject could neither enjoy it nor make use of it. Knowledge would be, so to speak, a dead-end street, leading nowhere. With regard to activity, beings endowed with cognitive powers would not be better than nonknowing beings.

The elicited appetite is *really distinct from the nature of its subject.* As we have seen above, the natural "appetite" is not really distinct from that of which it is the appetite, because it is nothing but the natural order of a thing to its purpose. The elicited appetite, however, is really distinct from the nature of its subject. For by knowing the subject possesses a form which is really distinct from his own form or nature; hence the inclination which is consequent upon such a form will be an appetite that is really distinct from the nature of the subject.

The elicited appetite is *really distinct also from the cognitive potency* which it follows, because the formal objects of the appetitive and the cognitive potencies are different. While a cognitive potency is concerned with things insofar as they are sensible or intelligible, an appetitive potency has as its object things insofar as they are known to be desirable or suitable for the subject. Hence the only object of the elicited appetite is the known good.

Concerning elicited appetite the following should be noted.

1) The appetite elicited by cognition is to be distinguished from the *natural appetite of the cognitive potency*. By its very nature a cognitive potency tends to its acts as its own good or end; e.g., sight tends naturally to the act of seeing. But in addition to this natural appetite there is the elicited appetite which tends to the perceived object as a good that is desirable for the knowing subject as a whole.

2) The elicited appetite is a *passive* potency in the sense that it needs to be determined to its action by a good apprehended by a cognitive potency.[3]

3) Although the elicited appetite is really distinct from the cognitive potency which it follows, the two are *closely related*. The appetitive function naturally complements the cognitive function by making it possible for the subject to act in accordance with its knowledge. Moreover, the real distinction does not mean that the two operative potencies exist or act as autonomous beings—they are merely distinct immediate principles by means of which one and the same subject acts.

Historical Notes

*93. The existence of appetites is denied by the materialists who do not admit any purposive tendencies.

The real distinction of the elicited appetite from the nature of the subject is denied by the nominalists and the empiricists, who reject really distinct operative potencies.

According to the ancient Stoics and some modern philosophers, such as *Herbert Spencer* (1820–1903), ap-

[3] Cf. St. Thomas, *Summa theol.*, Ia–IIae, q.22, a.2.

petite in general is reducible to cognition; according to *William James* (1842–1910) sense appetite is nothing but the sum total of sensations produced by physiological conditions, and therefore not really distinct from sense cognition; according to *Spinoza* (1632–1677) the will and the intellect are not really distinct.

SUMMARY

94. By appetite in general is meant any inclination towards an end. A natural appetite is the nature of a thing considered as ordered to its end. An elicited appetite is an inclination called forth by an act of cognition or to an object as known.

Experience shows that appetite follows cognition. Moreover, in cognition the knower possesses a form, and any form is for an end and orders its subject to this end; therefore, cognition is followed by appetite.

The elicited appetite is really distinct from the nature of its subject, because it is consequent upon a form which is distinct from the natural form of the knower. It is distinct also from the cognitive potency upon which it is consequent, because its formal object is the thing as desirable, while that of the cognitive potency is the thing as knowable.

SUGGESTED READINGS

95. Aristotle, *De anima,* bk. II, chap. 3.

Thomas Aquinas, *In II De anima,* lect. 5, nos. 286–291; *Summa theol.,* Ia, q. 80, a. 1; *De veritate,* q. 22, a. 3.

Henri Renard, *The Philosophy of Man,* chap. 7.

CHAPTER 10

Sense Appetite

Nature and Kinds of Sense Appetite

*** 96. *Feelings, Emotions, and Passions.* Apart from cognitive actions there are other sense experiences which are of an affective nature, such as hunger and thirst, pleasure and joy, love and hatred. These affective experiences of the sense appetite find their origin in sensation; yet they are not mere sensations but inclinations or tendencies towards or away from a sense object. They are accompanied by certain physiological changes, called the "bodily resonance," such as accelerated heartbeat, blushing, visceral changes ("butterflies" in the stomach), and glandular secretions. According as this bodily resonance is strong or relatively weak, modern psychologists speak of *emotions* and *feelings* or sentiments. In this context the term "feeling" does not indicate an act of sense cognition but an act of appetite based upon sense cognition. The difference between feelings and emotions is merely a matter of degree of bodily resonance, and therefore Thomistic philosophers correctly classify both under the general term "*passions.*" In Thomistic philosophy passion simply indicates any movement of the sense appetite, and does not have the derogatory implication attached to it in ordinary language.

Organic Nature of the Sense Appetite. As has been said, the sense appetite takes its *object* from sensation, for it is an appetite flowing from sense cognition. Accordingly, it will always be concerned with the sensible good or the sensible evil, i.e., with something that pleases or displeases the animal body on the level of sense experience.

Because of the sensible character of the object, the *organic nature* of the sense appetite should be clear. Operative potencies are specified by their objects. But the object of the sense appetite is the concrete and material good perceived by the senses. Such a good can be attained only by means of an operative principle which is composed of a psychical and a corporeal or organic element. Therefore, the sense appetite is of an organic nature.

Concupiscible and Irascible Appetite. The sense appetite may be divided into the concupiscible and the irascible appetite or, to use more modern expressions, into the propensity to enjoy and the propensity to fight, mild or emergency emotions. The *concupiscible* appetite has as its object the sensible good or evil simply taken as such, while the *irascible* appetite is concerned with the sensible good that is difficult to obtain or the sensible evil that is hard to avoid. These two appetites are *really distinct* operative potencies, as is evident from the fact that they can counteract and be opposed to each other. For example, the concupiscible appetite may incline a sensing subject to enjoy its present state of peace and quiet, while the irascible appetite drives it to fight against obstacles opposing the acquisition of a new good.

It is to be noted that the movements of the irascible appetite arise from those of the concupiscible appetite and tend to terminate in them. For instance, anger arises from sadness over a present evil, and after overcoming this evil terminates in joy.

Fundamental Movements of the Sense Appetites

97. The good to which the sense appetite tends may be either something which is good in itself or the deliverance from an evil. Accordingly, both the concupiscible and the irascible appetites have two contrary terms, good and evil. The *concupiscible* appetite may be concerned with both terms in a threefold way, namely, as they are in themselves (as such), as present, and as absent. This gives rise to six ways in which this appetite may refer to its term. To each of these ways corresponds a passion, as indicated in the diagram below. The *irascible* appetite may be concerned with a difficult evil in three ways, viz., as present, as absent or threatening but conquerable, and as absent or threatening and unconquerable. With a difficult good the irascible appetite is concerned as either attainable or unattainable. A present good is not difficult; hence there is no movement of the irascible appetite which is directed to a present difficult good. Thus there are five ways in which the irascible appetite may refer to its term. In all, this gives us eleven fundamental movements of the sense appetite or eleven passions. Other passions exist, but they are combinations of fundamental passions; for instance, pity is a combination of love and sadness.

The following classic diagram indicates the opposed passions and their objects.

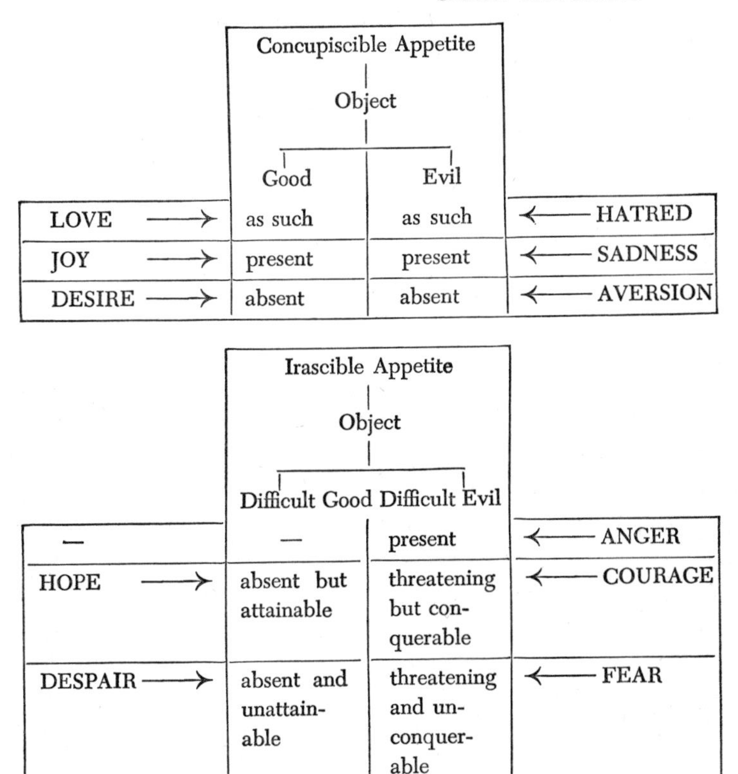

Concupiscible Appetite — Object	Good	Evil	
LOVE →	as such	as such	← HATRED
JOY →	present	present	← SADNESS
DESIRE →	absent	absent	← AVERSION

Irascible Appetite — Object	Difficult Good	Difficult Evil	
—	—	present	← ANGER
HOPE →	absent but attainable	threatening but conquerable	← COURAGE
DESPAIR →	absent and unattainable	threatening and unconquerable	← FEAR

Role of the Passions. The passions play a very important role in the life of both rational and irrational animals. Animal activity is less determined by nature than that of purely vegetative life, because in animals the cognitive potencies give rise to activities which are not found in plants. However, the energy of any organism is limited and therefore has to be used with moderation and care. If all is well organically the passions show themselves in a feeling of well-being. If the organs are overtaxed or perhaps not sufficiently exercised, the passions urge the sensing subject to remedy the defect by means of rest or exercise. In emergency situations they are the driving forces by means of which the animal is capable of acting as directed by its estimative and memorative sense powers.

Irrational animals do not have any suprasensitive principle to direct their passions. In man, however, the passions may be, and should be subjected to the control of reason and will, for otherwise man will lower himself to the level of the brute. As controlled by reason man's passions can contribute powerfully to support the activities of intellect and will, because they can intensify man's tendency to the object of his desire.

Muscular Motion

98. Nutrition accumulates chemical energy in the muscles. When released energy produces local movement of the muscles. Such muscular motion is automatic, reflex, or spontaneous. If the motion occurs independently of any stimulation of the sense organs, it is called *automatic;* e.g., heartbeat and breathing. A *reflex* motion results from the stimulation of a sense organ (or from a phantasm [1]), but is not, or at least not perfectly, under the control of the appetite; for instance, the contraction of the pupil of the eye under strong light; the "knee jerk." Muscular motion which results from an act of cognition and is under the control of the appetite is called *spontaneous;* e.g., the movement of an animal towards perceived food.

Some psychologists try to explain all muscular motion as

[1] So-called psychic or conditional reflexes. For instance, the mere *sight* of tasty food may cause the secretion of saliva, because the imagination combines the sight with previously experienced flavors.

purely reflex or automatic motions. Yet our own experience shows that many of our movements are controlled by the rational appetite or will. It is likewise not possible to explain all animal motions as pure reflexes.[2] Hence the occurrences of spontaneous motions in man and animals cannot reasonably be denied. And because all motion requires a principle of motion, it should be clear that moving organisms possess a potency of locomotion.

*Whether or not this locomotive potency is a *distinct active potency* of sense life is a matter of dispute. Some philosophers, as Suarez, John of St. Thomas, and Mercier, affirm its real distinction from the appetite as an active potency which elicits its own acts. Others, however, such as St. Thomas, Froebes, and Renard, hold that the appetite itself produces the motions and that the parts of the body can be said to have a locomotive potency only insofar as they are able to receive the movement imparted to them by the appetite. To quote St. Thomas: "The power of locomotion is not only in the sense and the appetite as commanding the motion, but also in the parts of the body insofar as they are able to obey the appetite of the soul which moves them." [3] And: "The power of locomotion is twofold. One commands the motion, namely the appetite. . . . The other locomotive power is the one which executes it, through which the members of the body are rendered capable of obeying the appetite: its act is not to move but to be moved." [4]

In man the locomotive potency, like all other powers of his sensitive nature, is subservient to the intellect and

[2] Cf. Thomas V. Moore, *Dynamic Psychology,* pp. 55 ff.

[3] *Summa theol.,* Ia, q.78, a.1, ad 4.

[4] *Op. cit.,* q.75, a.3, ad 3. Cf. *Contra gentes,* bk. II, chap. 82; *De potentia,* q.3, a.11, ad 20.

will, and thus can become an instrument of his thinking and willing. For instance, man's tongue is an instrument of speech and serves to express his thoughts; his hands are instruments of his practical intellect and serve to embody the creations of his mind.

Historical Notes

*99. The organic nature of the sense appetite is denied by *Descartes,* who holds all life to be immaterial. According to *Tongiorgi* the organs of the appetite are merely a condition but not an essential element of sense life.

The real distinction of the irascible and the concupiscible appetite is denied by *Suarez,* but affirmed by *Aristotle, St. Thomas,* and most Thomistic philosophers.

The division of the appetite into eleven fundamental passions is the traditional Thomistic division. *Descartes'* division has only six primary passions, that of *Spinoza* only three. Modern psychologists have proposed several other divisions.

SUMMARY

100. The movements of the sense appetite are called passions, which embrace both the feelings and emotions of modern psychology. Feelings differ from emotions only in degree of bodily resonance.

The sense appetite takes its object from sense cognition and is concerned with a sensible good or evil. Sense appetite is organic in nature, for its object can be attained only by a principle of operation which is composed of a psychic and a corporeal element.

The concupiscible appetite, the propensity to enjoy, is

concerned with the sensible good as such. It is really distinct from the irascible appetite, the propensity to fight, which refers to the difficult or arduous good or evil, as we know from the fact that these two appetites can be opposed to each other.

The fundamental movements or passions of the concupiscible appetite are love, joy, desire, hatred, sadness, and aversion. Those of the irascible appetite are hope, despair, anger, courage, and fear.

The passions play a very important part in the life of an animal because they give the animal the inclination to act as required by the conditions of its organs or the emergency situations reported by the senses. In man they support the activities of intellect and will, because they intensify man's tendencies to the object of his rational desire.

Motions of the animal body are automatic (independent of sensation), reflex (dependent on sensation, but not controlled by the appetite), or spontaneous (arising from sensation and controlled by the appetite). Spontaneous motions require a principle of motion which is capable of executing the motion as directed by sensation and appetite.

SUGGESTED READINGS

101. Aristotle, *De anima,* bk. III, chaps. 9–10.

Thomas Aquinas, *Summa theol.,* Ia, q. 81, a. 2; *De veritate,* q. 25, a. 2; *In III De anima,* lect. 14. Concupiscible and irascible appetite.

——— *Summa theol.,* Ia–IIae, qq. 22, 23, 25, a. 1. The passions in general.

George P. Klubertanz, *The Philosophy of Human Nature,* chaps. 9, 11.

Robert E. Brennan, *General Psychology,* chap. 18. Emotion and outer behavior.

Thomas V. Moore, *Dynamic Psychology,* Part II, pp. 55 ff. Reflexes. Part III, pp. 101 ff. The affective mental states.

——— *The Driving Forces of Human Nature* (New York: 1950), Part III, pp. 107 ff. Human emotional life.

CHAPTER 11

The Nature of the Sensitive Soul

*** 102. Before considering the nature of the animal soul, we must first investigate whether or not there is any necessity to raise this question. If animals are not essentially different from plants, there will be no need to investigate their soul's nature in a special way, for it will have to be the same as that of plants. If, on the other hand, animals are essentially different from plants, they will need an essentially different soul.

The Distinction Between Plants and Animals

To discover whether or not plants are essentially different from animals, we must attend to the vital activity of plants and animals. Action always follows being; therefore, essentially different activities will require essentially different natures. And because the soul is the formal principle of nature, which gives to the nature its specific perfection, essentially different natures will require essentially different souls.

From the preceding chapters it is clear that plants have no sensation nor sense appetite, while animals have both.

But sensation and appetite are operations which are essentially different from nutrition, growth, and reproduction, for they are more perfectly immanent and irreducible to vegetative operations. Therefore, cognitive beings are essentially different from noncognitive beings. Hence animals are essentially different from plants and superior to them.

The Sensitive Soul

103. *Its Existence.* There should be no doubt regarding the existence of a sensitive soul in animals. Animals have vital operations and potencies, which can exist only in a body endowed with a vital principle or soul. The soul of an animal is essentially different from that of plants, because its vital operations of sensing and appetency are essentially different from the operations of vegetative life. The type of soul required by the specific activities of animal life is called a sensitive soul.

The Sensitive Soul Is the Substantial Form of the Body. The proof of this assertion is as follows:

If the body and the sensitive soul together are one principle of operation, the sensitive soul is the substantial form of the body. But the body and the sensitive soul of the animal are one principle of operation. Therefore, the sensitive soul is the substantial form of the body.

The *minor* of this argument was proved in the preceding chapters. With respect to the *major,* in order to be one principle of operation or one nature, body and soul must be related to each other as potency is to act in the order of nature, i.e., as matter is to substantial form. Otherwise, they could not constitute one nature, but would be two beings that are accidentally united (cf. chap. 2).

In view of the fact that animals are endowed not only with sensitive life but also with vegetative life, the question may be asked whether or not there are two souls in the animal, one vegetative and the other sensitive. The answer is that there is *only one soul* in the animal, the sensitive soul, but this soul is at the same time the principle of the vegetative operations of the animal. The animal soul is called sensitive because it is quite natural to name a thing after that which is most perfect in it. Two souls in one animal would mean two substantial forms, which is impossible, as we have seen in Chapter Two.

The Sensitive Soul Is Dependent Upon the Body for Its Existence. By a sensitive soul we mean here the soul whose highest activity consists in the operations of sense life.[1] The proof of the assertion is as follows: If the sensitive soul intrinsically depends upon the body for all its operations, it is dependent upon the body for its existence. But the purely sensitive soul is intrinsically dependent upon the body for all its operations. Therefore, this soul depends upon the body for its very existence.

The *major* premise follows from the principle that action follows being. The *minor* is clear, because the operations of the sensitive soul are either vegetative or sensitive, both of which are organic.

From the intrinsic dependence of the sensitive soul upon the body it follows that this soul *cannot continue to exist* after the death of the animal. At the moment of death, the sensitive soul is indirectly corrupted, as was explained in Chapter Five.

[1] The question whether or not so-called irrational animals have an intellect will be considered in Chapter Fifteen.

Historical Notes

*104. *Descartes,* who conceived animals as complex machines which "act naturally by springs like a watch," did not admit any principle of life in irrational animals. Likewise, those materialists who explain all life as purely mechanical and chemical reactions.

Tongiorgi and *Palmieri* (1829–1909) admitted a soul in animals, but denied that the soul is the substantial form of their bodies.

Plato, Palmieri, and *Tongiorgi* denied that sensitive souls cannot exist independently of the body. This view would imply that sensitive souls are spirits and therefore endowed with an intellect and immortal.

SUMMARY

105. The operations of sense life are irreducible to those of vegetative life and differ from them in immanence; hence animals are essentially different from, and superior to plants.

The existence of a sensitive soul follows from the fact that animals have sense operations, for action follows being. The sensitive soul is the substantial form of the body, because together with the body it constitutes one principle of organic operations, which is possible only if body and soul are related to each other as potency and act, or as matter and form. The sensitive soul is the principle also of the vegetative activities in the animal, for it is impossible for one body to have two substantial forms.

The sensitive soul is dependent upon the body for its very existence, for it depends upon the body for all its operations. Consequently, the sensitive soul comes into existence in dependence upon the body, i.e., is educed from the potency of matter, and ceases to be by indirect corruption when the sensing organism dies.

SUGGESTED READINGS

106. Aristotle, *De anima,* bk. III, chap. 4.

Thomas Aquinas, *Summa theol.,* Ia, q. 75, a. 3; *Contra gentes,* bk. II, chap. 68; *De potentia,* q. 3, a. 11. Intrinsic dependence of sensitive soul upon body.

——— *Summa theol.,* Ia, q. 118, a. 1. Origin of the sensitive soul.

——— *Contra gentes,* bk. II, chap. 82. Corruption of the sensitive soul.

SECTION IV

Intellectual Life

107. From the preceding chapters it is clear that both men and animals possess the vital operations of sense cognition and sense appetite. In the present section we must investigate whether or not men and perhaps also animals have other vital operations which exceed the vegetative and sensitive orders, and therefore require a different kind of a vital principle or soul. The operations to be considered are those of intellect and will. Regarding the intellect we shall first study its existence and nature, then the origin of ideas and the object of the intellect, and finally the question of subhuman intelligence. Concerning the intellectual appetite or will, we shall have to investigate its existence, nature, as well as its freedom of operation.

In the course of these studies it will become evident that the intellect and the will are operative potencies of an inorganic nature. Therefore, it becomes necessary to devote our attention to the nature of the soul demanded by these potencies, its union with the body, its origin and duration.

Schematic Division

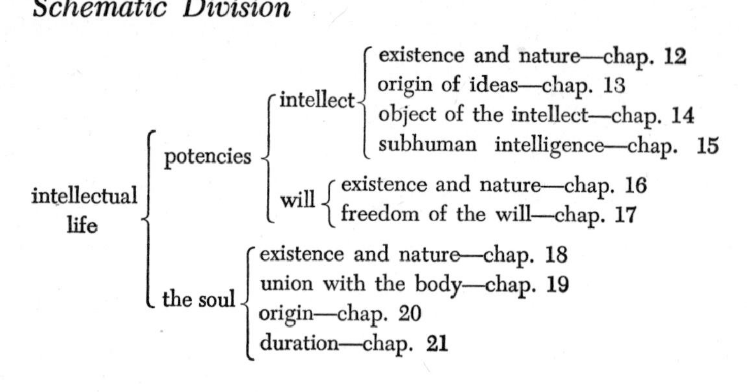

CHAPTER 12

Existence and Nature of the Intellect

Existence of a Suprasensible Cognitive Potency

*** 108. *Man's Excellence in the Cognitive Order.* Even the most confirmed materialist will be willing to admit that man's achievements distinguish him from all other animals. While other animals continue to live, generation after generation, without any remarkable changes in their general pattern of life, man largely determines his own pattern and constantly tries to improve his way of life by deliberately searching for new and better ways of, and tools for doing things. Moreover, alone among animals man has developed an ingenious way of letting others know what is going on in his mind—by means of arbitrarily chosen sounds, gestures, and other signs he expresses his ideas. These two, the deliberate use of tools and the invention of language to communicate his ideas, set man apart from the rest of the visible world. From these two have sprung culture and civilization, the arts and the sciences, the law and order which normally prevail in human society. They are activities which manifest that man has an "intellect."

Reserving a more profound examination of the nature of this intellect to the second part of this chapter, we want to show at present that these activities prove that man is endowed with a cognitive potency which surpasses the capacities of sense life described in the preceding chapters.

The Deliberate Use of Tools. By a tool we mean anything used by an agent to reach a desired purpose. The term "deliberate" indicates that the agent uses the tool neither at random, on a hit or miss basis, nor according to a fixed pattern that is the same for all; but with the intention of attaining a desired purpose by means of a tool selected for this purpose by the user. Such a deliberate use of tools implies that the user knows the *tool as a tool,* the *purpose as a purpose,* and the *relationship* of one to the other. It implies also that the user is able *to judge* whether or not a thing is suitable as a tool for the desired purpose. But the knowledge of tool as tool, purpose as purpose, and relationship, as well as the personal judgment of the suitability of the tool for the purpose, cannot be had by a sense power. As we have seen in the preceding chapters, sense powers are limited to the apprehension of concrete and individual phenomena, the concrete combination of sense data, and a concrete estimation of good and evil. On the other hand tools, purpose, and relationship as such, are abstract and universal; a personal judgment is an affirmation or negation of identity, and therefore above the capacity of a sense power. Accordingly, man's ability to make deliberate use of tools shows that he has a suprasensible power of cognition.

The Invention of Language. Language consists in the manifestation of thoughts by means of deliberately and arbitrarily chosen symbols. An arbitrary symbol is any material thing, such as a sound, gesture, or mark, which the user selects to replace and designate something other than itself. For instance, of itself the sound "horse" does not indicate anything else than itself. As a sign, however, it stands for the animal known as a "horse." To use such symbols one must understand that a material thing can stand for, and indicate something else with which it has no natural relation. Such an understanding requires knowledge of *signs as signs* and *relationship as relationship*. But no sense power is capable of knowing a sign as a sign and a relation as a relation, because the senses are limited to the concrete and individual, while a sign as sign and relation as relation are abstract and universal. Therefore, again, we may conclude that man has a cognitive potency which exceeds the level of the senses and cannot be reduced to them.

The Nature of the Intellect

109. What is the nature of this suprasensible cognitive potency which is called the human intellect? Is it merely suprasensible in the meaning that it surpasses all other cognitive potencies observed in animals, or is it a cognitive potency of a different order—suprasensible in that it is inorganic and immaterial? The answer to this question has more than a purely academic value, for upon it will depend the answer to be given to such practical questions as the immortality of the soul and the foundation of the social and moral order. Yet, practical considerations should not influence our answer, which has to be given in accordance with the own internal exigencies of the problem.

Senses of the Term "Immaterial." Before examining the problem let us first recall the exact meaning of certain terms. Immaterial, as we have seen in no. 65, may be taken to mean *"not limited to a purely passive reception of forms."* Obviously, in this sense of the term there is no special problem concerning the immateriality of the intellect, because all cognitive potencies are immaterial in this sense. Immateriality may mean also spirituality, i.e., *intrinsic independence of matter* in operation and existence. An operation which is immaterial in this sense is not performed by the body or any of its organs, but can spring only from a spiritual principle. It is in this sense that the term should be understood when there is question of the immateriality of the intellect. However, this *intrinsic* or subjective independence of matter does not preclude the possibility of *extrinsic* or objective dependence upon the body, i.e., the possibility that the intellect cannot function until a certain material condition is fulfilled because it depends upon matter for the object of its action. This extrinsic dependence will be discussed in the next chapter.

In the following pages we intend to show that the intellect is immaterial in the sense explained above. Because of the importance of the problem, several proofs will be offered for the immateriality of the intellect.

110. *The Immateriality of the Intellect Follows from Its Object.* This proof, which presupposes the admission of realism, may be formulated as follows:

If the intellect knows the immaterial, the intellect is immaterial.

But the intellect knows the immaterial.

Therefore, the intellect is immaterial.

The *major* premise is clear, because a cognitive potency must be proportionate to its object (cf. no. 66). No organic potency which is intrinsically dependent upon matter can reach an object which is intrinsically free from matter. The action of an organic potency takes place through its organ, which is something concrete and extended and therefore affected by space, time, and the individual determinations of matter; hence this action cannot reach an object which is not concrete and extended in space and time. Claiming that the immaterial can be grasped by the material is tantamount to claiming that an effect can be greater than its cause. To use a comparison, it would be like trying to put a spirit literally into chains, or tying a piece of string around that which is understood by the terms "intelligibility," "being," or "freedom."

Regarding the *minor,* the intellect knows the *universal,* as in man, house, animal, and action; the *abstract,* as humanity, truth, and principle; the *immaterial,* as being, substance, spirit, and relation. But the universal is immaterial, because it transcends the limits of time and space which characterize matter; the abstract is immaterial, because it leaves behind the concrete world of matter; the immaterial is wholly free from matter either absolutely (as a spirit) or at least because it can be found without matter (substance).

The Immateriality of the Intellect Follows from Its Self-Reflection. Reflection may be proper or improper. By *improper* reflection is meant that a subject knows the acts of one cognitive potency by means of another. In this way the central sense reflects upon the acts of the external senses. Likewise, our intellectual knowledge of the activity of our senses may be called reflection in this improper signification. Reflection is *proper* if a cognitive potency is formally conscious of its own acts and itself. In this description of proper reflection the term "formally" indicates that we are not concerned with the implicit consciousness which accompanies every act of understanding, but with the cognitive activity in which the intellect takes itself and its action as objects of its consideration. Proper reflection is possible only in a cognitive potency which is inorganic or immaterial. The proof is as follows:

If the intellect is capable of proper reflection it is inorganic.

But the intellect is capable of proper reflection.

Therefore, the intellect is inorganic.

Regarding the *major* premise, in proper reflection a cognitive potency knows itself and its act, so that the principle and the term or object of the operation are identical. Identity excludes any intermediary, for nothing can come between a thing and itself. But in an organic potency the object is received through the organ, so that the organ is between the potency and the object. Hence in an organic potency the object cannot be identical with the potency itself. Moreover, an organ is something material and extended, having parts outside parts. But in self-reflection, the whole applies itself (*re*-flects upon) to the whole, which is impossible for an extended reality. A piece of paper, for instance, cannot be folded in such a way that the whole covers the whole. Therefore, a cognitive potency which is self-reflective cannot be organic.

The *minor* premise is clear from experience. Man is capable of being formally and intellectually self-conscious, i.e., knowing himself intellectually by paying explicit attention to his intellect and its activity.

*The objection could be raised that experience shows merely man's awareness of his intellectual activity, but not that this awareness is proper self-reflection. In other words, perhaps man has another cognitive potency by means of which he is aware of his intellect through *improper* reflection, just as through the central sense he is aware of the actions of the external senses. To this we may answer that if such a cognitive potency of reflection is admitted, a third power has to be admitted by means of which man reflects upon his reflective potency, for man is capable also of reflecting upon his power of reflection (we are doing it now); and a fourth to reflect upon the third; and so on without end. Thus we should be bound to admit an almost unlimited number of reflective powers, most of which would never be used.

111. *The Immateriality of the Intellect Follows from Its Extension to All Bodies.* This argument, which is of a profound metaphysical nature, is the one which St. Thomas preferred above all others. It may be proposed as follows:

If the human intellect were an organic potency it could not know the nature of all bodies.

But our intellect is capable of knowing the nature of all bodies.

Therefore, the human intellect is not an organic potency.

With respect to the *major* premise, as we have seen in Chapter Six, in a finite being cognition is an act by which the knower becomes the object to be known. But it is impossible to become what one already is. Before the act of cognition, the cognitive subject is in potency to become the object, but is not yet actually the object. If the intellect were organic it would actually be of a definite corporeal nature. But that which actually is of a definite corporeal nature cannot be at the same time in potency with respect to all corporeal nature. Therefore, if the intellect were organic it could not know the nature of all bodies. How being of a definite corporeal nature limits the capacity of a cognitive potency may be illustrated by a comparison. If the sense of sight were of a definite color, say, blue, its actuation would always result in the sensation of blue and no other color could be sensed.

The *minor* is clear from experience. Note, however, that we do not claim actual knowledge of the nature of all bodies for the human intellect, but merely that it is capable of knowing this nature. Moreover, in claiming that our intellect is capable of such knowledge, we do not mean that it can know exactly in all details what the nature of a given body is, but only that the intellect can know the nature of all bodies at least insofar as they are bodies.

**Further Analysis of This Proof.* Several points in this argument deserve further investigation. In the first place, one may say that an intellect which is *physically* of a corporeal nature could still be cognitively or *intentionally* in potency to the form of other bodies. To this, we may reply that the form of other bodies would have to actuate such a corporeal intellect through its organ; hence the form of this organ would first actuate the intellect, so that it would no longer be in potency to the intentional reception of form. As a result, an organic intellect could know only its own organ.

But is it not true that the senses are organic; and therefore would not it follow by analogy that the *senses can know only their organs?* The answer is that the senses do not know the nature of their organs, but are limited to the sensation of certain definite material qualities of the external object, and *these qualities do not exist in the organs.* The eye, for instance, is colorless and thus can be actuated by the material quality of external objects which is called "color"; the organs of heat and cold have a definite temperature and therefore can sense only those material qualities of the object which may be indicated by the term "hotter or colder than the organs of heat and cold." Accordingly, the actuation of an organic sense by a material quality which does not exist in its organ will not result in the sensation of its own organ by the sense, but in the sensation of the material quality of the external object which stimulates the organ.

Again, it may be urged that if the reasoning of this proof is correct, one could argue: If the intellect is a being it *cannot know the nature of all beings,* because any actuation of the intellect could result only in the intellect knowing itself. Therefore, either the intellect cannot know all beings, which is false, or the intellect is a nonbeing, which is ridiculous. The reply is: Our argument does not deny that the intellect has a definite nature, but merely a definite *corporeal* nature, because matter is the principle of limitation and therefore whatever is material or corporeal cannot be actuated by more than one form of the same kind. If, however, the intellect is not material but spiritual, this limitation is not present. Hence we may admit that if the intellect were a material being, it could not know all beings; but this conclusion does not follow with respect to an intellect which is spiritual. Moreover, it may be admitted that our intellect has no direct knowledge of spiritual beings, but knows them only in the way of corporeal natures.

112. *Modern Difficulties.* From modern psychology two difficulties can be raised against the inorganic nature of the intellect. In the first place, psychologists have devised various methods for the *measurement* of human intelligence. But only that which is quantified can be measured. And since quantity is a property of matter, it would seem to follow that the intellect is material.

Secondly, intellectual activity does not occur without very definite *changes in the body,* such as an increase in rate of heart-beat and temperature. Moreover, it is a well-known phenomenon that thinking causes tiredness, i.e., a decrease in bodily energy. Therefore, again, it would seem that the activity of the intellect is organic.

With respect to the first of these difficulties, the measurement of intelligence, so-called intelligence tests indicate a person's ability by means of his achievements as compared to those of others belonging to the same social or racial level, age-group, etc. In other words, these tests do not measure the intellect in the strict sense by indicating its quantity, but merely *express quantitatively the qualitative appreciation* of one's intellectual achievements relatively to others. Keeping in mind that man knows the spiritual in the way of corporeal things, there is no reason to be surprised at his efforts to express spiritual qualities in terms of quantity.

Regarding the second difficulty, the occurrence of mental fatigue and bodily changes during the process of intellectual activity is not subject to debate. However, these facts cannot prove the organic nature of the intellect unless it be established that they really form part of the very process of intellection. Certain organic activities, as we shall see in Chapter 13, are a necessary *condition* for the activity of the intellect, which is extrinsically dependent upon organs. As a result, our intellectual activity is accompanied by body changes, and excessive intellectual endeavors may produce fatigue in the organs which prepare the operation of the intellect.

113. *Some Consequences of the Immateriality of the Intellect.* From the fact that the intellect is intrinsically

independent of matter we may at once draw the following conclusions with respect to the intellect:

a) In a purely material being there cannot be any intellectual activity in the proper sense of the term. As to intelligence in a wider sense, see Chapter 15.

b) Intellection is an act of the soul alone in which the body has no part. Obviously, we mean intellection itself and not any activity which prepares intellection, such as that of the external sense, the central sense, and the imagination. In saying that the soul alone is the principle of intellection, we do not affirm that the soul is the principle *which* understands; we mean only that the soul is the sole remote principle *by means of which* man understands. The principle which understands is the supposite or man himself.

c) Because the intellect is inorganic no part of the body can be called the seat of the intellect. Hence it is not true that we think with our brain. Nevertheless, it must be admitted that the brain, which is the seat of the internal senses, is more intimately connected with the activity of the intellect than, say, our big toe. For this reason the brain may be called the *extrinsic organ* of the intellect.

Each Man Has His Own Intellect. This point, which in the Middle Ages was the subject of much discussion, needs to be discussed only very briefly. From internal experience each one knows that it is he himself who understands and thinks, that he has his own acts of intellection, as is exemplified by Descartes' principle: "I think, therefore I am." But if the acts of intellection are not produced by a principle which belongs to me as a cognitive power flowing from my nature, they would be intellectual acts of another being *in me,* but never acts which I experience as *my* acts.

To use a comparison, the situation would be similar to that of a man who has swallowed a tiny watch: the watch keeps ticking in him, but by no stretch of imagination could one justify the statement that he is ticking.

Historical Notes

*114. The immateriality of the intellect is defended by many philosophers of widely different schools of thought —by *Plato, Aristotle, Averroes* (*ibn-Roshd,* 1126–1198), *Thomas Aquinas,* as well as *Descartes, Kant, Hegel,* and *Bergson* (1859–1941). It is denied by the materialists, who explain intellection as atomic vibration (*Democritus,* c. 460–360 B.C.) or physico-chemical reactions. As *Huxley* (1825–1895) expressed it, "the brain secretes thought as the liver secretes bile." The behaviorists (*Watson*) attempt to explain thought as movements of the larynx; the sensists try to explain it as a combination (*Locke,* 1632–1704) or transformation (*Condillac,* 1715–1780) of sense images; the structuralists (*Titchener,* 1867–1927) reduce it to vague sensations; etc.

In the Middle Ages there was a lively controversy concerning the unity of the intellect in all men. *Averroes,* the great Arabian commentator of Aristotle, asserted that there is only one intellect for all, while *St. Thomas* maintained that each man has his own intellect. Both appealed to *Aristotle,* but the latter's exact position has never been definitely settled.

SUMMARY

115. Man's excellence above other animals reveals itself most strikingly in his deliberate use of tools and the invention of language to communicate his thoughts. The deliberate use of tools implies that the user knows what is meant

by tool and purpose and their relationship, and that he is able personally to judge the suitability of a tool for the desired purpose. Because the sense powers are capable neither of knowing the meaning of tool, purpose, and their relationship, nor of pronouncing judgment about the suitability of one for the other, it follows that man has a cognitive potency which is suprasensible. Now the invention of language proves that man knows the meaning of signs as signs, and relationship as relationship. But the cognition of such abstract and universal things is beyond mere sense powers. Therefore, again, man has a cognitive potency which surpasses the level of sensation.

This cognitive potency, called the intellect, is suprasensible in the sense that it is strictly immaterial and inorganic. By "immaterial" here is meant that it is intrinsically independent of matter. However, this independence does not exclude the possibility of extrinsic or objective dependence upon matter.

The immateriality of the intellect follows from the fact that the intellect knows the immaterial, for a cognitive potency must be proportionate to its object. But the intellect can know the universal, which transcends the limits of space and time that characterize matter; the abstract, which leaves behind the concrete world of matter; the immaterial, which is free from matter. An organic potency operates through its organ and therefore can reach only that which is extended in space and time. Therefore, the intellect is inorganic.

The ability of the intellect to reflect upon itself also shows its immaterial nature. Self-reflection means that the principle and the object of the act of knowing are identical. But identity excludes any intermediary; hence there can be no organ through which the intellect knows itself.

The immateriality of the intellect follows also from its capacity to know the nature of all bodies. In a finite being cognition is an act by which the subject becomes the object to be known. But it is impossible for a thing to become what it already is. Therefore, if the intellect were of a corporeal nature, it would no longer be in potency to corporeal nature. As a matter of fact, however, the intellect is capable of knowing all bodies.

From the immateriality of the intellect it follows that no purely material being can have an intellect in the proper sense of the term; that intellection is an act of the soul alone; and that no part of the body can be called the seat of the intellect.

Each man has his own intellect, for otherwise each one would not experience his acts of intellection as his very own acts.

SUGGESTED READINGS

116. Aristotle, *De anima,* bk. III, chap. 4.

Thomas Aquinas, *De veritate,* q. 10, a. 8; *Contra gentes,* bk. II, chaps. 49, 66. First proof.

——— *Contra gentes,* bk. II, chaps. 49, 66. Second proof.

——— *Summa theol.,* Ia, q. 75, a. 2; *In III De anima,* lect. 7, no. 680; *De anima,* a. 14. Third proof.

——— *Summa theol.,* Ia, q. 76, a. 2; *Contra gentes,* bk. II, chaps. 73, 75; *De unitate intellectus.* Each man has his own intellect.

George P. Klubertanz, *The Philosophy of Human Nature,* chap. 8, pp. 158–164.

CHAPTER 13

The Process of Intellection

The Origin of Ideas

*** 117. *Dependence of the Intellect Upon the Phantasm.* In Chapters 3 and 6 we saw that the human intellect is in potency to understanding before it actually understands, and needs to be actuated by an impressed species. This impressed species is called the intelligible species. Experience shows that the actuation of the intellect somehow comes from the senses, specifically from the phantasm of the imagination. The following facts may be adduced in proof of this assertion:

a) If the working of the imagination is disturbed through injury to the brain, poisoning (narcotics or alcohol), or other causes, the intellect itself does not function properly even with respect to problems which previously were understood.

b) When we have to explain a difficult intellectual problem we try to find sensible examples or analogies, so that phantasms may be formed which can aid the intellect in the understanding of the problem.

c) If the phantasm of a sensible thing is completely absent, the intellect cannot form a proper idea of this thing;

for instance, it is impossible to give a proper idea of color to a man who has been blind from birth.

Accordingly, it is clear that our intellect does not operate without the phantasm. In some way the intellect obtains its necessary species from the senses.

This dependence of the intellect upon the senses gives rise to a great problem. A sense image is an image produced by an organic potency and therefore intrinsically material. The intellect, on the other hand, is inorganic or intrinsically immaterial and therefore can be acted upon only by a species which is immaterial. Otherwise the material would produce an immaterial effect, and the effect would be greater than the cause. Thus we are faced with the apparently impossible: How can the material impress itself upon the immaterial? How can a material phantasm actuate and determine an immaterial intellect?

Existence of an Agent Intellect. To solve the difficulty we must admit that *the phantasm is not the sole cause* of the actuation and determination of the intellect by an intelligible species. Another cause must be acting together with the phantasm, and this cause must be *immaterial*, for it will have to explain the immateriality of the intelligible species. This cause cannot be the intellect itself which understands, because the intellect which understands is a passive potency and needs to be actuated by the species before being fully able to act. Therefore, we must admit the existence of another immaterial agent, distinct from the intellect which understands, as the cause of the immateriality of the intelligible species. This immaterial agent is called the *agent intellect.* To distinguish it from the intellect which understands, the latter is called the possible or *potential intellect.*

The existence of the agent intellect may be proved as follows:

If the phantasms alone cannot produce the species which is necessary to actuate the potential intellect, there is an agent intellect.

But the phantasms alone cannot produce this species.

Therefore, there is an agent intellect.

The *major* premise is clear from the foregoing: if the phantasms exercise causality in the production of the intelligible species, but their causality cannot explain the immaterial nature of this species, then another cause must be admitted to explain this immateriality; which cause cannot be organic, because otherwise it would not explain anything.

The *minor* premise was proved at the beginning of this chapter.

The same conclusion will be reached if, instead of considering the necessity of the intellect to be actuated by a species, we pay attention to the intelligibility of the phantasm. A phantasm is not actually but only *potentially* intelligible, because it is material in the sense that it is the image of an individual material being with its individual determinations. Therefore, a phantasm is not proportionate to the immaterial intellect. To become *actually* intelligible, the phantasm has to be dematerialized, i.e., stripped of its material conditions. But only an immaterial entity can dematerialize the phantasm. Therefore, we must admit the existence of such an immaterial entity, called the agent intellect.

118. *Nature of the Agent Intellect.* What is the nature of this immaterial agent which together with the phantasm actuates and determines the potential intellect? Is it to be

identified with God Himself? Or a separate substance which operates in all men? Or an operative potency of each man? And if it is an operative potency, is it merely a different name expressing another function of one and the same intellectual potency or really distinct from the potential intellect?

A brief consideration should be sufficient to show that the *agent intellect is not God* Himself. If God's intervention were needed every time our intellect understands something, to understand would be beyond man's natural powers. God would have given him an intellectual nature which somehow never is in working order. Being intellectual he would have been ordered by nature to understanding, yet deprived of the necessary natural means to understand. Thus God would have created a nature which is essentially deficient, which is against divine wisdom.

For a similar reason we must say that the *agent intellect is not a separate spiritual substance,* for otherwise man would naturally be unable to understand. Moreover, if the agent intellect were a separate substance its causality would be independent of man; hence man would have no control over his acts of understanding, which is against experience.

By exclusion, therefore, it follows that the agent intellect is an *operative potency* of man, and consequently that there are as many agent intellects as there are human beings.

The agent intellect and the potential intellect are *really distinct.* For otherwise the intellect would have to be in act and in potency at the same time and with respect to the same. As an agent intellect, it would have to be in act with respect to the intelligible species, because it produces this species; as a potential intellect it would have to be in potency with respect to this species, because it receives this species. Therefore, the agent and potential intellect are not merely different names indicating different functions of one and the same intellectual potency, but really distinct operative powers.

Role of the Agent Intellect and the Phantasm in the Production of the Intelligible Species. As we have seen above the agent intellect and the phantasm "together" produce the intelligible species which actuates the potential intellect. We must now determine more accurately the relationship between the agent intellect and the phantasm in the production of this species.

In the first place, it is to be noted that not only the agent intellect but also the phantasm acts as the *efficient cause* of the species. The intelligible species requires an adequate efficient cause, i.e., a cause which can explain why it is both immaterial and of a determinate nature. But the agent intellect merely dematerializes; it always acts in the same way and thus cannot explain why the species is of a determinate nature. The phantasm, on the other hand, can explain why the species is of a determinate nature, for it represents something which is of a determinate nature, but cannot explain why the species is immaterial. Therefore, both the agent intellect and the phantasm are efficient causes of the species.

Secondly, the phantasm is not a coordinate principal cause, but acts as an *instrument of the agent intellect.* The phantasm cannot be a principal cause of the intelligible species, because being material it cannot act, by virtue of its own power, upon the immaterial intellect. Therefore, its causality is merely instrumental.

*As an instrument of the agent intellect, the phantasm

receives a premotion of the agent intellect by virtue of which it is transitorily raised to the immaterial level and thus is able to act upon the potential intellect.[1] Ordinary instruments, such as the tools of a craftsman, exercise their instrumental causality through the medium of their own action upon the subject; e.g., a chisel produces a statue through its action of cutting the wood. The phantasm, however, cannot act in this way upon the potential intellect—the material cannot act, by virtue of its own power, upon the immaterial—but exercises its instrumental causality by supplying the agent intellect with a determinate image that can be raised transitorily and passively to the immaterial level, and thus instrumentally produce an immaterial impression of a determinate nature in the potential intellect.

Comparison of the Agent and the Potential Intellect. Both the agent and potential intellect are immaterial potencies of the soul and both belong to the cognitive order. Both also are necessary for intellection. The action of both is immanent. But while the action of the potential intellect is strictly immanent, for it remains in this intellect as its perfection, that of the agent intellect is immanent only in a wider sense, because it remains in the same supposite but terminates in another potency (the potential intellect).

Only the potential intellect is an intellect in the proper sense of the term, because only the potential intellect elicits acts of understanding. The agent intellect is an intellect only in an improper and analogous sense, inasmuch as without its causal influence there can be no act of under-

[1] Cf. St. Thomas, *De veritate,* q.10, a.6, ad 8; q.27, a.4, ad 5; *In IV Sentent.,* d.1, q.1, a.4, sol. 2, ad 4 (no. 148 in Moos ed.); *Summa theol.,* IIIa, q.62, a.4, ad 1.

standing. The proper act of the agent intellect is to dematerialize phantasms by stripping them of their material conditions and presenting their essence to the potential intellect.[2]

The potential intellect is in potency and needs to be complemented by the intelligible species before being fully able to elicit its act of intellection. For this reason it is called a passive potency. The agent intellect, on the other hand, does not need to be complemented, but is always fully ready to act and by its action changes its object; hence it is said to be an active potency.

*The agent intellect is not active in the sense that its essence is its act, for nothing finite is its own act, but only in the sense that it elicits its act at once when a phantasm is present.[3] The phantasm, however, does not actuate the agent intellect—the material cannot act upon the immaterial—but is a necessary condition for the action of the agent intellect. The agent intellect does not reduce itself from potency to act, which is impossible, but connaturally passes from potency to act under the influence of the motion by which the First Cause moves all finite causes to their action. This influence can be either direct or through man's will. It should be clear that the First Cause moves also the potential intellect to its action.

[2] The action of the agent intellect may be compared to X rays showing the hidden structure of an object. For this reason the agent intellect is sometimes called the intellectual light. Because the agent intellect strips the phantasm of its material conditions, it is also called the abstractive power. This abstraction of the agent intellect differs from that of the potential intellect, which alone is formally cognitive.

[3] Cf. St. Thomas, *Summa theol.*, Ia, q.54, a.1, ad 1; *In III De anima*, lect. 10, no. 739.

Schematic Comparison

	Agent Intellect	*Potential Intellect*
points of agreement	belongs to the cognitive order is a potency of the soul is something immaterial. is necessary for intellection *needs to be moved to its act by the First Cause	
points of difference	causes understanding action is immanent only in a wider sense is an active potency is always fully ready to act	formally understands action is strictly immanent is a passive potency needs to be complemented before being fully ready to act

119. *Expressed Species of the Intellect.* When the agent intellect and the phantasm produce an intelligible species in the potential intellect, this intellect elicits its act of understanding. The act of understanding unites the knower with the object known and therefore must terminate in something corresponding exactly to that which is known. But the external object may not even be present; and even if present does not correspond exactly to that which is understood, for the external object, which exists concretely and individually, is understood as separate from the individual determinations of matter. Therefore, in the absence of a term corresponding exactly to that which is understood, it is necessary for the intellect to express in itself an image of that which it understands. This image is called the expressed species of the intellect, the mental word, or concept. In this species the intellect knows the external

object. Experience shows the existence of such a species, for in our intellectual life we are aware of the fact that we form concepts, definitions, and judgments of the things understood, and these concepts, definitions, and judgments are forms of expressed species.

*The expressed species of the intellect is *really distinct from the impressed species.* The impressed species is a principle of the act of intellection, while the expressed species is a "product" of this act.

*The expressed species is *really distinct from the act of intellection.* It is "produced" by this act, and that which produces is always really distinct from that which is produced.

*Finally, the expressed species is *really distinct from the object understood,* for to understand an object is quite different from understanding its concept. The concept is merely a means in which the object is known. The intellect understands the object when it considers the object, but understands the concept of the object only when it reflects upon the "product" of its understanding. What we understand is not primarily the concept of the object, but the object of which the concept is an image. Any theory which holds that our intellect merely understands concepts but not things is idealistic.[4]

120. *Summary of the Process of Understanding.* The whole process of understanding may be summarized as follows, although care should be taken not to interpret the sequence of events too mechanically.

The phantasm from which all intellectual knowledge takes its origin, is only potentially intelligible, because it

[4] It is beyond the scope of this study to show the fallacy of idealism. The question is considered professionally in epistemology.

is not wholly free from the conditions of matter and therefore not proportionate to a cognitive potency which is intrinsically immaterial. The agent intellect dematerializes the phantasm and thus makes it actually intelligible. The intellectual potency of understanding is only potentially understanding and needs to be actuated before being fully able to understand. The dematerialized phantasm, i.e., the phantasm as acted upon by the agent intellect, is proportionate to the potential intellect and acts upon it, thereby producing an intelligible species in it and thus making it fully capable of eliciting its act of understanding. The actuated intellect now elicits its act of understanding. The object itself of this act not being present in the intellect exactly as it is understood, the intellect expresses in itself a species or image of that which it understands, and this species is called the concept or mental word.

The Various Acts of the Intellect

121. The human intellect does not acquire perfect knowledge of its object by the first act performed after the reception of the intelligible species. With respect to the acquisition of knowledge there are three kinds of intellectual actions, which are called simple apprehension, judgment, and reasoning.

Simple Apprehension. By an act of simple apprehension the intellect grasps the essence of an object, but does not affirm or deny anything. In saying that the intellect grasps the "essence" of the object, we do not mean that a first apprehension is sufficient to make the intellect know the nature of the object in all its specific details. All that is implied is that the intellect has some idea of the object, although this idea may be very general and vague.

Judgment. Subsequently to its first apprehension the intellect has other apprehensions, and thus is in a position to compare the objects apprehended and to affirm or deny that they form a composite. This is called the act of judgment, in which the intellect understands the subject and the predicate as one inasmuch as they are parts of one proposition.

Reasoning. The intellect is capable also of proceeding from the understanding of one truth to that of another so as to gain explicit knowledge of another truth implied in the first. This is called reasoning. The power of reasoning is not a special potency but merely a different function of the potential intellect. The object of both reasoning and understanding is one and the same; only the way of attaining the object is different. Reasoning is compared to understanding as motion towards an object is to rest in the object reached, for by reasoning the intellect arrives at the understanding of an object. Obviously, motion and rest do not refer to different potencies but to one and the same.

Intellectual Memory. Experience shows that man has not only the power to acquire intellectual knowledge, but also the power to retain it, and to recognize intellectual knowledge as possessed in the past. The capacity to retain intellectual knowledge corresponds on the intellectual level to the imagination on the sense level, while the capacity to recognize intellectually corresponds to the memorative potency on the sense level.

The *capacity to retain* intellectual knowledge (by retaining the intelligible species) is another function of the intellect and does not require a distinct cognitive potency. A simple consideration of the nature of the intellect will show the reason. Operative potencies are specified and distinguished according to their formal objects. As long as the formal object is the same there is no need to admit a different potency. Now the range of the intellect is not limited but extends to everything which is or can be, for whatever is or can be is intelligible. In other words, as we shall see more extensively in Chapter Fourteen, being is the formal object of the intellect. Therefore, no matter how being is diversified, it can always be known by the intellect and consequently there is no need to admit a distinct potency to retain intellectual knowledge.

*Against the existence of an intellectual power of retaining one could object that if an intelligible species is retained by the potential intellect, this intellect is actuated and consequently man would *actually* know all the time what this species represents. But it is manifest that we do not actually know here and now everything our intellect has learned in the past. Therefore, it would not seem possible for man to have a memory which retains intelligible species. To this difficulty we may answer that there are three ways in which an intelligible species may be present in the intellect—namely, in a *purely potential* way, and then the intellect has not yet any knowledge of that which the species represents; in a *completely actual* way, and then the intellect actually knows what the species represents; in a *habitual* way, i.e., in a way which is intermediate between purely potential and completely actual presence, and then the intellect knows habitually, which is the same as saying that it retains the species. Once a species is received in the intellect it cannot cease to exist in it, because being immaterial it is not subject to corruption.

Regarding man's *capacity to recognize* the past intellectually, a distinction must be made between the act of understanding and the object understood. The intellect alone cannot recognize an *object* as understood in the past, because the intelligible species of the object is immaterial and therefore does not include time. Man is able to recognize an object as understood in the past insofar as his intellect acts together with his sense which attains the past. On the other hand, the intellect, by means of its own activity, can know its *acts* and their succession and thus is able to know the past as past.

*Is it possible for the intellect to use a retained species without having recourse to a phantasm? Is there any so-called *"imageless thought"*? Philosophically speaking we must answer in the negative. The potential intellect needs to be actuated before it elicits its act of understanding. This actuation cannot come from the retained species alone, because the retained species is merely habitually present. The actuation cannot be given by the agent intellect acting upon the potential intellect, through the retained species, because of itself the agent intellect is equally related to all retained species, so that there would be no reason why one species would be used in preference to others. The only remaining possibility, therefore, is that the actuation comes from the agent intellect and the phantasm which can serve as the foundation of the retained species.[5]

*The data of experience referred to above in no. 117, show that phantasms are needed even for the use of acquired knowledge. Moreover, experimental psychologists, such as Binet and Marbe, who investigated imageless thought, could find no cases in which no image whatsoever accompanied *concepts.* With respect to *judgments* they could find no images distinct from those of the con-

[5] Cf. St. Thomas, *Contra gentes,* bk. II, chap. 73.

cepts used in the judgments. In view of the fact that a judgment consists essentially in the affirmation or negation of a relationship of identity between a subject and an object, and that the apprehension of a relationship is something strictly proper to the intellect,[6] it should not be surprising that a judgment is not accompanied by a special image of this relationship. Nevertheless, a judgment is not imageless, because its subject and predicate are not imageless.

The assertion that phantasms are present in all activity of the intellect should not be understood as if these phantasms are always direct "images" of the thing understood. Very often, e.g., with respect to such things as potency and act, cause, relativity, and unified field theory, the phantasm used by the intellect is nothing but the phantasm of the spoken or written symbol.

Historical Notes

122. From the time of the Greeks there have been three trends of thought with respect to the origin of ideas, which we may call sensism, intellectualism, and senso-intellectualism.

Sensism holds that the origin of ideas can be adequately explained by sensation alone, so that there is no need of an agent intellect. Intellectualism maintains that ideas originate independently of sensation. Senso-intellectualism assigns a double cause to the origin of ideas, one organic (the phantasm) and the other inorganic (the agent intellect).

*Sensism originated with *Democritus,* who held that all cognition must be explained by means of tiny images flowing from material objects. In more modern times sen-

[6] Cf. St. Thomas, *De veritate,* q. 1, a. 3.

sistic theories of understanding have been proposed by the associationists (*Hartley,* 1705–1757), the empiricists (*Locke*), the sensists (*Condillac*), the positivists (*Comte,* 1798–1857), the structuralists (*Titchener*), the behaviorists (*Watson*), and the gestaltists (*Koehler,* born 1887). To sensism can be reduced also the opinions of *Henry of Ghent* (ca. 1210–1293), *Palmieri,* and more recently *Romeyer* who hold that the phantasm alone can explain the origin of ideas, although these authors do not deny the immateriality of the intellect.

*Among the Greeks intellectualism was defended by *Plato,* according to whom the soul contemplated everything intelligible in the World of Ideas before its imprisonment in the body; hence ideas are innate in the human intellect. A limited form of innatism was held by *Descartes,* for whom so-called primitive ideas, such as God, truth, and being, are innate. Apart from the innatists, intellectualism embraces the idealists (*Kant* and *Hegel*), who claim that ideas are neither innate nor derived from sense experience, but created by the intellect; also the ontologists (*Malebranche,* 1638–1715), who say that our mind has intuitive knowledge of God's ideas. *St. Augustine* held that our ideas come from a special illumination by the Uncreated Intellect, but it is not too clear whether or not he excludes the causality of sense experience.

*Senso-intellectualism was first proposed by *Aristotle,* who was followed by the Arabian philosophers (*Avicenna, Averroes*), *St. Thomas, Duns Scotus, Suarez,* etc.

*Regarding the nature of the agent intellect *Avicenna* considered the agent intellect to be a separate substance. *Scotus* and *Suarez* deny the real distinction between the agent and the potential intellect.

*With the exception of *Suarez,* who defends a kind of

exemplary causality, scholastic philosophers admit that both the agent and the phantasm exercise efficient causality in the production of the intelligible species; they also agree almost unanimously that the agent intellect is the principal cause, and the phantasm the instrumental cause. The further explanation of the instrumental causality of the phantasm is colored by the view taken of instrumental causality in general.

*Concerning the expressed species of our intellect, its necessity is generally admitted, except that *Rosmini* (1797–1855) denies it in direct understanding. The idealists make the expressed species the very object understood. According to *Scotus* and *Suarez* the act of intellection is not really distinct from the expressed species.

*The existence of an intellectual memory which can retain intelligible species was denied by *Avicenna,* who admitted only a certain facility to receive again the impressed species.

SUMMARY

123. Our intellect is in potency to understanding before it actually understands and needs to be actuated by an intelligible species. Experience shows that this actuation somehow comes from the phantasm. It is certain, however, that the material phantasm alone cannot actuate the intellect, for the effect cannot be greater than the cause. Hence it is necessary to admit the existence of an immaterial agent which can raise the phantasm to the level of the intellect. This agent is called the agent intellect. The agent intellect is not a separate substance (God or a created spirit), for otherwise man would be naturally unable to understand, and every act of understanding would require a special intervention of an outside agent. Therefore, the agent

intellect is a potency of man. It is distinct from the potential intellect because it is related to the intelligible species as act, while the potential intellect is related to this species as potency.

The agent intellect and the phantasm act in the order of efficient causality. Together they produce an intelligible species in the potential intellect. The agent intellect explains why this species is immaterial, and the phantasm why it is a species of a determinate nature. The phantasm, however, is not a principal coordinated cause of the species, for by virtue of its own power the material cannot act upon the immaterial; but it is the instrumental cause of the agent intellect, which alone is the principal cause.

When the potential intellect is actuated by the intelligible species it elicits its act of understanding. In the absence of a term corresponding exactly to that which is known, it will be necessary for the intellect to express in itself an image of that which is known as a means in which it knows the object. This image is called the concept, mental word, or expressed species of the intellect.

The intellect does not acquire at once by its first act perfect knowledge of the object considered, but is capable of perfecting its knowledge by successive acts. By the first act, called simple apprehension, the intellect grasps something of the essence of the object, without affirming or denying anything. Subsequently, after other acts of apprehension, the intellect can compare its apprehensions and thus is led to affirm or deny their composition. This is called the act of judgment. Various judgments can be arranged in such a way as to lead to the discovery of a new truth, implicitly contained in them. This is called the act of reasoning. The act of reasoning is merely a different function of the intellect and not of a new distinct potency, because its object is not distinct from that of understanding; reasoning is merely a way of arriving at understanding.

Intellectual memory is the capacity to retain and recognize intellectually. To retain intellectual knowledge, by retaining the intelligible species, is another function of the intellect and not the act of a new potency. For the object of the intellect extends to everything intelligible, i.e., everything which is or can be, and therefore to being itself. Accordingly, the intelligible species does not require one potency *qua* received and another *qua* retained.

Man's capacity to recognize intellectually understood objects is a function of his intellect together with his sense power. But, by means of its own activity, the intellect is capable of knowing past acts of intellection and their succession, and thus it can know the past as past.

SUGGESTED READINGS

124. Aristotle, *De anima,* bk. III, chap. 5, the agent intellect; chap. 6, apprehension and judgment; chap. 7, necessity of the phantasm.

Thomas Aquinas, *In III De anima,* lect. 10–12; *Summa theol.,* Ia, q. 79, aa. 2–5; potential and agent intellect.

——— *Summa theol.,* Ia, q. 79 aa. 6 and 7; *De veritate,* q. 10, aa. 2, 3; intellectual memory.

——— *Summa theol.,* Ia, q. 79, a. 8; reasoning.

——— *Summa theol.,* Ia, q. 84, aa. 3–7; *De veritate,* q. 10, a. 6; origin and necessity of species.

——— *Summa theol.,* Ia, q. 85, a. 2; *Contra gentes,* bk. I, chap. 53 and bk. IV, chap. 11; expressed species.

Henri Renard, *The Philosophy of Man,* chap. 6. Nature of the intellect.

Robert E. Brennan, *Thomistic Psychology,* chap. 7, pp. 179 ff. Origin of ideas.

George P. Klubertanz, *The Philosophy of Human Nature,* chap. 8, nos. 91–99. Process of knowledge.

Peter Dunne, "The Production of the Intelligible Species," *The New Scholasticism,* 1953, pp. 167–197.

J. de la Vaissière, *Elements of Experimental Psychology* (St. Louis: 1927), chap. 6. Imageless thought.

Thomas V. Moore, *Cognitive Psychology* (New York: 1939), Part V, chaps. 3,4. Psychology of judgment and reasoning.

Robert E. Brennan, *General Psychology* (New York: 1952), chaps. 21–24. The intellect and its functions.

Hubert Gruender, *Experimental Psychology* (Milwaukee: 1935), chaps. 14, 15. Psychology of ideas. Chap. 16. "Psychology of judgment and reasoning.

CHAPTER 14

The Object of the Intellect

*** 125. Because operative potencies are specified by their objects, the study of the object of the intellect will give us a more profound insight into the nature of this cognitive potency. In studying the object of a cognitive power care has to be taken to distinguish the material and the formal object. By the *material* object is meant anything which in any way whatsoever is knowable by the cognitive power. In the case of the intellect the material object embraces reality as well as purely logical entities; substances as well as accidents; bodies as well as pure spirits, for all these things can be objects of our thought. The *formal* object is that "aspect" or "formality" to which the cognitive potency is essentially ordered and under which it attains its objects; e.g., color is the formal object of sight.

In this chapter we shall first devote our attention to the formal object of the intellect, and then consider how man's intellect knows the various things which fall under its material object.

The Formal Object of the Intellect

Common and Proper Object. As we have seen in the preceding chapters, the human intellect is inorganic and intrinsically independent of matter. Nevertheless, it is an obvious datum of experience that man's intellect somehow is united with a body and to a certain extent dependent upon the body for its operation. Accordingly, the intellect may be considered either in itself, i.e., insofar as it is an intellect, or insofar as it is united with a body. Thus the inquiry concerning the formal object of the intellect may refer either to the object of the intellect as an intellect or to the object of the human intellect which is united with the body. In the first alternative the question is concerned with the *common* or adequate object of the intellect; in the second, it refers to the proportionate, specific or *proper* object of man's intellect as united to the body. The proper object of our intellect is that "formality" which the intellect attains primarily and directly and in relation to which it knows all other objects.[1] It should be clear that this proper object cannot be anything but a further determination of the common object.

The Common Object of the Intellect. To what is the intellect ordered by its very nature? Or what is intelligible? Nonintelligible is only that which is absolutely impossible, that which cannot *be*. Intelligible is whatever *is* or at least *can be*. In other words, nonbeing is unintelligible, and being is intelligible. Regardless of the condition in which the intellect is found, its object will have to be being. And it is precisely the relationship of a thing to "to be" which makes the thing intelligible. Consequently, it is *being* which is the common formal object of the intellect.

[1] By "primarily and essentially" is meant that the object is known in itself and not under the aspect of, or in relation to another object. In sight, for instance, the extended is known, but not primarily and directly, but under the aspect of color.

Concerning the common object of the intellect, the following may be noted.

a) As explained in general metaphysics,[2] being in relation to the intellect is called "the true." Therefore, one could also say that the *true* or truth is the common object of the intellect.[3]

b) Although, in principle, whatever is can be known by the intellect, it does not follow that our intellect actually knows all being, or even that our intellect as united with a body can know all being. Our intellect, as united to the body, takes its object from the senses and thus, as a matter of fact, is unable to know that which no sense object does represent in any way.

c) Because no other cognitive power extends to all being, it is only to the intellect that applies in all its fullness the saying of Aristotle: "The soul in a way becomes all things."

d) From the fact that the object of the intellect is being itself, it follows that the intellect is not divided into a number of really distinct potencies.[4] Therefore, the power to form judgments, reason, intellectual memory, the speculative and the practical intellect are not really distinct, but merely different functions of one and the same cognitive potency.

The Proper Object of the Intellect. As is known from general metaphysics [5] being is an analogous perfection and

[2] Cf. the author's *Introduction to the Science of Metaphysics,* chap. 2, sect. 4.

[3] Cf. St. Thomas, *Summa theol.,* Ia, q.55, a.1.

[4] Cf. St. Thomas, *Summa theol.,* Ia, q.79, a.7; and above, no. 121.

[5] Cf. the author's *Introduction to the Science of Metaphysics,* chap. 1, sect. 3.

found to exist in many different modes; e.g., as substance, accident, spirit, body, finite and infinite. Hence the question arises whether these various modes of being are equally intelligible to our human intellect or one of them is more intelligible than others. In other words, must any qualification be added to being as the formal object of the intellect when we consider the human intellect which exists in a body? The answer is that our human intellect is directly ordered to the understanding of *being existing in matter*[6] or, as it is usually expressed, the *abstracted essence of sensible things,* and that our intellect understands other things in relation to this essence. This should be clear from the following considerations.

If we enumerate the kinds of beings that can be known by our intellect we find that they are individual sensible beings, the abstracted essences of sensible beings and suprasensible beings. Of these three classes it is evident that the last, *suprasensible beings,* are known only in relation to sensible beings. Our concepts of them are purified concepts of material beings, as is implied by the very etymology of the terms by which they are indicated. "Spirit," for instance, comes from a Latin term meaning "breath"; "angel" from a Greek word meaning "messenger"; "to reflect" from a Latin verb meaning "to bend back"; "to comprehend" from a Latin term meaning "to take hold of." *Individual sensible things,* on the other hand, cannot be the proper object of our intellect, because our intellect does not even know what makes the individual sensible being this being and no other. It understands the individual sensible being only by paying attention to its accidental determinations and considering these together with its essence (cf. no. 126). Therefore, it follows by ex-

[6] Cf. St. Thomas, *Summa theol.,* Ia, q.87, a.3, ad 1.

clusion that the proper object of our intellect is constituted by the abstracted *essence of sensible beings.*

*A careful consideration of the nature of the intellect leads to the same conclusion. The proper object of our intellect must be directly and immediately proportionate to our intellect; for the knower becomes the object to be known, and in knowing its proper object the knower becomes this object directly and immediately. But our intellect is an immaterial entity existing in matter. Therefore, its object must be an immaterial entity existing in matter, i.e., the essence of material being as abstracted from matter. It is to be noted, however, that this argument has binding force only after it has been proved that the intellectual soul is the substantial form of the body.

When we say that the proper object of the intellect of man is the essence of material being, this assertion should not be understood as if the intellect had perfect knowledge of all material beings. In many cases the intellect knows the essence of the material object only in a very general way, such as that it is a body, a substance, or a being.

Knowledge of Material Objects

126. *The Singular Material Being.* From experience it is evident that man knows singular material beings by means of his senses. But, in addition to this pure sense knowledge, man has also *intellectual knowledge of the singular material thing;* otherwise he would not be able intellectually to distinguish the singular from the universal, to make judgments concerning singular material beings, and reason about them. Moreover, his will is often concerned with singular material things and therefore somehow these things must be known by the intellect, for the will is an appetite which is consequent upon intellectual

cognition. Accordingly, the fact of our intellectual knowledge of the singular material should not be subject to doubt.

The question, however, is how it is possible for our intellect to know the singular material thing. Our intellect does not grasp the singular material *directly*, because the principle of singularity in material beings is individual matter, while intelligibility is based upon immateriality.[7] There is no way in which our intellect can grasp the singular material being in its sole formal object, because the formal object of our intellect, the essence of material being, abstracts from the individual.

Nevertheless, the fact that our intellect has knowledge of the singular material can be explained if we keep in mind that the intellect receives its species from the senses. The sense image, or phantasm, represents the singular material being in its singularity. If, therefore, the *intellect and the senses combine their activity* into a unified complex act of knowing, the result will be intellectual knowledge of an essence that is restricted to a singular material being. Language itself shows the existence of such complex acts of knowing the singular material being, for we speak of "this man" and "that cat," thereby indicating that our intellectual knowledge of the object in question is a complex of an essence ("house" or "man") and the added limitation of this essence to the singular ("this" or "that").[8]

Moreover, it is possible for our intellect to know the existence of the singular material thing by a *kind of reflection* upon the steps leading to its understanding of the essence

[7] Note that "intelligibility is incompatible with the singular, though not with the singular *qua* singular, but *qua* material; for nothing can be understood unless immaterially." *Summa theol.*, Ia, q. 86, a. 1, ad 3.

[8] Cf. George P. Klubertanz, in the places referred to in no. 130.

of material being. Reflection upon the act of understanding shows the necessity of an impressed species coming from the phantasm, and this phantasm is a representation of the singular material being. Nevertheless, even this reflection does not enable the intellect to understand more of the singular material being, *qua* singular, than the bare fact of its existence.

127. *Suprasensible Reality*. Because immaterial realities cannot be presented to our intellect by proper phantasms, we cannot directly know immaterial realities. Nevertheless, our intellect can arrive at an *indirect* and *imperfect* knowledge of them. In the first place, from the knowledge of material beings the intellect can be led to affirm the existence of immaterial reality, such as God. In the second place, the intellect can attain to a very imperfect and analogous knowledge of the nature of the immaterial reality by conceiving this nature as if it were the nature of a material reality, and negating in it all the imperfection and limitations of materiality. Obviously, in this way, the intellect knows rather what immaterial reality is not than what it is. How imperfect such analogous knowledge of the immaterial is may be illustrated by a comparison with the analogous knowledge of a reflection in a mirror possessed by a person who is blind from birth. If we want to tell such a person that there is a likeness of himself in the mirror, we should have to use the term "statue," for the only likenesses known by him are those of statues. For him, there would be a statue of himself in an analogous sense in the mirror. Obviously, the blind man can have only a very dim knowledge of the image in the mirror, for he has no proper knowledge of his image as a statue in an analogous sense. Or, to use another example, a person who is deaf from birth will form an idea

of sound as if it were a color; for instance, a loud sound will be conceived as fiery red, a soft sound as light green or pink, and a beautiful harmony of sounds as a masterpiece of painting or the harmonious flow of different beams of colored lights.

It may be noted that our inability to form proper ideas of immaterial reality is *not caused by the nature of the object*. The immaterial is perfectly intelligible in itself, but it is not perfectly intelligible for our intellect which has as its proper object the essence of material things represented by phantasms.

The Intellect and Its Subject. Whenever we elicit an act of understanding we are implicitly and, as it were, concretely conscious of the *existence* of this act and its subject. At present, however, we are not concerned with this implicit knowledge of intellection and its subject, but with explicit knowledge which takes the *nature* of the intellect and its subject as the objects of its considerations. Regarding this knowledge we must deny that the intellect *directly* knows itself and its subject. The reason, again, is that the proper object of the intellect is the essence of material being which is presented to the intellect by the phantasm. But neither the intellect nor its subject [9] (the rational soul) can be properly represented by a phantasm. Therefore, our intellect does not have any direct knowledge of itself and its subject.

Nevertheless, our intellect is capable of knowing its own nature and that of its subject *indirectly* and *analogously*. Man can take his own acts of intellection as the object of his consideration, as is done in philosophy, and by studying the nature of these acts arrive at certain conclusions con-

[9] The term "subject" is used here in the broad sense.

cerning the nature of the intellect and its subject. But when he takes his acts of intellection as the object of his study, he must make use of phantasms to obtain the impressed species without which his intellect cannot operate. However, no phantasm can properly represent the immaterial acts of intellection; therefore, all knowledge obtained in this way will be improper or analogous, because in it the immaterial is known in the manner of the essence of the material. Because of its analogous character, clear knowledge of the nature of the intellect and its subject is difficult to obtain. It requires a very careful and prolonged study.

Historical Notes

*128. All philosophers who deny the immateriality of the intellect deny also that the formal object of the intellect is the essence abstracted from material things. Likewise, those who claim that man has intuitive knowledge, whether by means of innate ideas (*Plato, Descartes*) or through immediate intuition of God (the ontologists).

Scotus held that being as being is the formal object of our intellect in all its states, while *St. Thomas* distinguishes a common and a proper object of the intellect.

The singular material being is claimed to be directly intelligible by *Scotus, Suarez,* and the nominalists. *Cajetan,* on the other hand, held that the singular material can be known intellectually only by means of a process of reasoning. Most Thomists admit that the singular material is known intellectually without reasoning, by a kind of reflection upon the intelligible species and the phantasm.

Materialistic philosophers deny that our intellect can know suprasensible realities. According to *Scotus* knowledge of the suprasensible is not analogous.

SUMMARY

129. By the material object of the intellect is meant anything which in any way can be known by the intellect. By the formal object is meant that object to which the intellect is essentially ordered. The common object of the intellect is the formal object of the intellect as an intellect, i.e., regardless of its union with, or separation from the body. The proper object of the intellect means here the formal object of the human intellect which is united with a body. It is that formality which our intellect attains primarily and directly, and in relation to which it knows all other objects.

By its very nature the intellect is ordered to understand the intelligible. But intelligible is that which is or can be. Therefore, being is the common object of the intellect.

The proper object of the human intellect is the being existing in matter, or the abstracted essence of material being which is represented by phantasms. The reason is that the suprasensible is not known directly but only in relation to the sensible; the individual sensible in its individuality is out of reach of the sole intellect; therefore, there remains only the essence of sensible or material being.

The singular material being is known concretely by means of the senses. It is known also intellectually, for man is able to make judgments concerning the singular. However, it is not known directly to the intellect, because the principle of its singularity, which is matter, is not intelligible in itself. The intellect knows the singular material being insofar as the operations of the senses and the intellect together form one complex act of knowing an essence as restricted to the singular. Moreover, the intellect can arrive at knowledge of the singular material being by reflecting upon its act of understanding the essence of a material being. This reflection shows the necessity of an impressed species coming from a phantasm representing a singular material being. In this way it arrives at knowledge of the singular, although it does not acquire any intellectual insight into the singular *qua* singular.

SUGGESTED READINGS

130. Aristotle, *De anima*, bk. III, chaps. 4, 8.

Thomas Aquinas, *Summa theol.*, Ia, q. 79, a. 7. The common object.

——— *Summa theol.*, Ia, q. 84, a. 7; q. 85, aa. 1, 5; *In III De anima*, lect. 8, nos. 705–713. The proper object.

——— *Summa theol.*, Ia, q. 86, a. 1; *De veritate*, q. 2, aa. 5, 6; q. 10, a. 5. Knowledge of the singular.

——— *Summa theol.*, Ia, q. 87, aa. 1, 3; *Contra gentes*, bk. II, chap. 75. Self-knowledge of the intellect.

——— *Summa theol.*, Ia, q. 88, aa. 1, 2; *De veritate*, q. 10, a. 11; *De anima*, a. 16. Knowledge of the suprasensible.

George P. Klubertanz, "St. Thomas and Knowledge of the Singular," *The New Scholasticism*, 1952, pp. 135 ff. "The Unity of Human Operation," *The Modern Schoolman*, 1950, pp. 75 ff. (especially pp. 85–89).

Jacques Maritain, *The Degrees of Knowledge* (New York: 1938), pp. 252 ff. The objects of the intellect.

E. Gilson, *The Spirit of Mediaeval Philosophy* (New York: 1940), chap. 12. Knowledge of things. Chap. 13. The intellect and its object.

CHAPTER 15

Subhuman Intelligence

*** 131. The question concerning subhuman intelligence may be understood in two ways. In the first place, it may be taken to refer to the possibility of intellectual life at a lower level than that of man. In this sense the question is equivalent to the problem whether the human level of intellect is the lowest possible grade of intellectual being. This question is strictly philosophical, for it is concerned with the ultimate *nature* of intellectual life. Usually, however, the question is understood as referring to the existence of intellectual life in those animals which man himself calls irrational. In this sense the question is not concerned with the nature of intellectual life but with its *subjects*. It tries to determine whether intellectual life is found only in individuals belonging to the species of mammals called "man" or also in individuals belonging to other species of animal life. This question may be called a mixed problem to which both animal psychology and philosophy contribute. Animal psychology is needed to supply the necessary data, obtained through a long and controlled process of observation for signs of intellectual life in many individuals belonging to many species. Philosophy is needed to supply a clear idea of intellectual life, because without such an idea one will not know exactly what to look for in the observation of animals. Moreover, the interpretation of the data is likely to be strongly influenced by philosophical preconceptions, so that it is quite possible that a certain conclusion will be presented in the name of science, while in reality this conclusion is based upon a philosophical position. An evolutionist, for instance, who holds that man descends from nonhuman ancestors, will be inclined to interpret the data in a sense which favors his theory. For these reasons the question of the extension of the intellect to nonhuman subjects may be treated in philosophy.

In the following pages we shall briefly consider, first, the existence of intellectual life in nonhuman animals, and then the possibility of intellectual life on a level lower than that of man.

Existence of Intellectual Life on the Subhuman Level

132. When the question is raised whether or not man is the only animal endowed with an intellect, we cannot define man as "rational animal," for this definition will be correct only if other animals are not rational. The best we can do will be to give a provisional description of man in terms of the general physical characteristics which distinguish him from all other animals. For this purpose we could appeal to man's dentation, but the age-old primitive description of man as a "featherless biped" will be quite sufficient. The question, therefore, is whether or not these featherless bipeds are the only animals having an intellect.

Because the nature of a being is known from its operations, only a careful study of animal activity can provide the answer to this question. If the activity of animals shows no signs of being directed by an intellect of their own, the only reasonable conclusion will be that they do not have an intellect.

"Intelligent" Animal Activity. As evidence for brute animal intelligence the following two categories of facts may be appealed to:

1) Many animals show a capacity to *learn from experience.* This capacity varies from one species to another and from individual to individual, so that some animals are commonly called "stupid" and others "intelligent." Animal training offers numerous examples, but even without being taught by man, animals often show remarkably "intelligent" activities based upon experience. They succeed in finding new ways of reaching a purpose, as is illustrated by the chimpanzee, Sultan, described by Dr. Koehler in his book *The Mentality of Apes,* which joined two sticks to reach a distant banana; and Peckham's wasp, which used a pebble to pack the soil used in closing the entrance to her nest and thus made the nest invisible.

2) Many animal activities commonly attributed to "instinct" are of such a complex and difficult nature that they cannot be explained without an *intellectual insight into the problems* involved. For instance, bees solve a problem of applied geometry in the construction of their honeycombs; ants solve a problem of social organization in setting up community life in such a way that every individual is assigned a specific task benefitting the whole of the community; hunting wasps show a perfect knowledge of the anatomy of their victims and a superb operating technique when they sting the victim in such a way that paralysis sets in but death does not follow.

Ambiguity of the Term "Intelligence." Do the facts pointed out above prove the existence of intellectual life in animals? Before the question can be answered it is important to remove all ambiguity with respect to the term "intelligence." In the *strict* sense of the term, intelligence means the activity of the intellect and thus refers to universal ideas, judgments, and reasoning.[1] In a *wider* sense, intelligence may be used to include any capacity to learn. In the present problem we are concerned with intelligence in the strict sense, for no one will deny that many animals show a remarkable ability to learn from experience.

Moreover, the activity of a being may show the guidance of an intellect, even if the being in question itself does not have any intellect. One has only to consider some of the machines produced by modern techniques to admit this assertion. For instance, unquestionably the working of a modern motorcar shows intellectual insight into the problems of combustion, friction, dynamics, etc. Yet no one will claim that the motorcar is intelligent. We must distinguish, therefore, intelligent activity resulting from the *insight of the acting subject* itself, and intelligent activity resulting from the *insight of another being* which moves or directs the acting subject.

Principle of Economy. To prove that animals are intelligent in the strict sense of the term, it will be necessary to prove that their activity cannot be explained unless they have an intellect of their own. The point at stake is not whether their activity can be explained by means of a personal insight into the problems involved, but whether such an insight is *the only possible explanation.* We must be guided here by the so-called principle of economy, accord-

[1] These activities are those of an imperfect intellect which does not understand an object fully by a single act. A perfect intellect would have complete understanding of its object by a single act.

ing to which it is unreasonable to assume that a higher principle or cause is the source of an activity for which a lower principle can offer an adequate explanation. It was in the name of the same principle that in Chapter 11 sense life was excluded as the explanation of tropism. Accordingly, only unequivocal signs of intellectual life will prove that animals have an intellect.

The Capacity to Learn from Experience. This capacity will be on the intellectual level if it implies the formation of universal concepts and judgments. Without universal concepts, the learning is on the purely sensory level; if no judgments are formed there is no possibility to advance intellectuality (to learn) or to apply one's intellectual insight to a given situation (to act intelligently). The question, therefore, is whether acquired animal behavior proves the presence of universal concepts and judgments. We must answer in the negative, because there is not a single case of allegedly "intelligent" behavior learned by animals which cannot be explained upon a purely sensory basis.

With respect to the "intelligent" behavior animals have learned through *human training*, the assertion is evident. In training sense images are associated in a pattern determined by the trainer. Some animals are capable of retaining the association more easily than others and therefore are said to be more "intelligent" than others.

With respect to "intelligence" revealed in the *invention of new means* for reaching a purpose, the examples usually appealed to are not unequivocal evidence of a true intellect. As is clear from Dr. Koehler's own book, his chimpanzee joined the sticks accidentally. The subsequent rush to the railing in an effort to reach the banana can be interpreted as a mere repetition of its previous effort, except that now it happened to have in its hand a suitable tool for reaching the banana. Subsequent repetitions of the action of joining sticks and reaching the banana can be explained by the association of sense images in the first accidental use of the joined sticks. The use of a pebble by Peckham's wasp to pack the soil was not the invention of a new tool, for other wasps use pebbles and bits of hard material for the same purpose. The only thing special about Peckham's wasp was the repeated use of the same pebble, which may be explained by the scarcity of pebbles around the nest or even as quite accidental.

Learned animal behavior would provide an unequivocal proof of intelligence if the acquired behavior implied the *purposive selection* of new means to solve a problem, for this would involve an insight into the nature of means, and purpose, and their relationship. Although animal behavior is not so stereotyped as not to admit any variation at all in the selection of means, the differentiations resulting from experience are not sufficiently pronounced to allow only an explanation based upon intellectual insight. The great danger in the interpretation of animal behavior lies in anthropomorphism, or the misuse of the argument from analogy: in a given situation, man would act in this or that way under the guidance of his intellect; therefore, if an animal acts in a similar way, it, too, is guided by its intellect.

133. *Instinctive Animal Activity*. The examples referred to in no. 131 leave no doubt that animal activity which is guided by instinct often shows a profound insight into the problems involved. The question, however, is whether or not this insight is "personal." By "personal" here is meant that the insight is arrived at by the efforts of the individual to solve the problem, or at least that the solution of the

problem is understood by the individual animal.[2] A personal insight into the problems implied by their instinctive activity must be denied for the following reason. Instinctive activities are performed perfectly, even when done the first time, and in the same way by all individuals of a species. If they depend upon a personal insight *acquired* by the individual's efforts, it follows that animals are far more intelligent than man, who arrives only by repeated efforts and many failures at the solution of similar problems. Moreover, there would be no explanation why all individuals solve the problems involved in their activity in the same way even when different solutions are possible. If, on the other hand, an appeal is made to *innate* intellectual insight of the animal into the problems involved, there is no explanation for the very limited range of problems covered by this insight. So-called instinctive activity is limited to whatever is necessary, within the range of normal conditions, for the preservation of the individual and the species. In different conditions the animal acts very stupidly. For example, under normal conditions there is nothing solid between a source of light and the seeing subject, so that, say, a fly is not prevented from flying towards the source of light. If man places a glass pane between the fly and the source of light, the fly keeps bumping into the glass in a futile effort to fly into the direction of the light. It is not conceivable that an animal which has its own power of understanding would continue to act so stupidly. Whether innate or not the understanding of a problem implies the understanding of universal ideas and certain principles, such as the relation of means and end, of cause and effect, and others which play a role in its solution. Because

[2] We may not a priori exclude the possibility of innate animal understanding.

of their very nature, these ideas and principles apply also to other problems, so that their application to problems to which they are not innately applied is not beyond the capacity of an individual which really understands them. Therefore, an appeal to innate intellectual insights of animals into the problems involved in their instinctive activity leaves the limited range of this insight without an explanation.

Our conclusion, therefore, is that the intelligent nature of animal instinctive activity cannot be accounted for by an appeal to personal insight, whether acquired or innate. Whatever intelligence reveals itself in animal instinctive activity must be attributed to the Author of nature who has provided animals with concrete sense-conditioned patterns of intelligent behavior, as far as is required by the preservation of the individual and the species under normal conditions.

The Absence of Language. To these considerations we may add that if animals had an intellect they would have devised some form of language to communicate their ideas. Very few animals live a completely solitary life; most of them live in more or less social groups. But in a social group of individuals endowed with an intellect, language is a necessity, because whoever has ideas wants to express them, at least when their expression is very important for his own good or that of his society. Even the most backward social groups of human beings have developed some kind of language. Animals, however, do not have any language expressive of ideas. They are able to express their emotions, such as rage and love, by means of natural signs, but have no system for the communication of ideas. Yet many animals possess the physical organs necessary for a kind of speech similar to that of man. Many efforts have been made to teach them a language, but the only success has been a mere mechanical repetition of sounds without any realization of their meaning. Therefore, we may safely conclude that the absence of true language among animals is a sign of the absence of ideas and intellectual life.

A last remark. Some advocates of animal intelligence in the strict sense of the term seem to be driven by the desire to prove that man is not essentially above the beasts and therefore not subject to any other obligations than a mere animal. If animals had a true intellect man would not be lowered to their level, but animals would be raised to the level of man, and therefore would be subject to all the rights and obligations that flow from human nature.

The Possibility of Intellectual Life on a Subhuman Level

134. A few words will be sufficient concerning this question. Intellectual life on the level of man is characterized by its dependence upon the body. Although the intellect in itself is independent of matter, yet the activity of the human intellect is conditioned by matter. Technically this is expressed by the formula: Man's intellect is intrinsically independent of matter, but extrinsically dependent upon it. Intellectual life on the subhuman level would mean an intellect which is more dependent upon matter than that of man. The question whether such a life is possible must be answered in the negative. The reasons are as follows:

a) No true intellect can be *intrinsically* dependent upon matter, for by its very nature the intellect is inorganic.

b) No true intellect, it seems, could have a *greater extrinsic* dependence upon matter than that of man. In the first place, man's intellect depends upon the body for *all its acts*. It must be actuated through the agency of a phantasm, which is material, before being completely able to act. Secondly, man's intellect depends upon matter for *all its objects*. It does not have within itself any species, but receives all its species from the material phantasm.

How *imperfect* man's intellect is may be seen from the following:

a) Man's intellect is not its own act, but a *potency* for understanding.

b) Man's intellect is *passive*, in the sense that it needs to be acted upon before being fully able to act.

c) The actuation of man's intellect comes about through the agency of a *material* agent (the phantasm).

d) Because of its actuation and determination by the phantasm, man's intellect can properly understand only the essence of *material* beings. The immaterial, which in itself is perfectly intelligible, is known only vaguely and in the way of the material (analogously).

e) Man's intellect progresses by a slow and painstaking process from confused knowledge to more exact knowledge. *Even in the material world,* which forms the proper object of his understanding, there remain uncharted thousands of *mysteries* whose nature he has not yet understood, although the greatest of mankind have spent their lives in the investigation of these mysteries.

Historical Notes

*135. Many psychologists who admit brute animal intelligence understand the term "intelligence" in the broad sense as any capacity to learn from experience, and therefore cannot be considered to oppose our thesis. The sensists, however, deny that man has a higher kind of knowledge than mere animals and admit only a difference of degree.

Quite a few evolutionists following *Darwin* (1809–1882), defend a progressive evolution of all cognitive powers and have tried to prove that animals possess a kind of intellectual life.

SUMMARY

136. The assertion that so-called brute animals are intelligent could be supported by an appeal to the capacity of animals to learn from experience and the fact that many of their instinctive activities are practical solutions of very complex problems, which cannot be solved without an insight into the principles involved.

To prevent misunderstandings one should distinguish between intelligence in the strict sense, which implies ideas, judgments and reasoning, and intelligence in the wider sense, which means any capacity to learn from experience. The point at issue is only intelligence in the strict sense. Moreover, with respect to intelligent activity, one should investigate whether the activity results from the insight of the acting subject itself or is directed by another. Only the first type will require a true intellect in the acting subject.

Animal intelligence in the strict sense can be proved only by animal activity which cannot be explained otherwise than through the personal insight of the acting subject. But the proofs offered do not satisfy this condition. The allegedly intelligent activities which animals learn from experience can be explained upon a purely sensory basis; animal instinctive activities, on the other hand, reveal a profound insight into the problems involved, but this insight is not personal. If it were personal it would be either acquired or innate. If acquired, there is no explanation why all individuals of the same species solve the problem in the same way even when many solutions are possible; if innate, there is no explanation why the insight into the solution of the problem is not applied to other problems. Moreover, if animals had an intellect they would have devised a kind of language to communicate their ideas; for most of them lead a more or less social life, and in a society the communication of ideas is a necessity.

Regarding the question whether any intellectual life on a subhuman level is possible, we must answer in the negative. To be truly intellectual, cognition has to be intrinsically independent of matter. On the other hand, no intellect can have a greater extrinsic dependence upon matter than that of man, for man's intellect depends upon matter both for its actuation and its object.

SUGGESTED READINGS

137. Thomas Aquinas, *Summa theol.*, Ia–IIae, q. 13, a. 2, ad 3; *Contra gentes*, bk. II, chap. 66. Animal intelligence.

——— *Summa theol.*, Ia, q. 79, a. 2; q. 85, a. 1; *Contra gentes*, bk. IV, chap. 11. Grades of intellect.

J. de la Vaissière, *Elements of Experimental Psychology* (St. Louis: 1927), Section Three of Animal Psychology, pp. 25 ff. Experiments on intellectual life in animals.

Hubert Gruender, *Experimental Psychology* (Milwaukee: 1935), chap. 12, pp. 252 ff. Animal intelligence.

W. Koehler, *The Mentality of Apes* (New York: 1925).

J. H. Fabre, *The Hunting Wasps* (New York: 1915), chaps. 9, 10.

John A. Frisch, "Did the Peckhams witness the invention of a tool by *Ammophila Urnaria*?" in *The American Midland Naturalist*, Sept. 1940. May be found in Anable, *Philosophical Psychology*, Reading VI.

CHAPTER 16

Existence and Nature of the Will

Existence of the Will

*** 138. Concerning the existence of intellectual appetencies or acts of appetite, there cannot be any serious doubt. It follows not only from the a priori argument by which above, in Chapter 9, it has been proved that cognition is followed by appetite, but is also a datum of experience. Such things as freedom, justice, mercy, and honor cannot be apprehended by the senses, but are objects of intellectual cognition. This intellectual knowledge gives rise to a desire for the possession of freedom, honor, etc. Accordingly, experience shows that there are appetencies based upon intellectual cognition. These appetencies are called acts of will.

Acts of will occur intermittently; e.g., in a condition of sleep or unconsciousness the will does not act. Therefore, in accordance with the principles explained in Chapter 3, we must admit the existence of an operative potency of intellectual appetency. This potency is called the will.

Nature of the Will

139. The general principles formulated above (chap. 9) for elicited appetite apply also to the will. It may be worthwhile to recall these principles as applied to the will.

The will is *really distinct from the nature* of its subject; for in a finite being nature and operative potency are always really distinct.

The will is *really distinct from the intellect;* for will and intellect have specifically different formal objects.

The will is a *passive* potency; for it needs to be determined to its action by an object apprehended by the intellect. On the other hand the will may be called *active,* because, as we shall see, it moves the intellect and the sensitive potencies to their acts.

Although really distinct from the intellect the will is closely related to it. It *complements* the intellect by making it possible for the subject to act in accordance with its intellectual apprehensions.

Although the will is really distinct from the nature of its subject, it is *not an autonomous entity.* It does not act in its own right, but is merely an operative principle by means of which the subject acts. Expressions, such as "the will acts," or "the will chooses" are nothing but brief expressions for "man acts or chooses by means of his will" (cf. chap. 3, no. 46).

The will is *really distinct from the sense appetite.* This distinction follows from the fact that the intellect is really distinct from the senses. An elicited appetite is a passive operative potency and needs to be actuated by an object apprehended by the cognitive potency from which it flows. But the objects apprehended by the intellect and the senses are formally different.

The will is an *inorganic potency*. The reason should be clear. The will is an appetite which is consequent upon the intellect, which is inorganic, and therefore must belong to the same level as the intellect itself.

The Object of the Will. Any appetite is a tendency towards a good. As an appetite following the intellect, the will tends to objects apprehended as "good" by the intellect. Because of its immaterial nature the intellect is not limited to the cognition of the concrete and particular, but apprehends things in their universal nature. Accordingly, the *formal* object of the will, or the aspect under which the will tends to anything, is the good in general. The good is realized concretely in existing things, although not to the same extent, and these things constitute the *material* objects of the will. Unlike sense appetite, which of itself is limited to the particular sensible good, the will can tend to anything which in any respect is apprehended as good by the intellect, whether universal or particular, material or immaterial. Experience confirms this assertion; for the will can tend to the particular and material, such as this piece of meat or that work of art, as well as to the universal, such as "liberty and justice for all."

The Acts of Will. An important distinction with respect to the activity of the will is that between acts directly done by the will and acts done by other operative potencies under the command of the will. The will is capable of moving other operative potencies to their acts, because the object of the other potencies is a particular good and therefore included in the object of the will. An action which is executed by another operative potency as moved by the will is called a *commanded* act. For instance, if a soldier shoots an enemy the acts of taking aim and pulling the trigger are commanded acts, but the decision to shoot comes directly from the will. Both kinds of acts are "voluntary," but only the direct act of will is *elicited* by the will. Commanded acts are voluntary only in an analogous sense —namely, inasmuch as they have been caused by an act of will.

*Elicited acts of will may be concerned either with the end to be attained, the good or happiness in general, or with the means to this end. With respect to the end, the will not only loves it, but also desires to attain it and to rejoice in its possession. These acts of will correspond on the intellectual level of appetite to the movements of the sense appetite called love, desire, and joy. To distinguish the acts of will from the corresponding acts of sense appetite, they are often called *volition, intention,* and *fruition.* Regarding the means to the end, there is *choice* or the selection of one particular good in preference to another; *consent* or the desire of the will for the object chosen as a means to happiness; and *use* or the actual utilization of the means to attain the end. Sometimes the movements of the will are given the same names as the passions corresponding to them on the sense level, but these names do not apply to the movements of the will in the proper sense.[1]

Historical Notes

*140. In general, those philosophers who admit the immateriality of the intellect admit also that the will is inorganic. Accordingly, the opponents of this thesis are the same as those who opposed the immateriality of the intellect.

The real distinction of the will from the intellect is denied

[1] Cf. St. Thomas, *De veritate,* q.25, a.4.

by *Spinoza,* who considers thinking and willing as two functions of the same power.

SUMMARY

141. The existence of intellectual appetencies is evident not only from the fact that cognition is followed by appetite, but is also a datum of experience. Because these intellectual appetencies occur intermittently they require a real operative potency, which is called the will.

The will is really distinct from the nature of its subject, because in any finite being nature and operative potency are really distinct. It is really distinct from the intellect, because its object is specifically different from that of the intellect. The will is passive in the sense that it needs to be determined to its act, but active in the sense that it moves other operative potencies to their act. The will naturally complements the intellect, for it makes it possible for man to act in accordance with his understanding.

The will is really distinct from the sense appetite, because it flows from the intellect, which is really distinct from the senses from which the sense appetite flows.

The will is inorganic, because it belongs to the same level as the intellect which is inorganic.

The object of the will is the good apprehended by the intellect. Because the intellect is not limited to the apprehension of the particular and concrete, it knows the good in general; hence the formal object of the will is the good in general.

A commanded act of will is an act done by another operative potency under the command or control of the will; an elicited act of will is an act directly done by the will, such as the acts of desire and love.

SUGGESTED READINGS

142. Thomas Aquinas, *Summa theol.*, Ia, q. 59, a. 1. Object of the will.

——— *Summa theol.*, Ia, q. 80, aa. 1, 2; *De veritate,* q. 22, aa. 3, 4; *Summa theol.*, Ia–IIae, q. 9, a. 5. The nature of the will.

——— *Summa theol.*, Ia–IIae, qq. 8–17. The acts of will.

J. de la Vaissière, *Elements of Experimental Psychology,* chap. 7. Experimental evidence of voluntary activities.

CHAPTER 17

The Freedom of the Will and Its Limits

*** 143. Contrary to animals, whose course of action is dominated by patterns determined for their species by nature, man appears in this world as a being endowed with a large amount of self-determination, capable of deciding for himself what course of action he will take. This capacity of self-determination is usually indicated by the term "freedom." Because action which is based upon intellectual cognition is directed by the will, we must examine whether or not man's will is really free, and if so, to what extent.

The Freedom of the Will

The Concept of Freedom. Freedom in general means the absence of determining influences. It is the opposite of necessity. Necessity may be either intrinsic or extrinsic. By extrinsic necessity, or coercion, is meant that an external agent exercises a determining influence upon the operative potency of a subject in the order of efficient causality. Hence with respect to the will, *freedom from coercion* means that no efficient cause forces the will to act against its inclination.

By intrinsic necessity is meant that the very nature of a thing determines it to act or not to act, to act in this way or that way, under a given set of conditions. For example, by its very nature hydrogen is determined to combine with oxygen into water when the required conditions are fulfilled. The elements have no "choice" in the matter. With respect to the will, *freedom from intrinsic necessity* means that the will is not determined to act or not to act, to act in this way or that way, even when all the necessary conditions for action are given.

In addition to freedom from coercion and intrinsic necessity, we speak of *moral freedom,* by which is meant that the right order to the ultimate end does not impose an obligation upon the will with respect to action. Moreover, there is also so-called *social freedom,* which refers to the concrete conditions that are necessary for the exercise of human freedom.

At present we are not concerned with moral freedom, the nature and limits of which are studied in ethics, nor with social freedom, which is discussed in the political and social sciences, but only with freedom from coercion and intrinsic necessity. In addition, our problem is limited to the elicited acts of will and does not extend to the commanded acts. With respect to commanded acts, it should be clear that powers which are normally controlled by the will may be subjected to external forces over which the will has no effective control. Freedom from coercion and intrinsic necessity in the elicited acts of will is called *freedom of choice.* It may be defined as the capacity of self-determination by virtue of which the will remains master of its own acts even when all other necessary conditions are fulfilled.

Reserving the investigation of the extent to which the will is free to the second part of this chapter, we must now see whether the will has freedom of choice in the sense explained above. However, before doing so we must first make an important distinction with respect to the judgments of the intellect.

Speculative and Practical Judgments. As we have seen above, the object of the will is the good apprehended by the intellect. But in judging whether or not an object is good the intellect may proceed either speculatively or practically. *Speculatively good* is that which the intellect judges to be good in a universal way, i.e., without applying the judgment to the concrete conditions affecting the subject here and now; for instance, a son ought to honor his parents. *Practically good* is that which the intellect judges to be good in the concrete circumstances affecting the subject here and now; for example, I am the son of this man and must show him here and now this act of honor.

144. *The Will is Not Subject to Coercion.* Coercion means that one is made to act against his inclination. But an act of will is always and by its very nature an inclination to something. Hence a forced act of will would be an actual inclination of the will to something to which it is actually not inclined, which is a contradiction in terms. Therefore, the will cannot be forced to elicit its own act.

The Will is Endowed with Freedom from Internal Necessity. The proof is as follows:

If the intellect has practical judgments which are changeable, the appetite following these judgments is undetermined or free.

But the intellect has practical judgments which are changeable or undetermined.

Therefore, the will is free.

The *major* premise of this proof follows from the nature of the will. The intellectual appetite follows the judgment of the intellect and therefore corresponds to the nature of these judgments. Accordingly, if the intellect has practical judgments which are not determined, the will also will not be determined or free.

Regarding the *minor* premise, a practical judgment is always a judgment concerning a particular good. But any particular good, as apprehended by a practical judgment, is imperfect or evil in some respect. Therefore, my intellect does not have to consider such a good as good for me here and now, but may consider it as evil. For instance, I am offered a highly paid position. I need the money, and therefore this position is good for me. On the other hand, it will imply much responsibility and may disturb my usual peace of mind, so that in this sense it is evil for me. Accordingly, my practical judgment does not have to be that the position is good for me, but may be that it is evil for me. Not even God Himself, as He is known to man, is good in all respects. For example, I may be faced with the choice between God and money to be obtained in a dishonest way. Choosing God will imply that I do not get the money, and in this respect God is evil for me here and now. Consequently, whether a particular good will be judged as good for me here and now will depend upon the aspect under which the intellect considers the good. In other words, the particular goods considered by our intellect are not capable of determining the intellect to one practical judgment, so that the intellect is undetermined or free from the necessity to approve the particular good.

Confirmation of This Proof by Experience. The preceding metaphysical proof of freedom is confirmed by experience, which shows that in the case of conflicting motives the issue is often settled by the "active interposition of the Ego," i.e., by an act of will. In many cases, before choosing, I am conscious that alternative courses of action are open to me; in choosing, that I actively determine the course to be taken; and after choosing, that I am sorry or glad over my choice.

Of course, we do not intend to say that our capacity to choose freely is directly experienced, i.e., that we experience what we can do or could have done. Nevertheless, we do experience that we here and now settle an issue by the active interposition of the Ego, by choosing freely. From this fact of free choice we may legitimately infer that we have the capacity to choose freely.

Moreover, if one admits—and in practice everyone does —that man differs from mere animals because he is morally responsible at least for certain actions, one must admit also the basis of this responsibility, which is man's control over these actions, or his freedom to determine whether or not he will do them.

The Foundation of Freedom. From the preceding considerations it is clear that the *immediate* foundation of our freedom of choice lies in the fact that the will is an appetite following the intellect, and therefore has as its formal object the good in its universality. *Ultimately,* however, the foundation of freedom lies in the inorganic nature of the intellect, for it is precisely because of its spiritual nature that the intellect apprehends the universal. Whenever the intellect apprehends a particular good it perceives something good in it, but not the good without any limitation or restriction. As a result, it is not necessitated to judge the particular good as good here and now, because it may focus its attention upon the other aspect of the particular good. Thus, in the words of St. Thomas, "of necessity man has freedom of choice because he is rational." [1] And, "only a being endowed with an intellect can act with a free judgment, inasmuch as it knows the good in its universality and thus is able to judge this or that to be good. Hence wherever there is an intellect, there is free choice." [2]

145. *The Role of Intellect and Will in Free Choice.* As we have seen above, with respect to the particular good the intellect is not necessitated to judge it as good here and now, but may judge it as either good or evil according as it focuses its attention upon different aspects of the particular good. Thus the question arises as to what finally determines the intellect to cease considering the particular good under different aspects and pronounce a definite judgment. The answer is that the will puts an end to the deliberation of the intellect and chooses one practical judgment as the *ultimate* judgment: "This is good for me here and now," or, "This is evil for me here and now." It has to be the will that determines which judgment will be ultimate, for otherwise the will would be determined by a judgment over which it has no control and therefore would not be free.

From this we may conclude that as long as no deliberation precedes the act of will, there can be no question of free choice. Hence an act of will elicited under such circumstances would not be free. Such nonfree acts of will often are the first reaction of the will when a particular good is presented to it and the intellect has not yet had the time to deliberate over the matter. Moreover, a situation may arise sometimes in which passion so captivates man that

[1] *Summa theol.*, Ia, q.83, a.1.

[2] *Op. cit.*, Ia, q.59, a.3.

only one aspect of a particular good is presented to the consideration of the intellect and no deliberation is possible.

The objection may be made that there seems to be a *vicious circle* in the roles assigned to intellect and will with respect to free choice—on the one hand, it is claimed that the ultimate practical judgment of the intellect determines the will, and on the other, that the will determines the ultimate practical judgment.

To this difficulty we may reply that there would be, indeed, a vicious circle if the assertion is made that the act of selecting a judgment as ultimate *precedes in time* the determination of the will to this act by this ultimate practical judgment. Such an assertion would be similar to claiming that the chicken develops from the egg it has laid. Likewise, there would be a vicious circle if the acts of will and intellect were conceived as prior to each other by a mere priority of nature and not of time, but *in the same genus of causality*. Such an explanation would be similar to an attempt to explain the motion of two geared wheels by asserting that wheel A moves wheel B, and that B is the cause of the motion of A. But the Thomistic explanation of the roles of intellect and will in bringing about the determination of the will, places the mutual causality and precedence of intellect and will *in different genera*. The ultimate practical judgment of the intellect precedes the act of will insofar as it proposes an object to the will and thus moves the will to act; the act of will, on the other hand, precedes the ultimate practical judgment insofar as it moves the intellect to pronounce this definite judgment. Thus the will is the *efficient* cause of the election of a practical judgment as ultimate, but this same judgment is the *formal* cause of the will's act of election, because it specifies the object of the will. In the order of efficient causality the act of will is prior to its determination by the ultimate practical judgment, but in the order of formal causality the ultimate practical judgment is prior to the act of will. This mutual priority of intellect and will is not a priority of time, but merely a priority of nature. In the order of time, both causes act simultaneously.[3]

Although at first this explanation may seem very difficult and almost unintelligible, the difficulty will disappear if careful attention is paid to the fact that it is in different orders that will and intellect are said to be prior to each other in exercising their causality. A similar mutual priority exists also in the causality of matter and form, for matter limits form, while form specifies matter; also in the causality of agent and end, because the end determines the agent to act, while the action of the agent produces the end. Or, to give a more familiar example, an athlete limbers his muscles by running, while by limbering his muscles he is aided in running.

146. *The Freedom of the Will and Its Movement in the Order of Efficient Causality.* Above, in no. 144, we have seen that no external agent can force the will to act. On the other hand, it is clear that in the order of efficient causality the will needs to be moved. Man's operational capacities are *potencies*—they pass from potency to act, and according to general metaphysical principles nothing can pass from potency to act unless it be moved by an agent. Therefore, *the will needs to be moved by an external agent.* This necessity of the will to be moved by another gives rise to two questions: 1) Which external agent can move the will without forcing it?, and 2) Does the movement of the will

[3] For the problem of reciprocal causality, see the author's *Introduction to the Science of Metaphysics,* chap. 15.

by an external agent take away its internal indetermination?

Regarding the first question, if the will is made to move by an outside agent without being forced, it must be moved in accordance with its nature. But only that which is the cause of the nature of a thing can cause natural movement in it. Any other cause would do violence to it. Therefore, only the being which is the cause of the will can move it to act. But the will is an inorganic potency and therefore its subject is the soul alone. The cause of the human soul, as we shall see in Chapter 21, is God. Therefore, *only God can move the will as an efficient cause.*

Regarding the second question, the movement of the will by God does not take away its freedom. To use the words of St. Thomas: "God moves all things *in accordance with their condition* in such a way that from necessary causes the effects follow of necessity, but from contingent causes the effects follow contingently. Since, then, the will is an active principle which is not determined to one thing but indifferent to many, God moves the will in such a way that He does not determine it to one thing of necessity, but its movement remains contingent and not necessary, except in those things to which it is moved as a nature [i.e., the good in general]. . . . It would be more repugnant to the divine movement if the will were moved of necessity, which is not in accordance with its nature, than for it to be moved freely in accordance with its nature." [4]

147. *Interaction of Will and Other Operative Potencies.* If by action we mean the exercise of *efficient causality,* it should be clear that *no other operative potency can act*

[4] *Summa theol.,* Ia–IIae, q. 10, a. 4c and ad 1.

upon the will. In the first place, as we have seen above, only God can move the will as an efficient cause. Secondly, the other operative potencies are either organic or inorganic. If they are organic they cannot act upon the will, which is inorganic. The only inorganic potencies other than the will are the agent and the potential intellect. But the action of the potential intellect is strictly immanent and therefore does not produce any effect outside itself. The action of the agent intellect, on the other hand, is to dematerialize, and therefore does not apply to the will.

However, it is possible for other operative potencies to act upon the will in the order of *formal* or *final* causality. Regarding the intellect, this should be clear from the preceding part of this chapter. With respect to the operative potencies of sense life, it follows from the fact that the objects apprehended by sense cognition may please man's sense appetite and therefore be recognized by the intellect as suitable for man. Experience shows the same —under the influence of emotion or passion man sometimes judges and desires here and now a sensible good, which he does not approve and will when he is not influenced by passion.

Experience shows also that *the will is able to move other operative potencies to their act as an efficient cause;* for instance, I often think about a problem because I will; I decide (will) to see a movie or to hear a speech. The metaphysical reason why the will is able to act as an efficient cause upon other operative potencies is that the object of the other operative potencies is contained in the object of the will; for the universal good includes the particular goods that are objects of the other potencies. Hence the other potencies can be moved by the will, unless one admits that man's nature is vitiated to such an extent that his specifically human powers of intellect and will have lost all possibility of control over his lower powers. Such an admission, however, would be tantamount to saying that man has been lowered to the level of the brute animal.

Not all potencies are equally subject to the control of the will. Activities which are regulated by a natural appetite allow but little control. For instance, the operations of growth and nutrition can be influenced only in a very indirect way, such as by determining the quantity and quality of food to be made available to them. Likewise, the sensitive and intellectual potencies naturally tend to their act; therefore, when the necessary conditions for their action are fulfilled, the will cannot prevent their action from taking place. However, the will is often able to prevent, by means of commanded acts, the fulfillment of these conditions and in this way can control the powers of sense life. Specifically, with respect to sense appetite, the will has no control over the fact that sensible goods attract the sense appetite, but under normal conditions the will is able to dominate these attractions and choose a good which is less attractive, or even not attractive to the sense appetite.

The Limits of Freedom

148. In the preceding part of this chapter we have established that man's will is endowed with freedom of choice, but we did not determine whether or not this freedom has any limits. This question has to be considered now. In this matter it will be necessary to distinguish the things with respect to which there can be question of freedom in our acts of will. They are the act of willing

itself, the object which is willed, and the relationship of this object to the end intended. With respect to the act of willing, the will may be free to act or not to act. This freedom is called *freedom of exercise* or contradiction. With regard to the object, the will may be free to choose between objects that are different, such as eating, sleeping, studying, or relaxation. This is called *freedom of specification.* Regarding the relationship to the end, the will may be free to choose objects which as a matter of fact do not lead to the good in which man will find perfect happiness, i.e., morally evil objects. This freedom is called *freedom of contrariety.* It is the physical power to choose moral evil.

Moreover, with respect to the objects of the will, we must distinguish between the perfect good and imperfect goods. The *perfect good* is, as it were, the incarnation of the formal object of the will—it is a good which fully realizes the formal object without any limitation whatsoever, and its possession means complete happiness or the satisfaction of all desires. The perfect good is the ultimate *end* of the will. While there is disagreement as to what concretely constitutes the ultimate end and perfect good, there cannot be any doubt that it must satisfy all our desires and thus give perfect happiness. Because there is disagreement concerning what concretely is the perfect good and cause of complete happiness, we shall use the term here in a general sense without specifying what exactly this good is. *Imperfect goods,* on the other hand, realize the formal object of the will in a limited way only. Their possession may give some satisfaction and lead to the perfect happiness which in themselves they do not possess. Such goods are *means* to the ultimate end of the will.

After these preliminary distinctions we must now consider the question of the limits of freedom.

The Will Has Freedom of Exercise, but Not of Specification with Respect to the Perfect Good or Happiness. Regarding freedom of *specification,* the perfect good and the happiness flowing from its possession are good in all respects and therefore can never be presented to the will as evil. The intellect has only one judgment concerning them and therefore there is no possibility of rejecting them when they are presented to the will. Moreover, by its very nature the will is ordered to the perfect good as its ultimate end and thus has no control over it as the object of its acts.

The objection may be raised that Christian philosophers consider God the perfect good satisfying all desires; yet even a Christian can reject God and choose a good which is opposed to God and therefore morally evil. To this, we answer that God, considered as He is in Himself, is the perfect good. Man, however, does not know God as He is in Himself, but only in His effects. Therefore, man may judge God to be evil insofar as some of these effects may be held to be evil for man here and now; e.g., the restrictions God imposes upon man's tendency to sensible goods.[5]

On the other hand, the will has freedom of *exercise* even with respect to the perfect good and happiness, for man can abstain from considering them and consequently cease to will them.

The same rules apply to freedom of specification and exercise with respect to the *necessary means* for the attainment of the ultimate end. Whoever wills the end by

[5] Cf. St. Thomas, *De veritate,* q.22, a.2, ad 3.

the same token wills the means that are of necessity connected with the end. Such are, for instance, to be and to live. The fact that some people commit suicide and seem to will not-to-be does not militate against this assertion. The suicide does not directly intend not-to-be, but to-be-without-trouble, and not-to-be merely happens to be connected for him with his to-be-without-trouble.

What has been asserted above concerning the necessary means to the ultimate end applies also to the *unique means to any nonultimate end,* once this end has been chosen and as long as this choice is adhered to. For instance, once a student wills to obtain grade A in his examinations and sees that constant study is the only way in which this grade can be obtained, his will to obtain an A implies by consequent necessity the will to study constantly.

The Will Has Freedom of Specification and Exercise with Respect to All Other Goods. Regarding *specification,* all other goods are nonperfect goods which are not considered to be of necessity connected with the attainment of the perfect good or happiness. Because the nonperfect good is good only to a certain extent, the intellect is able to consider it as either good or evil. It does not of necessity have to present the nonperfect good as desirable here and now, so that the will is not necessitated.

There is also freedom of *exercise* with respect to these goods, because man's will can refuse to exercise any act at all with respect to them.

Man's Will Possesses Freedom of Contrariety. Although man is not free to reject the perfect good in which he finds happiness, he does not see the necessary connection between the perfect good and the means by which it can be reached. As a result, he may choose as a means to happiness something which as a matter of fact leads away from the perfect good, i.e., something which is morally evil.

It is to be noted that so-called "freedom" of contrariety is not really freedom in the true sense of the term.[6] True freedom means self-determination and self-control, while the choice of the morally evil means that man allows his will to be determined against the very judgment of reason. Hence the choice of evil means less self-determination.

Problems Raised by Free Will

149. Several difficulties may be raised against the admission of a free will. Some of these flow from modern science.

Conservation of Energy. One may argue that freewill activity would result in an increase of energy, which is against the law of conservation of energy.

To this, we may reply that the *commanded* acts of free will are executed by the body in accordance with the law of conservation of energy and therefore do not result in an increase of physical energy. *Elicited* acts of will, on the other hand, are inorganic actions and therefore do not directly result in a change of physical energy. It is true, however, that the will does not elicit its actions without changes in organic conditions and that these changes need physical energy. But these changes take place in the body, so that the needed energy can be supplied by physical forces operating in the body in accordance with the law of conservation of energy.

[6] Cf. St. Thomas, *De veritate*, q.22, a.6.

Determinism. It could be urged that the material components of the body always obey the same deterministic laws of nature, whether they are inside a human body or outside it. Hence the bodily activities occurring in a commanded act of will are subject to these laws. Therefore, there are no truly free commanded acts, so that freedom is largely an illusion.

In reply to this difficulty, we may admit that the physico-chemical reactions occurring in a commanded act of will take place in accordance with the deterministic laws of nature. However, the fact that the physico-chemical aspects of these acts follows these laws does not imply that the principle directing these acts is a *physical part* of a physico-chemical system and subject to the same laws. The physico-chemical reactions of a motorcar rigidly follow deterministic laws; yet this does not mean that no driver directs the operation of the car. No more than the driver is part of the car, is man's will a physical part of the human body. Accordingly, the material components of the body may obey deterministic laws, while at the same time they are directed by an "outside" principle which is not subject to these laws, although, of course, the scope of its directive ability may be confined within certain limits by these laws. In calling the will an "outside" principle, we do not intend to say that the will is external to man or even to the human body. It is external merely to the human body considered precisely as a physico-chemical unit, but internal to man and to his body taken precisely as a *human* body.

Statistical Predictability. If man has a free will, it would be impossible to predict what course of action he will take, for only that which is predetermined can be predicted. Yet it is possible to compile statistics of so-called "free actions," and upon the basis of these statistics to predict how many people will "freely" perform a certain action.

To this objection we reply in the first place, that in order to predict it is necessary to know *what* will happen, but not *how* it will happen. Secondly, statistics do not allow the prediction of what this individual man will do, but merely how many in a large group, *on the average,* will do a certain act. The constancy of the statistical datum can be explained by the fact that men are fundamentally alike, subject to the same drives and *likely* to react in the same way under the same conditions.

We are willing to go even further than the objection and admit that it is possible to predict with moral certainty free decisions which will be taken by certain *individuals.* For instance, one can be morally certain that if a lazy man has to choose between a difficult and an easy job, both offering the same pay, he will choose the easy job; or that a very religious man, faced with a choice between dishonest riches and honest hard work, will choose hard work.

One could even claim that in many instances there is only an infinitesimally small chance that free human behavior will not be in accordance with what is foreseen and that the very structure of social life is based upon this kind of predictability. For example, everybody eats in a good restaurant without fear of being intentionally poisoned, because the behavior of the cook and the waiters can be predicted; a professor stands in front of his class, even on examination days, without fear of being murdered, because the behavior of students can be predicted; traffic is possible because one can predict that drivers in opposite directions will stick to their side of the road; etc. It is possible even to go to the absolute extremes of predictability and to claim with Ach that after an experimental study of an individual a multiple choice of activity can be arranged in such a way that his selection can be predicted with one hundred percent accuracy. All this, however, does not prove that there is no free choice, but merely that *free choice is not an act without a motive* and that it is often possible to predict from a knowledge of one's character and surroundings which motive will prevail.

The Greater Good. Another difficulty which is often made is that the "greater good" prevails. When there is a choice between various goods, the one which has the strongest appeal for the individual determines the act of will. Therefore, there is no such thing as a truly free choice.

In reply, we point out the *ambiguity* of the terms "greater good" and "strongest appeal." If these terms are meant to indicate the good or motive proposed by the ultimate practical judgment, it is unquestionably true that the greater good always wins. But we should not forget that it is the will which in the order of efficient causality freely makes the practical judgment ultimate (cf. nos. 144 f.). If, on the other hand, by "greater good" is meant that which is considered greater by any other judgment, we deny that it determines the will. Of course, it may be granted that most people will decide in favor of that which most people would consider to be the greater good. The question, however, is not what most people will do, but rather, whether or not they do freely whatever they do.

Historical Notes

150. The freedom of the will is defended by *Plato, Aristotle, St. Thomas, Scotus, Descartes, Locke,* and many others of very different schools of thought. *Kant* denies it in the noumenal world, but admits it in the phenomenal world as a postulate of practical reason. The freedom of the will is denied by the determinists and the fatalists, who in one way or another hold that the will is necessitated either from within or from without. Several forms of determinism may be distinguished.

Mechanical determinism is defended by extreme materialists, such as *Epicurus* (341–270 B.C.), *Hobbes* (1588–1679), and *Stuart Mill* (1806–1873). In general, they admit that understanding and willing are purely material processes, subject to the same mechanical laws which govern the whole cosmos.

Biological (physiological) *determinism* is defended by many psychoanalysts who follow *Freud* (1856–1939), and by the behaviorists (*Watson*). In general, they admit that man's activity is rigidly fixed by biological determinants, such as the activity of the endocrine glands, hereditary factors, surroundings, etc. While it cannot be denied that hereditary factors, glands, etc., exercise influence upon the will, and that in abnormal cases can prevent deliberation and therefore also free choice, we deny that these factors normally necessitate the will.

Psychological determinism derives its origin from *Leibnitz,* who did not deny the freedom of the will, but explained it in such a way that determinism resulted. According to psychological determinism there is an intrinsic necessity for the will to choose the greater good. While we are willing to admit that the greater good exercises a powerful attraction, so that more often than not the greater good is chosen, we deny that the will is necessitated by the greater good.

Metaphysical determinism asserts that the freedom of the will must be rejected because it would imply a violation of the principle of causality. On the one hand, the will would be the cause of its free choice, and, on the other, the will is not sufficiently determined to make this choice and therefore not its cause. However, from the preceding considerations it should be clear that the Thomistic explanation does not violate causality, for the will is sufficiently determined by the ultimate practical judgment to be the cause of the choice. Moreover, the concept of cause does not imply that the effect follows of necessity, but merely that the effect has a cause.

Theological determinism, as defended e.g., by *Calvin* (1509–1564), denies the freedom of the will, because when God moves the will He determines its act in such a way that there can be no free choice. While we admit that God moves the will, we deny that He moves anything against its nature, so that the freedom of the will is safeguarded. How God can move the will without taking away its freedom is one of the most famous problems in the history of philosophy and theology. Its discussion, however, belongs to theodicy and theology. Under theological determinism we may classify also the pantheism of *Spinoza,* according to whom the divine causality necessitates all other modes of being; and fatalism, which holds that everything happens of necessity as decided by fate.

Regarding the explanation of the freedom of the will, *Scotus* and *Suarez* maintain the so-called theory of liberty of equilibrium or indeterminism. According to this theory, whenever the intellect judges two things to be good, the will is able to choose either of them without being determined by the intellect. However, such indeterminism loses sight of the true character of the will as a rational appetite. The will does not know anything and, therefore, if not guided by the intellect, cannot act as a rational appetite. We should never forget that the will is not an independent entity whose freedom is to be safeguarded, but keep in mind that it is really man who is free and decides freely, by means of his will, under the guidance of his intellect.

SUMMARY

151. Freedom in general means the absence of any determining influences. With respect to the will, freedom from coercion means that no external agent makes the will act against its inclination. Freedom from intrinsic necessity means that the will is not determined with respect to its action by its own nature. Freedom of choice implies that the will is free from coercion and intrinsic necessity in its elicited acts.

Speculatively good is that which the intellect judges to be good in a general way, without applying the judgment to the conditions affecting the judging subject here and now. Practically good is that which the intellect judges to be good in the concrete conditions affecting the subject here and now.

The will cannot be coerced. To coerce means to make one act against his inclination. But an act of will by its very nature is an actual inclination to something. Therefore, a forced act of will would be an actual inclination of the will to something to which it is actually not inclined, which is a contradiction.

The will is free from internal necessity, because the will follows the practical judgments of the intellect, and the practical judgment regarding particular goods is changeable or undetermined. Any particular good is good only in certain respects but evil in others, so that it does not have to be judged as good.

Experience confirms this proof of freedom, for in case of conflicting motives the issue is often settled by the active interposition of the Ego, i.e., by an act of will.

The immediate foundation of freedom lies in the fact that the will follows the intellect and therefore has as its object the good in its universality; hence it is not necessitated to judge good anything whose goodness is limited. Ultimately, however, the foundation of freedom lies in the immateriality of the intellect, for it is precisely because of its immaterial nature that the intellect apprehends the universal.

Because the deliberation of the intellect over the particular good could go on indefinitely but has to cease if action is to follow, the will stops the deliberation by electing one practical judgment as ultimate. It has to be the will which makes this election, for otherwise the will would follow a judgment over which it has no control and therefore would not be free.

The assertion that the will follows and therefore is determined by the ultimate practical judgment does not contradict the statement that it is the will which elects one judgment as ultimate. In the order of time, the determination of the will by the judgment does not precede the election of this judgment by the will, but both are simultaneous. There is, however, a priority of nature inasmuch as the will needs to be determined to its act by the intellect, while the intellect needs to be determined to its judgment by the act of will. But this mutual priority is not in the same genus of causality, but refers to different orders of causes. The will is the efficient cause of the election of one judgment as ultimate, but this same judgment is the formal cause of the will's election because it specifies the object of the will.

The human will needs not only to be determined in the order of formal causality, but also to be moved in that of efficient causality, for the will passes from potency to act. Because the will cannot be forced, this movement of the will must be in accordance with its nature. Therefore, it can be given only by that which is the cause of the will, for only the cause of a nature can cause natural movement in it. This cause is God, who moves the will in such a way that its freedom is safeguarded.

No other operative potency of man can act upon the will, but they are able to act upon the will in the order of formal or final causality, inasmuch as their objects can be apprehended by the intellect as suitable for man. The will can act efficiently upon other operative potencies, because the object of the other powers is contained in the object of the will.

Regarding the limits of freedom, the will is not free to reject the perfect good or ultimate end and the happiness flowing from it, because they cannot be apprehended as evil. However, the will has freedom of exercise with respect to them, because man can abstain from considering them. The same rule applies to the means that are apprehended as of necessity connected with the attainment of the perfect good and happiness. Regarding all other goods, the will is free to accept or reject them and to abstain from any act. Moreover, man is able to choose the morally evil, because he does not see the necessary connection between happiness and the means by which it can be attained, and therefore may choose as a means to happiness something which as a matter of fact leads away from it.

Free will does not violate the law of conservation of energy, because the elicited acts of will are inorganic and in themselves do not require any physical energy. The organic changes, on the other hand, which are necessary conditions for the activity of the will take place in accordance with the law of conservation energy.

Freedom is not reduced to an illusion by the fact that the commanded acts of will are subject to the deterministic laws of nature. Although these laws limit the scope of freedom, narrowing the field of man's possible free actions, they do not eliminate freedom, because the will, as a directive principle of body activities, is outside the sphere of physico-chemical reactions.

Statistical predictability of man's free actions is not against freedom. Statistics do not indicate how actions occur, but only which actions are likely to occur. In general, they do not apply to the individual but only to a group. If they are accurate with respect to the individual, their accuracy flows from the fact that the will does not act without a motive and that the motive which will prevail often can be predicted from a knowledge of one's character.

The greater good may be said to prevail if by this expression is meant that which is judged to be greater by the ultimate practical judgment. What is the "greater good" in any other judgment will often prevail, but does not do so of necessity.

SUGGESTED READINGS

152. Aristotle, *Ethica Nicomachea,* bk. III, chap. 5.

Thomas Aquinas, *Summa theol.,* Ia, q. 82, aa. 1, 2; q. 83, a. 1; Ia–IIae, q. 10, aa. 1, 2; q. 13, a. 6. Freedom and its limits.

——— *Summa theol.,* Ia, q. 82, a. 3; Ia–IIae, q. 9, a. 1. Interaction of intellect and will.

——— *Summa theol.,* Ia, q. 105, a. 4; q. 106, a. 2; q. 115, a. 4; Ia–IIae, q. 9, q. 10, a. 4. Movement of the will in the order of efficient causality.

——— *Summa theol.,* Ia, q. 81, a. 3; Ia–IIae, q. 9, a. 2; q. 10, a. 3; q. 17, a. 7; *De veritate,* q. 26, a. 10. The will and other operative potencies, especially the passions.

Robert E. Brennan, *Thomistic Psychology,* chap. 8. The volitional life of man.

George P. Klubertanz, *The Philosophy of Human Nature,* chap. 10. The will.

Robert P. Sullivan, *The Thomistic Concept of the Natural Necessitation of the Human Will* (River Forest: 1952).

Henri Renard, *The Philosophy of Man,* chap. 7. The appetites of man.

Gerard Smith, "The Nature and Uses of Liberty," *The New Scholasticism,* 1952, pp. 305 ff.

Hubert Gruender, *Experimental Psychology,* chap. 17. Experimental studies of voluntary activity.

Yves R. Simon, "The Foreseeability of Free Acts," *The New Scholasticism,* 1948, pp. 357 ff.

Andrew G. Van Melsen, *The Philosophy of Nature* (*Duquesne Studies, Philosophical Series,* no. 2, Pittsburgh, 1954), chap. 7, esp. pp. 247 ff. Determinism and free will.

P. Henry Van Laer, *Philosophico-Scientific Problems* (*Duquesne Studies, Philosophical Series,* no. 3, Pittsburgh, 1953), chap. 5. Determinism and previsibility.

CHAPTER 18

The Existence and Nature of the Intellectual Soul

*** This chapter will be brief, because most of its conclusions follow immediately from the nature of man's intellect and will.

The Existence of the Intellectual Soul

153. There cannot be any serious doubt regarding the existence of an intellectual soul in man. Man has vital actions and therefore must have a vital principle or soul. Because man has the vital activities of understanding and willing, which transcend the level of sense life and cannot be reduced to it, man must have a soul which differs from that of mere animals. Man's soul must be proportionate to the intellectual kind of life found in man. This principle of life is called the rational or intellectual soul. However, in speaking here about the existence of a rational soul in man, we do not yet mean to claim that this soul is the substantial form of man's body, but merely that it is the first principle of man's intellectual life.

The Nature of the Intellectual Soul

154. *The Intellectual Soul Is a Substance.* The reason for this assertion is that the acts of understanding and willing are accidents and therefore do not exist in themselves but in a substance. But understanding and willing are acts of the intellectual soul alone. Therefore, this soul is a substance.

The Intellectual Soul Is One Substance. By this statement we mean that one and the same intellectual soul remains as a permanent principle throughout the succession of acts of understanding and willing. Internal experience shows the truth of this assertion, inasmuch as we experience our acts of intellect and will as acts of the same Ego which remains throughout their succession. To the objection that some people experience their activity as belonging to different Ego's (so-called split personalities), we answer that this phenomenon of abnormal psychology can be explained by a disturbance of the memorative and imaginative potencies.

The Intellectual Soul Is Simple. By calling the soul simple, we mean that its essence is not composed of parts, viz., matter and form, which are the constituent principles of a composite essence. The intellectual soul is simple, because it is the principle of operations that are intrinsically independent of matter. But if this principle were composed of matter and form, its operation could not be intrinsically independent of matter, because action follows being.

If the intellectual soul is essentially simple it follows that it has *no quantitative parts,* for quantitative extension can be found only in something material.

The Intellectual Soul Is Spiritual. Spiritual is that which can exist independently of matter. From the fact that intellection and willing are intrinsically independent of matter it follows that the soul, which is the principle of these actions, is independent of matter, for action follows being.

The Intellectual Soul Is Really Distinct from the Body. This follows at once from the fact that the intellectual soul is spiritual, while the body is material.

The Intellectual Soul Alone Is Not Man. Our own experience shows that man has not only acts of understanding and willing, but also of vegetative and sense life. But the intellectual soul alone cannot be the principle of vegetative and sensitive acts, because these acts are organic. Therefore, the intellectual soul alone is not man.

Each Man Has His Own Intellectual Soul. That each man has an intellectual soul is clear from the fact that each man is capable of intellection, although the use of this capacity may be impeded by the disturbance of the extrinsic organ of intellection. Each man has his own intellectual soul, because internal experience reveals to each man that he is an understanding and willing Ego, which is distinct from other understanding and willing Ego's.

There Is Only One Soul in Each Man. Man experiences himself as *one* living being which grows, senses, understands, and wills. But if there were more than one soul in a man he would not be one but several living beings, because it is the soul which makes a being living. The fact that the rational and sensitive appetites are often in opposition does not militate against the assertion that they belong to the same principles of life. For these opposite appetites are experienced as appetites pulling one and the same living subject in different directions.

Moreover, if there were several souls in man, it would be impossible to explain why the functions of one soul would aid or impede those of another soul. Yet experience shows that these functions, if properly balanced, aid one another, while the intensification of one may impede the others. For instance, the stimulation of the nutritive function by a copious meal is not conducive to intellectual pursuits; absorption in thought dims sense perception, as is well illustrated by the proverbial distracted professor; excessive worry may cause stomach ulcers.

If there is only one soul in man it follows that the rational soul is not only the principle of intellectual life, but also that of vegetative and sensitive life. Hence the rational soul is sometimes said to be *virtually sensitive and vegetative.*

In man vegetative life is the foundation of his sense life. It is the vegetative life which forms and maintains his sense organs. On the other hand, vegetative life in man could not sustain itself without man's sense life, for, unlike a mere plant, man must make use of his senses to find the necessary food. Both vegetative and sense life are a necessary condition for man's intellectual life, because man cannot function intellectually without the imagination, whose organ must be nourished by man's vegetative life.

Historical Notes

*155. The existence of any soul in man is denied by all those who deny that there is an essential difference between living and nonliving bodies (cf. no. 28). The existence of a specifically rational soul is denied by those who reduce intellection to sensation (cf. no. 114).

The substantial nature of the soul is denied by all those who reject substances, such as the phenomenalists and the associationists (*Stuart Mill*). For *Mill,* instead of a soul, there is a stream of consciousness. Phenomenalism as applied to psychology is called the theory of actuality, which is defended by *Wundt* and *James.*

The spiritual nature of the rational soul is defended by philosophers of widely different schools, such as *Plato, Aristotle, St. Augustine, Averroes, St. Thomas, Descartes, Leibnitz, Kant, Hegel,* and *Bergson.* It is denied by all those who deny that the intellect is inorganic. The simplicity of the soul was denied by some medieval philosophers, e.g., *St. Bonaventure* (1221–1274), who admitted a kind of "spiritual matter" in all finite beings in order to distinguish the finite from the infinite.

The real distinction of body and soul was denied by *Spinoza,* who considered body and soul as different expressions of one and the same reality.

The intellectual soul was identified with man by *Plato,* for whom man is a soul clothed or enclosed in a body.

That each man has his own intellectual soul was denied by *Averroes,* who identified the soul with the sole agent intellect he admitted for all men.

The unicity of the rational soul in man was denied by some Neo-Platonists, who admitted a vegetative, a sensitive, and an intellectual soul in man; also by *Appollinaris* (*ca.*310–*ca.*390) and *Ockam,* who admitted a sensitive and a rational soul; and by the Manicheists, who asserted that man is composed of a body, a soul which is a principle of good, and a soul which is a principle of evil.

SUMMARY

156. Man has an intellectual soul, because he has intellectual life. This soul is a substantial principle, for its acts of intellection and willing are accidents. The soul is one substance, for the acts of intellect and will are experienced throughout life as acts of the same substantial Ego.

The intellectual soul is simple, i.e., without matter, because otherwise its operations could not be intrinsically independent of matter. It is spiritual, because it exists independently of matter, as is clear from the fact that it can act independently of matter. It is really distinct from the body, because it is immaterial, while the body is material.

The intellectual soul is not man, because man has also acts of sensing and vegetative life, which are organic and therefore cannot have the soul alone as their principle.

Each man has an intellectual soul, because each man is capable of understanding. This soul is each man's own soul, because man experiences himself as a thinking and willing Ego which is distinct from all other thinking and willing Ego's. There is only one soul in each man, because man experiences himself as one being which grows, senses, and thinks.

SUGGESTED READINGS

157. Aristotle, *De anima,* bk. III, chap. 3. Spirituality of the soul.

Thomas Aquinas, *Summa theol.,* Ia, q. 75, aa. 1–5; *De anima,* a. 6. Nature of the soul.

——— *Summa theol.,* Ia, q. 76, aa. 2, 3; *Contra gentes,* bk. II, chap. 58; *De anima,* a. 11. Each man his own soul and only one soul in each man.

Etienne Gilson, *The Spirit of Mediaeval Philosophy,* chap. 9.

Hubert Gruender, *Psychology Without a Soul* (St. Louis: 1912), chaps. 1–3; *Problems of Psychology* (Milwaukee: 1937), chaps. 1, 5, 6. Critical studies of modern views of the soul.

Thomas V. Moore, *Cognitive Psychology* (New York: 1939), chap. 4, pp. 34 ff. Multiple personalities.

CHAPTER 19

The Union of Soul and Body

*** 158. It is not subject to doubt that in some way or other man's body and soul are united, but the precise nature of this union constitutes a difficult problem, because it is a union of body and spirit, of the material and the immaterial. The same difficulty was not encountered with regard to the union of body and soul in plants and animals, because their souls are intrinsically dependent upon matter, so that their union remains entirely within the material order. In man, however, the soul, by itself, is a substance and intrinsically independent of matter; yet at the same time it is united with the body.

Three answers are possible with respect to the union of man's soul and body—this union is either merely apparent or real; if real, it is either substantial or accidental. But if this union is merely *apparent,* there is no question of union in the strict sense, but everything happens as if there were a union. If the union is *substantial,* body and soul are united in such a way that together they constitute one substance, existing by one "to be." If, on the other hand, the union is *accidental,* body and soul have their own substantial nature and their own "to be," and their actions are not actions of one and the same being. An example of an accidental union is that of a horse and its rider; of a substantial union that of body and soul in animals.

In the following pages we shall see that man's body and soul are substantially united in such a way that the soul is the only substantial form of the human body.

Substantial Union of Body and Soul

159. The nature of the union of man's body and intellectual soul is not open for an immediate inspection, but must be determined by a study of the activity of man. If man has any activity which requires a substantial union of body and soul, then we shall have to conclude to such a union.

Body and Soul Together Form One Nature. Man's body and rational soul together form one nature if there is human activity that can proceed only from body and soul together as one principle or nature, for nature is the same as the (remote) principle of operation. But, as we have seen in no. 154, the rational soul and the body together form the principle of the operations of vegetative and sense life, for these operations are organic and therefore can proceed only from an organic principle, i.e., a composite of body and soul. Therefore, body and soul are united into one principle of operation or one nature.

Note that one and the same *effect* can be produced by the joined activity of two or more causes acting in coordination without being united into one agent. For example, two horses pulling one cart produce one effect, viz., the motion of the cart. In arguing for the union of body and soul in one nature we do not proceed from the unity of the effect, but from the unity of *operation*, because one and the same operation cannot flow from distinct agents, but requires a unity of agent. Thus, in the example just given, each of the horses has its own operation of pulling.[1]

Body and Soul as One Substance. From the fact that man's body and rational soul together form a composite that is one principle of operation, we may immediately derive the conclusion that they are also one substance. For if they were distinct substances, they would also act as distinct substances and not as one principle of action. On the other hand, as we have seen in no. 154, the intellectual soul is a substance which does not depend upon the body for its existence, but is a substance in its own right. Now a substantial union resulting in one substance is possible only if the components are *incomplete* substances or substantial principles, for complete substances cannot be essentially united, but only accidentally, as by juxtaposition or unity of extrinsic purpose. Although the rational soul is independent of the body with respect to its existence and therefore *complete in substantiality,* nevertheless it is not an altogether complete substance. For the rational soul cannot exercise all its functions without the body, because in the operations of vegetative and sense life it is intrinsically dependent upon the body; therefore, it is said to be *incomplete in specific perfection.*[2] In this way the body and the rational soul constitute together one substance.

The Soul as the Substantial Form of the Body

160. Once it is admitted that body and soul together constitute one substance, we may ask what role each plays

[1] Cf. St. Thomas, *Contra gentes,* bk. II, chap. 57.
[2] Cf. St. Thomas, *De anima,* a.1, ad 12.

in the composite whole, called man. After the preceding considerations, the answer to this question should not be too difficult.

The Intellectual Soul Is the Substantial Form of the Body. The substantial form of a composite is that which gives the composite its specific perfection. But in man, the specific perfection is given by the rational soul, because it is this soul which makes man specifically human. Hence it follows that the rational soul is the substantial form of the body.

Consequences of This Thesis. From the fact that the soul is the substantial form of the body it follows that the soul by its essence is completely and *entirely in the whole body and in each part* of the body, although it does not exercise all its functions in each part. Some of these functions require special organs, while others are inorganic and therefore cannot be said to be exercised in any part of the body.

The soul is *individuated by the body* whose form it is; consequently, there are as many souls as there are human bodies. For, as we have seen in metaphysics,[3] any form is proportioned to, and limited by the matter whose form it is, and therefore multiplied according to the multiplication of matter.

Because the soul is individuated by the body whose form it is, it follows that the same soul does not inform different bodies in succession. Otherwise, it would be at the same time limited by the body whose soul it is and not limited by it, since it could be the form of another body. Therefore, so-called *transmigration* or reincarnation of

[3] Cf. the author's *Introduction to the Science of Metaphysics*, chap. 5.

souls (metempsychosis) into other human bodies is impossible. A fortiori, it is impossible for a human soul to be reincarnated in an animal body, for man and animal are specifically different.

The rational soul and body *do not need a common bond* to be united, for they are related as act and potency, which unite of themselves.[4] Moreover, the admission of such a common bond is useless to explain the union of matter and spirit. Such a bond would have to be either material or immaterial. If materal, one has still to explain how this bond can be united with the immaterial soul; if, on the other hand, it is immaterial, its union with the body remains unexplained.

Because the rational soul is the substantial form of the body, *body and soul exist by one "to be,"* are one being, composed of potency and act. Thus the dualism of matter and spirit is solved in the monism of being. The soul, which is subsistent and therefore has a "to be" of its own, communicates its "to be" to the body, so that the "to be" of the body is the same as the "to be" of the soul.

*The objection could be raised that if the body has the same "to be" as the soul, it must have also the same operations, because action follows being. Yet the soul is supposed to have operations in which the body does not share. To this we answer that the body would have to share in all the operations of the soul if the soul were totally immersed or encompassed by the body. But the very fact that understanding and willing are immaterial shows that the rational soul is not totally immersed in matter. Hence the body does not have the "to be" of the soul in the same way as the soul itself. The soul has it as the principle, and the body as the recipient which

[4] Cf. *op. cit.*, chap. 3.

participates in the "to be" to the extent of its capacity, but its capacity does not equal that of the principle.

Because the soul is the substantial form of the body rational *souls differ in perfection.* The perfection of a soul is proportioned to the capacity of the body, because a form is received according to the capacity of the receiver. According as the body is more or less perfectly disposed for the reception of a rational soul, this soul will be more or less perfect. This difference in perfection extends even to the proper functions of intellectual life, although these functions are intrinsically independent of the body. The reason is that the intellect depends for its operation upon the functioning of the senses, and the senses are more or less perfect in accordance with the disposition of the body.

*Because the rational soul is the substantial form of the body, there is *no need to raise the question as to why this soul is united with a body.* It is the very nature of the soul as a substantial form to enter into such a union, for only in such a union does the soul have the fullness of its perfection. If, however, the union of the soul and the body were merely accidental, a reason for the union would have to be assigned. This reason, it seems, could be only an act of will, either of the soul itself or of God. The first alternative is unreasonable, for a soul which is not naturally united with a body is in a more perfect condition when it is free from the shackles of the body and therefore does not seek to be united with it. The second alternative is unreasonable, for it implies that God, who first made the soul[5] as naturally without a body subsequently united it with a body against its nature, which would imply an imperfection in God's wisdom.

[5] Cf. below, chap. 20.

The Rational Soul Is the Only Substantial Form of the Body. This follows from the fact that body and soul together constitute one substance. In one substance there can be only one substantial form, because the substantial form gives a thing its perfection in the line of substance, so that any other form added to it will not be substantial but accidental.

Moreover, it would be useless to admit, in addition to the rational soul, any other substantial form, such as a sensitive soul or the form of corporeity. For the rational soul is the most perfect of all forms existing in matter and therefore can give matter all the perfections that could be given by the inferior forms.

It follows therefore that it is the rational soul which gives to man his *every grade of essential perfection;* it makes him not only a man, but also an animal, an organism, a body, a substance, and a being. Note, however, that the rational soul is not the efficient but the formal cause of these perfections.

Historical Notes

161. The problem of the union of body and soul has always been the subject of dispute among philosophers, mainly because of the difficulty of conceiving the union of the material with the immaterial.

The empiricists, who deny the existence of a spiritual soul, claim that the problem of union of body and soul is without a basis. Among them some, such as *Wundt* and *Bain* (1818–1903), proposed the theory of physicopsychical parallelism, according to which there are two series of actions, one physical and the other psychical, which are parallel but do not influence each other.

A merely apparent union is admitted by *Malebranche*

and other occasionalists, who reduce the union of body and soul to a mere coordination of the activities in the soul and the body, inasmuch as the First Cause, which produces the activity in one, uses this activity as the occasion to produce coordinated activity in the other. Somewhat similar is the position of *Leibnitz,* who admits activities in the body and the soul, but denies that they influence each other. He explains their apparent interaction as the result of a harmony established by God, who, foreseeing the activity of this soul and that body, united them with each other.

A real but accidental union was advocated by *Plato,* for whom the soul was merely the mover of the body; by *Descartes,* who reduced the union of body and soul to a united activity; and by *Bergson,* who made the body a kind of machine directed by the soul. A real union by means of a third intermediate substance was proposed by *Cudworth* (1617–1688) and *Le Clerc* (died 1736).

The substantial union of body and soul is defended by *Aristotle, St. Thomas, Scotus,* and many others. *Scotus,* however, admitted, in addition to the rational soul another substantial form, the "form of corporeity." A similar theory is held by those moderns, such as *Descoqs* (1877–1946), who say that the chemical elements in the body retain their substantial form.

The reincarnation of souls is admitted not only by certain Oriental religions (Buddhism), but also by *Plato* and the theosophists (*Annie Besant,* 1847–1933). *Plato* and the Buddhists assert even that in case a man leads an evil life his soul will be reincarnated in the body of a brute animal.

SUMMARY

162. Once the spirituality of the soul is admitted, the union of this soul with the body constitutes a difficult problem, because it means the union of matter and the immaterial. Three types of union are possible, viz., apparent, accidental, and substantial. Of these three the merely apparent and the accidental union are not acceptable, for they cannot satisfactorily account for those operations of man which require the body and the soul as their principle. Such operations are of an organic nature and therefore can proceed only from a principle which is a composite of body and soul. Therefore, it follows that the body and the rational soul are united into one substance, for they act as one substance. However, a union into one substance is possible only if the components are not complete substances but substantial principles. Although the soul is independent of the body for its existence and therefore a substance in its own right, it is not altogether complete, because without the body the soul cannot exercise all its functions. Therefore, the rational soul is called a substance which is incomplete in specific perfection but complete in substantiality. The soul is the substantial form of the body, because it is the soul and not the body which makes man specifically human.

As the substantial form of the body the soul is essentially present in the whole body and any of its parts, but it cannot exercise all its functions in each part, because some of these functions require very special organs, while others are not organic. As the substantial form of the body the soul is individuated by the body and multiplied in accordance with the multiplication of bodies; hence transmigration of souls is not possible. There is no need for a common bond uniting the soul and the body, because they are related as act and potency, or form and matter.

Because of their substantial union body and soul exist by one and the same "to be." This "to be" is the "to be" of the rational soul, which, being subsistent, has a "to be" of its own and shares it with the body.

Because the rational soul is the substantial form of the body, souls can differ in perfection, for a form is limited in perfection according to the capacity of the receiver.

The rational soul is the only substantial form of the body, because in one substance there can be only one substantial form. The substantial form perfects the receiving subject in the line of substance, so that any other form added to it can be only accidental. Moreover, it is useless to admit additional substantial forms in the human body, because the higher form contains all the perfection that could be given by the lower form. Accordingly, the rational soul gives to man his every grade of essential perfection—it formally makes him man, animal, organism, body, substance, and being.

SUGGESTED READINGS

163. Aristotle, *De anima,* bk. II, chap. 1.

Thomas Aquinas, *Summa theol.,* Ia, q. 76, aa. 1–8; *De spiritualibus creaturis,* aa. 2, 3; *Contra gentes,* bk. II, chaps. 56, 57; *De anima,* aa. 1, 2.

E. Gilson, *The Spirit of Mediaeval Philosophy,* chap. 9.

Henri Renard, *The Philosophy of Man,* sec. two, q. 2. Nature of the union of body and soul.

CHAPTER 20

The Origin of the Human Soul

*** In this chapter we shall investigate two problems. The first is concerned with the cause of the human soul; the second with the time at which the soul comes into existence.

The Cause of the Human Soul

164. The origin of the souls of plants and animals did not give rise to any special problem. Such souls are intrinsically dependent upon matter, and any form which is intrinsically dependent upon matter is educed from the potency of matter under the influence of an external agent which reduces matter from potency to act. The human soul, however, is intrinsically independent of matter and therefore cannot be said to be educed from the potency of matter, for it transcends matter. Hence the question arises: Whence comes the human soul?

The Human Soul Does Not Come from the Parents. If the human soul came from the parents it would have to come from their souls, their bodies, or the composites of body and soul. But the human soul cannot come from the *bodies* of the parents, for it is intrinsically independent of matter. For the same reason the human soul cannot come from the *composites* of body and soul, because the composite acts through the body, so that its activities are intrinsically material.

To come from the *souls* of the parents, the new soul would have to be generated, created or produced from a subject by the souls of the parents. *Generation,* however, is impossible. In generation, a part of the whole divides off from the whole; but the human soul is simple and therefore does not have any parts. *Production* from a pre-existing subject also is excluded. Such a pre-existing subject would be either a material or an immaterial substance. But from a material substance nothing immaterial can be made. An immaterial substance, on the other hand, is not subject to being transformed into another species of substance, because it is essentially without composition and therefore not subject to substantial change.[1] *Creation* of the new soul by the souls of the parents is impossible, for only God can create. To be able to create implies absolute control over "to be," and such a control is not possessed by any being which has its "to be" from another.[2] Therefore, there is no way in which the new human soul could come from the parents.

[1] The human soul is essentially different from all other spiritual substances, for a spiritual substance which is not the form of a body (i.e., a form received in, and limited by a potency) is essentially infinite and consequently cannot be multiplied in the same species. Cf. St. Thomas, *Summa theol.,* Ia, q.75, a.7, and the author's *Introduction to the Science of Metaphysics,* chap. 5.

[2] To create means to cause the "to be" of a thing in the absolute sense, and not merely the "to be" of this or that kind. But, however, no finite being can cause "to be" in the absolute sense in any other

For similar reasons we must exclude the possibility that the human soul would come from any other body or any other finite spiritual substance. Concerning the possibility of the human soul evolving from an animal soul, see Chapter 23.

*Although the parents do not generate the soul which makes their offspring specifically human, they remain its parents in the strict sense of the term. In a composite being the efficient cause does not have to produce all the component parts, but merely has to be the cause of their union. A carpenter, for instance, is the efficient cause of the table he makes, although he does not make the wood, because he causes the union of the various pieces of wood into a table. In the generation of a new human being the parents directly produce one of the components, namely, the body. The other component, the soul, is not produced by the parents, but its union with the body is caused by the parents inasmuch as they produce a body which necessarily requires a human soul as its act.[3]

*The objection could be raised that if the body necessarily requires a human soul as its act, the body is in potency to the soul, and therefore this soul must be educed from the potency of matter. As a result it could not be spiritual. The answer is that matter being in potency to a soul is not the same as this soul being in the

being, for otherwise it could cause its own "to be," which is absurd. The reason for this assertion is that "to be" is an act and therefore is limited only by the potency of the receiver. Accordingly, if a finite being could cause the "to be" of another being in the absolute sense, it could cause the "to be" of all finite beings, including itself; for the limitation of the "to be" is a finite being results from the potency of the receiving subject and not from the cause of the "to be."

[3] Cf. St. Thomas, *De potentia*, q.3, a.9, ad 6.

potency of matter or capable of being educed from the potency of matter. Matter is in potency to any form which can actuate it, but only a material form is educed from the potency of matter.

The Human Soul Comes into Existence Through Creation by God. From the preceding considerations it should be clear that the human soul can come only from God. This divine origin of the human soul offers the following possibilities: The new soul is a part of God's substance; God Himself becomes the form of the new human being; God creates a new human soul. But the first two of these three possibilities are not acceptable. God's substance is altogether simple because He is pure act; therefore, *no part of God's substance* can be a human soul. God Himself *cannot become the form* or soul of the new human being, for God is absolutely infinite, while the form of a human being is limited. Moreover, God is pure act and therefore cannot come to be anything. Accordingly, it follows that the human soul *is created* by God.

The same may be proved directly in the following way. The coming to be of a thing is proportioned to its "to be." But the human soul has a "to be" which is independent of a subject. Therefore, it comes to be independently of a subject, i.e., through creation.

Time of the Soul's Origin

165. When does the human soul come into existence? Does it exist before the human body or not? And if it does not pre-exist, when exactly is it created? At the first moment of conception or later?

No Pre-Existence of the Human Soul. A few philosophers have admitted that human souls exist before the bodies with which they are to be united come into existence. However, this view cannot be accepted. If souls were created before their bodies exist, they would have to be either specifically different or numerically the same. In the first alternative men would be specifically different; in the second, there would be only one soul for all men. Both alternatives are not acceptable. Therefore, the human soul does not exist before the body.[4]

Let us examine this argument. Why would pre-existing souls have to be either specifically different or numerically the same? The reason is that a soul which is created without the body is a form existing without being received in, and limited by potency; consequently, such a form could not be multiplied but would be unique in its kind. Therefore, if souls were created without bodies, they would have to be unique in their species. As a result, if such souls were many they would be specifically different; if they were not many they would be numerically one and the same. Neither alternative is acceptable—a man does not specifically differ from every other man, but human nature is essentially the same in all men; one soul in all men is impossible, as we have seen in no. 154.

Moreover, the human soul is the substantial form of the body and therefore it is not in accordance with its nature to exist separately from the body. Hence if God created human souls before their bodies, He would create them in an unnatural condition. It is irrational to suppose that God, who is the author of nature, would cause a soul to begin existence in a condition which is not in accordance with its nature. Therefore, we cannot admit that the human soul exists before its infusion into the body.

[4] Cf. St. Thomas, *In II Sentent.*, d.17, q.2, a.2; *De potentia*, q.3, a.10.

*166. *Time of Infusion of the Human Soul.* Regarding the question when exactly the human soul is infused into the body, it is not easy to give an apodictic answer. Many philosophers admit so-called "immediate animation," which means that the rational soul is infused at the very moment of conception, i.e., as soon as the sperm penetrates into the ovum and the fecundated ovum begins to live its own life. Their main argument would seem to be that any other solution gets involved in all kinds of unnecessary complications. If there is no human soul at the first moment of conception, there must be at least a vegetative soul, because the ovum nourishes itself and grows. After some time this vegetative soul will have to be corrupted and replaced by a sensitive soul, for the growing embryo begins to exhibit the typical structure of a sensitive organism. Finally, this sensitive soul will have to be corrupted, because the embryo begins to show the characteristic structure of a human being. Thus we should get a complex succession of vital principles, which can be avoided if one admits that there is a rational soul from the very first moment of conception. The fact that initially there are no signs of sensitive and intellectual life does not prevent the rational soul from being the soul of the embryo even in the initial stages of its development. For the rational soul is the principle also of vegetative life and therefore can exercise some of its functions even in a mere fecundated ovum.

Others, including St. Thomas himself, hold the view of "mediate animation" and argue that the initial organization of the fecundated ovum is not proportioned to a rational soul and exhibits only vegetative functions. Therefore, in accordance with the principle that action follows being, only a vegetative soul can be admitted in the fecundated ovum. Later, when the organization of the embryo becomes more perfect, this soul is corrupted and replaced by a sensitive soul, which, in its turn, gives way for a rational soul when the structural organization of the embryo begins to show the typical characteristics of man.

The arguments in favor of both positions are not unreasonable, and it does not seem possible to decide with certainty in favor of either opinion. However, the first position would seem to overlook the fact that the succession of souls is not eliminated but merely shortened; for, as we have seen in no. 53, in every generation of a living body there is a succession of souls. But if a succession of souls remains necessary, there would seem to be no compelling reason to abandon here the principle that the type of soul corresponds with the type of life manifested by the body. Moreover, recent embryological studies of identical (uniovular) twins show that a single ovum, fecundated by a single sperm, can be divided at different stages of its development into two or more separate embryos, each of which will develop into a complete human being.[5] If the fecundated ovum had a rational soul at the first moment of conception, one would have to admit either two rational souls in the ovum which will divide into distinct embryos, or the creation of an additional soul at the moment of division. The first alterna-

[5] The division may take place before the implantation into the uterus; after the implantation, but before the formation of the amnion; after the amniotic erosion of the uterus wall. Cf. M. M. Hudeczek, "De tempore animationis foetus humani secundum embryologiam hodiernam," *Angelicum*, 1952, pp. 162 ff.

tive cannot be acceptable, insofar as it would mean two substantial forms in one living body. The second labors under the following difficulties:

a) No reason can be given why the original soul should remain in one embryo rather than the other;

b) a new human being would be generated by the simple process of division;

c) the human soul shows itself infusable equally well into a mere fecundated ovum and an already partly developed embryo; yet the soul is the form of the body and as such requires that the body be proximately disposed for the reception of its form.

For these reasons it would seem preferable not to admit a rational soul in the embryo as long as its division into separate embryos is possible. Of course, even when such a division is still possible, there is a soul in the embryo, for it acts as a living body.

The objection that a vegetative soul cannot prepare the way for a sensitive soul because all its functions are purely vegetative is not too difficult to answer. Like the vital principles of the reproductive cells, the vegetative soul of the human embryo is of a transitory and instrumental nature, for its function is to serve the parents in the production of a new human being. But an instrument shares in the causality of the principal cause and therefore is capable of producing an effect of a higher nature than itself.

Accordingly, with respect to the time of the soul's origin, our answer is rather negative than positive. The human soul is not created before the body comes into existence and probably not as long as the embryo is capable of division into separate organisms. It is not possible to determine concretely how long such a division remains possible, because the genetic evolution of the embryo does not always proceed at the same rate.

Historical Notes

*167. The generation of the rational soul from a material source was admitted by *Tertullian* (160–240), who thought that man's soul comes from the semen. A similar view was maintained by those [6] who asserted that the vegetative soul of the embryo successively develops into a sensitive and a rational soul. In modern times a similar view is held by *Darwin* and other evolutionists who say that man wholly descends through evolution from nonhuman ancestors. *Rosmini* admitted that the sensitive soul becomes rational when God reveals the idea of being to it.

Others, such as *Frohschammer* (1821–1893) and *Hermes* (1775–1831), thought that the new soul is generated from the soul of the parents, which view *St. Augustine* had rather doubtfully proposed. But at least from the time of the Middle Ages, nearly all Christian philosophers have held that the rational soul comes into existence through creation.

Manes (third cent.) and *Priscillian* (fourth cent.) considered the soul as a part of the divine substance; *Marcus Varro* (first cent. B.C.) and *Amalric of Chartres* (eleventh cent.) held that God is the formal principle or soul of everything.

The pre-existence of human souls was admitted by *Plato, Origen* (185–254), and *Leibnitz.*

Regarding the time of infusion of the rational soul, *St. Thomas* and the more ancient Thomistic philosophers admitted the theory of mediate animation; nineteenth

[6] Cf. St. Thomas, *De potentia,* q.3, a.9, ad 9.

century philosophers generally favored immediate animation; many contemporary authors, such as *Hugon, Mercier, Remer, Messenger, Boyer,* and *Hudeczek,* are at least inclined to look with favor upon mediate animation.

SUMMARY

168. The rational soul can come neither from the bodies of the parents, because it is intrinsically independent of matter, nor from the souls of the parents, because the soul cannot create (it is finite), generate (it has no parts), or produce it from a pre-existing immaterial subject (such a subject is not substantially changeable). Nevertheless, the parents are truly the cause of their offspring, because they are the cause of the union of the human soul with the body.

The human soul comes from God, not through separation of a part from God's substance, because His substance has no parts; nor in the sense that God becomes the form of a body, because God is infinite while the form of the body is finite; but through creation. For coming to be must be proportioned to "to be," and the "to be" of the human soul is independent of a subject.

The human soul does not pre-exist; for pre-existing souls would have to be either specifically different or numerically the same, so that men would either be specifically different or all together have one soul. Moreover, pre-existing souls would have been created in a condition contrary to their nature, which would seem to be against divine wisdom.

SUGGESTED READINGS

169. Aristotle, *De generatione animalium,* bk. II, chap. 3.

Thomas Aquinas, *Summa theol.,* Ia, qq. 90, 118; *De potentia,* q. 3, aa. 9, 10; *Contra gentes,* bk. II, chaps. 83–89.

Robert E. Brennan, *Thomistic Psychology,* chap. 12, sects. 6, 7.

E. C. Messenger, Henry de Dordolot, Michael Browne, "The Soul of the Unborn Babe," *Theology and Evolution,* edited by Messenger (Westminster: 1950), pp. 217–332. Studies of the various aspects of the mediate animation theory.

CHAPTER 21

The Duration of the Human Soul

*** 170. It is an obvious datum of experience that man is subject to death. Death means the corruption of a living being, i.e., its decomposition into its component parts. The component parts of a living body are soul and body; hence man's death means the separation of his body and soul. When death occurs the "body" continues to exist in the sense that the matter which formerly had a human soul is now informed by other substantial forms corresponding to the distinct material substances existing in the corpse. We may continue to speak about the corpse as a "human body," but it should be clear that the corpse is not a human body in the proper sense of the term, because it is not, but merely was the body of a man.

What happens to the vital principle or soul of man when death takes place? With respect to the souls of plants and animals we have pointed out in previous chapters that they are (indirectly) corrupted, and thus cease to be when the plant or animal dies. Can the same be asserted of the human soul or does man's soul continue to exist after his death?

The question of the survival of man's soul after death contains four aspects. The first of these is concerned with the problem whether or not the human soul is subject to corruption. If the answer to this question is in the negative, we may not yet immediately conclude that the soul will continue to exist forever, because corruption is not the only way in which a thing can cease to exist. We shall have to investigate also whether or not the soul will perhaps be annihilated. If both these questions are answered in the negative, it will follow that man's soul will last forever. Once the survival of the human soul has been established, a further problem arises with respect to the condition of this soul. Will it survive as an independent being or lead a kind of impersonal existence as part of the Absolute? And if it continues to exist independently will it be able to exercise any function, or is its only possible survival a mere continuation of existence in a state of complete inertia?

The Immortality of the Soul

171. The immortality of the human soul will be established if we are able to prove that the soul is not subject to corruption or death. Because, as we have seen in no. 59, corruption may be either direct or indirect, both these types of corruption will have to be excluded to prove that the human soul is immortal.

The Human Soul Is Not Subject to Direct Corruption. Directly corruptible is only that which is composed of parts, for direct corruption means the decomposition of a composite whole into its parts. But the human soul is simple and therefore cannot be taken apart. Consequently, it is not subject to direct corruption. This immunity from direct corruption is not a special property of the human soul, but is found also in the souls of plants and animals and even in all other substantial forms. For any substantial form is one of the ultimate component principles of a composite whole, and no ultimate component principle can be decomposed.

The Human Soul Is Not Subject to Indirect Corruption. That is indirectly corruptible which depends for its very existence upon something which is subject to decomposition; e.g., the vital principles of plants and animals are indirectly corruptible. No such corruptibility can be admitted in the human soul. For the human soul is intrinisically independent of the body, both in its operations of understanding and willing and in its "to be"; hence the soul cannot be corrupted by the corruption of the living body.

*A confirmation of the soul's incorruptibility may be found in man's *natural desire for a continued existence.* "To be forever" is something which man's intellect knows and apprehends as necessarily connected with the attainment of his perfect happiness, and therefore everlasting existence is desired naturally. But a natural desire for an object means that a nature is ordered to this object. If, however, the object of this desire is not attainable, the natural desire itself is meaningless and shows a lack of wisdom in the Author of nature.[1]

Another confirmatory argument for the survival of man's soul after death may be found in a consideration of *the moral order.* This argument finds favor with many who are not moved by purely metaphysical arguments,

[1] Concerning natural desire, see H. van der Meulen, *Appetitus naturalis non potest esse frustra* (Gemert: 1953).

because it appeals to man's innate sense of justice. Briefly, it is as follows:

The moral order is either rational or not. If not, then good and evil, right and duty, and other similar concepts are meaningless; the whole foundation of human society crumbles, and mankind is reduced to the law of the jungle. If, on the other hand, the moral order is rational, living in accordance with this order must lead to the attainment of man's rational end, which is happiness. But, as a matter of fact, we see that doing what is morally good rarely, if ever, leads man to happiness in this life. Therefore, there must be a life after death in which the moral order finds the justification of its rationality. A similar argument could be formulated by starting with moral evil. It is to be noted, however, that this argument does not allow us to conclude to an *everlasting* life after death.

Everlasting Existence of the Human Soul

172. The preceding considerations permit us to conclude that the human soul is not naturally subject to corruption, and therefore will continue to exist unless an extrinsic cause annihilates it. Annihilation, in the strict sense of the term, means that a thing ceases to be in any way whatsoever.

The Soul Will Not Be Annihilated. Because annihilation implies absolute control over "to be" and "not to be," only the absolute cause of the "to be" in finite beings, i.e., God, needs to be considered when there is a question of annihilation. Hence the question is whether or not God will annihilate the human soul.

At first sight one would be inclined to say that only God Himself knows what He will do and that therefore man could have knowledge of the answer only through divine revelation, so that philosophy would have to end here with a question mark. Nevertheless, philosophy will be able to supply the answer if annihilation implies a contradiction in God, for what is a contradiction cannot be done at all, not even by God Himself. The question therefore is whether or not the annihilation of man's soul would imply a contradiction in God.

Unquestionably, the annihilation of a finite being is *not a contradiction in itself.* A finite being is a being whose essence is not its "to be"; it exists because something causes it to be. All that is needed to annihilate it will be that this cause ceases to cause its "to be."

Again, if we consider merely the *power of God,* there is no reason to say that God cannot annihilate the soul and any other finite being. For whatever is not a contradiction in itself falls, absolutely speaking, under the power of God.

The question, however, is different if we consider not merely God's power but also the other perfections which are implied in God's nature, specifically His wisdom. In God *power and wisdom,* as well as all other perfections, are one and the same reality; hence if the annihilation of the human soul would be against the perfection of wisdom, it would follow that God will not annihilate the soul, and even that He cannot annihilate the soul, because such an annihilation would imply a contradiction in God. Now it is easy to see that the annihilation of the human soul would imply a defect of wisdom in God. As we have seen in the preceding part of this chapter, the soul is created by God as a being which of its very nature is immortal, i.e., a being which God intended to remain forever. To reduce such a being to nonbeing would mean that God either changed His mind or did not know what

He was doing when He created the soul. But both of these alternatives are contrary to perfect wisdom. Therefore, it follows that God will not, and cannot annihilate the soul.

The Condition of the Surviving Soul

173. Granted that the soul continues to exist after man's death, what will be its condition? Will souls have a personal existence, or lose their identity and exist only as "parts" of the Absolute, or fused into one finite spiritual being?

Personal Survival. By saying that the soul survives personally we do not mean that this soul is a person. Personality, as has been seen in metaphysics,[2] implies a total incommunicability, while the human soul is essentially a substantial form and therefore communicable to the body. By personal survival we mean that the soul retains its identity as an individual intellectual substance.

It is beyond the scope of this study to show directly the irrationality of pantheistic systems which hold that the soul becomes a part of the Absolute. However, once it is accepted that the soul is something finite, it should be clear that it cannot become a part of the infinite Being, which is God.

The personal survival of the human soul follows from its very nature as a spiritual substance. A spiritual substance is not composed of matter and form but is essentially simple; therefore, it cannot be subject to such modification as would make it lose its essential identity.

*The main *difficulty* against personal survival may be formulated as follows:

To survive personally souls must remain different. But

[2] Cf. the author's *Introduction to the Science of Metaphysics,* chap. 9.

separate souls cannot be different either specifically or individually. Therefore, they cannot survive as distinct beings, but must be fused into one. Specific difference is excluded because all human souls belong to the same species and are not subject to essential change; individual differences are excluded because individual differentiation comes from the body, which is no longer united with the soul.

*To this difficulty we reply that separate souls are specifically identical but remain individually distinct, even though they are separated from their bodies. They remain individually distinct, because the individual soul is not caused, but merely conditioned by the body, upon which it does not depend for its "to be."[3] Only God can cause the soul and God causes the soul as it is, i.e., as this individual soul, proportioned to this body. Hence how long the soul will continue to be as an individual does not depend upon the body, but only upon God. On the other hand, separate souls remain specifically distinct, because specific diversity can result only from a formal principle, but not from the mere fact that souls are proportioned to different bodies.

*174. *Activity of the Soul After Death.* Is the soul which is separated from the body naturally[4] capable of

[3] Like other forms the human soul is multiplied according to the multiplication of the body. Unlike other forms, however, the human soul does not depend upon the body for its "to be"; therefore, the multiplication of other forms is caused by the multiplication of the body, but that of the human soul is merely conditioned by it. Cf. St. Thomas, *Contra gentes,* bk. II, chap. 81.

[4] We say "naturally," because we must make abstraction from knowledge gained through revelation, which is not a source of philosophical inquiry.

any action, or is it reduced to a state of complete inertia?

It should be obvious that the separate soul cannot exercise the functions of vegetative and sensitive life of which it was the source in the body. These functions are essentially dependent upon the body. But what about acts of understanding and willing? The intellect and the will are intrinsically independent of the body; does it follow, therefore, that they can still function after death? A reason for doubt would be that the intellect and will are extrinsically dependent upon the body, inasmuch as our intellect cannot operate without the phantasms of the imagination, which is an organic potency.

Regarding this question St. Thomas takes his guidance from the metaphysical principle that action follows being. While in the body the intellectual soul acts as an intellect that is in the body; once separated from it, it will act as an intellect that is by itself, i.e., without phantasms. Its object will be no longer the essence abstracted from matter, but its own substance.

Accordingly, the surviving soul will no longer be able to acquire new species by abstraction from sense images, although it may continue to use the species retained in the intellectual memory. Thus material objects and the future events of this world will be naturally unknown to it, at least insofar as direct knowledge is concerned. On the other hand, its knowledge of itself will be far more perfect than before death. Before death the soul knew itself only analogously, as if it were a material essence; after death it will know itself directly as a spiritual substance. And because the other separate souls are on the same level of immateriality as itself, there seems to be no reason why the surviving soul should not naturally be able to know them. Of God, the separate soul can have a more perfect natural knowledge than before death, because its own spiritual substance is closer to God than the essence of a material thing. Nevertheless this knowledge remains imperfect and analogous, for no finite substance can adequately represent the Infinite.

Will the soul ever be able again to exercise any of the functions for which it is intrinsically dependent upon the body? Or to put it more concretely, will the soul again be united with the body? Philosophy cannot supply a definite answer to this question, because it is faced with two inescapable facts—on the one hand, the body is mortal and offers no hope for a possible revival; on the other, the soul is the form of the body and therefore remains essentially incomplete without the body. To admit the resurrection of the body is philosophically unwarranted, because of the nature of the body, which cannot naturally come back; to deny it is philosophically unwarranted, because of the nature of the soul, which should not remain forever incomplete. This is a problem for which only God can provide a solution.

Historical Notes

*175. The immortality of the human soul is denied by the materialists and the positivists (*Comte*). Pantheists (*Spinoza*) and monists, who admit only the immortality of a transcendental Ego, deny personal immortality.

Personal immortality is admitted by *Plato, St. Thomas, Scotus, Descartes, Leibnitz, Kant, Bergson* (at least as highly probable), and in general by all Christian philosophers. Concerning *Aristotle*'s position there is no agreement, because it depends upon the interpretation given to his doctrine of the agent intellect.

The philosophical demonstrability of immortality is denied by *Scotus, Ockam, Henry of Ghent,* and perhaps *Cajetan. Hume* (1711–1776) and Stuart Mill denied that immortality can be demonstrated; *Kant* rejected its philosophical demonstrability, but admitted it as a postulate of practical reason.

SUMMARY

176. The human soul is naturally immortal. It cannot be corrupted directly, because direct corruption means the decomposition of a composite whole, while any substantial form is essentially simple. The soul cannot be indirectly corrupted, for it is intrinsically independent of the body and therefore does not cease to be when man dies. A confirmation of the existence of a life after death lies in the rationality of the moral order, inasmuch as this order, as a rule, does not lead to happiness in this life.

Because the soul is naturally immortal, it will not be annihilated by God, for otherwise God would reduce to nonbeing something which He had made to last forever, and thus show a lack of wisdom.

The human soul will survive personally. As a spiritual substance it is not subject to any modification which is an essential change. But to be reduced from a personal existence to an impersonal existence is an essential change.

SUGGESTED READINGS

177. Aristotle, *De anima,* bk. II, chap. 1 (413a 4–7), chap. 2 (413b 24–27); bk. III, chap. 5 (430a 22); Metaphysica, bk. XI, chap. 3 (1070a 26).

Thomas Aquinas, *Summa theol.,* Ia, q. 75, a. 6; *Contra gentes,* bk. II, chaps. 79–81; *De anima,* a. 14. Immortality of the soul.

——— *Summa theol.*, Ia, q. 89, aa. 1–8; *De anima*, aa. 15, 17–20. Knowledge of the separate soul.

Robert E. Brennan, *Thomistic Psychology*, chap. 12, sects. 8, 9.

George P. Klubertanz, *The Philosophy of Human Nature*, chap. 13, nos. 166–168.

Jacques Maritain, *The Range of Reason* (New York: 1952), pp. 54–65. Personal immortality.

SECTION V

The Origin of Life and Living Species

IN this section we shall consider two problems. The first will be concerned with so-called spontaneous generation, i.e., the origin of living bodies from inanimate matter. The second will be concerned with that of transformism or evolutionism, i.e., whether the existing species of life could possibly have evolved from common ancestors, or came originally into existence as distinct species.

CHAPTER 22

The Origin of Life

The Problem

*** 178. The question to be considered here is not how living bodies originate now. With respect to the present everyone admits biogenesis as a law, i.e., not a single instance is known of a living body which did not come into existence through a process of generation from another living body. The experiments of Pasteur and others have conclusively shown that in all instances where life seemed to originate from inanimate matter, microscopically small organisms gave rise to the new living bodies.

Our problem is concerned with the *possibility* of living bodies originating from inanimate matter. To a certain extent this problem refers to the future, but its main interest lies still in the past. It refers to the future insofar as the question can be raised whether or not laboratory experiments will ever succeed in producing a living organism, no matter how primitive, from inanimate matter. It refers to the past insofar as all available evidence points to the fact that once life on earth was physically impossible, so that at some time in the distant past living bodies must have made their first appearance on earth. Because observation of this first appearance is evidently impossible, the question how this life originated may be studied philosophically by an investigation of the various possibilities and the elimination of any position that is not in accordance with reason. In this way it will perhaps be possible to arrive at the conclusion that only one position is in agreement with the demands of reason, or that one position offers a greater degree of probability than others.

Possible Positions Concerning the Origin of Life. Omitting pantheistic and occasionalistic hypotheses with respect to the origin of life, the following may be formulated:

1) Living bodies did not originate in time, but have always existed.

2) The first living bodies came to the earth from other planets.

3) The first living bodies were created directly by God. By direct creation is meant that God produced from nothing both body and soul of the first living bodies.

4) The first living bodies were produced by God's positive intervention in the existing order of nature. Suspending the laws of nature, He directly produced in inanimate matter the conditions which made matter proximately disposed for actuation by a soul. This soul was educed from the potency of matter, except in the case of man, whose soul was created directly by God.

5) Living bodies can be produced from inanimate matter by the sole forces of matter, without any influence of extraneous causes. In this hypothesis, physical and chemical reactions are considered to be the adequate explanation for the origin of life.

6) Living bodies can originate from inanimate mat-

ter under the influence of the Primary Cause (God), acting through causes that are intrinsic to matter.

7) Living bodies can originate from inanimate matter under the influence of a secondary cause, extraneous to matter, acting upon inanimate matter.

Examination of the Various Positions with Respect to the Origin of Life

179. The first two of these positions need not be considered to any great extent. Even if living bodies had always existed they would need a cause to explain their existence, for their essence is not their "to be," and therefore they do not have in themselves a sufficient reason for their existence. Moreover, the earth has not always been suitable for life, because at one time in the past it was so hot that no living bodies could have existed upon it. To explain the origin of living bodies by claiming that they came from other planets, as is done by the second position, merely shifts the problem to another planet. Moreover, in passing from another planet to the earth, any form of physical life would have been exposed to certain death because of ultraviolet rays and the heat resulting from its passage through the atmosphere.

Direct Creation. There cannot be any doubt concerning the possibility that living bodies were directly created by God, for anything which is not a contradiction in terms can be done by God. The point, however, is that it would be unreasonable to suppose that God created new bodies when plenty of matter was available for the formation of these bodies. It does not seem in accordance with wisdom to make new material where an abundance of suitable material is available. But inanimate matter contains all the necessary material for the physical organization required by a living body.

Divine Intervention as the Sole Organizing Cause of Matter. Again, there cannot be any doubt that God has the power directly to organize matter in such a way that it is immediately disposed for actuation by a soul. However, it would seem unreasonable to attribute directly to God what can be brought about through the activity of the natural forces of inanimate matter acting in accordance with the laws of nature. *If* the Author of nature has endowed matter with forces that can naturally lead to the emergence of living bodies, it would seem unreasonable to suppose that He positively intervened in the process of natural development by suspending the activity of these forces and directly organizing inanimate matter. We say *if*, for it remains to be seen whether or not living bodies can have originated from inanimate matter acting in accordance with the laws of nature. Should the answer to this question be negative, then it would seem to be more consonant with divine wisdom to give rise to living bodies by organizing existing matter than by the creation of new matter.

Emergence of Life from Matter Alone. Can the physical forces of inanimate matter alone serve as an *adequate* explanation for the emergence of life? At first sight it would seem that the forces of inanimate matter can never give rise to a living body, because any material cause acts in accordance with its nature and therefore its effect cannot be greater than itself. But a living body is essentially more perfect than a nonliving body; hence it would seem that no forces of inanimate matter can give rise to a living body.

However, this answer fails to take into consideration the possibility of many material causes combining to produce an effect. Admittedly, if it is possible to introduce into a body the material dispositions making it proximately disposed for actuation by a soul, the cause or causes introducing these dispositions are the cause of a living body. The question, therefore, is whether or not it would be impossible for a combination of material forces to cause these dispositions in nonliving matter. The enormous complexity of the necessary dispositions excludes the possibility that a single line of material causality would ever produce these dispositions. But it is a well-known fact that physical causality, as it occurs in nature, is a very complex process in which many different lines of causality constantly interfere with one another. Now the interference of different lines of causality may result in an effect which is proportioned to none of the interfering causes taken separately. Conceivably such an effect could be even more perfect than any of the producing causes, precisely because the *combination* of these causes could happen to be equal to the material causality normally exercised by one cause of a higher nature. If the material forces operating in a living body, which the soul combines into a single unit, are able to cause the necessary dispositions for life and thus produce a new living body, why would it be *impossible* for these forces to be united "by chance" into an operational unit and thus give rise to a living body? If such a thing did happen a living body would have been produced from inanimate matter. Thus it would not be impossible for a combination of inanimate forces to give rise to a living body.

Granted that such a combination is a possibility, does

it provide an *adequate* explanation for the origin of life? An adequate explanation is one which takes into consideration *all* the causes that are at work in the production of an effect. No one admits that in the present state of science it is possible to indicate even all the *physical* forces that are necessary for the production of the dispositions of matter required for actuation by a soul. But supposing that a time will come when man will know all the material causes whose combination results in the production of a living body, will he have an adequate explanation for the origin of living bodies? The answer is in the negative, because he has failed to indicate the cause which led to the combination of these causes by unifying their activity. But could not this unification be brought about *by chance,* as was suggested above? We must answer that an appeal to chance is not an explanation, but a confession of ignorance of the adequate explanation. Chance refers to the unpredictability of an effect produced by causes whose combined action cannot be foreseen, because the cause of their combination is not known.[1] To deny that their combination has a cause is tantamount to a denial of the principle of causality. Therefore, an appeal to chance is an admission that the known physical forces of inanimate matter cannot explain the origin of life.

But, perhaps, at a future date science will discover the cause or causes which combine the forces of inanimate matter and make them produce in a nonliving body the necessary dispositions for actuation by a soul. Then, at least, science will have given an adequate explanation for the emergence of life by the sole forces of inanimate

[1] Concerning chance, cf. the author's *Introduction to the Science of Metaphysics,* chap. 14.

matter. Again, however, our answer has to be in the negative. Granted that perhaps a material agent causing the unification of these forces will be discovered, there still remains the *principle of finality,* i.e., the metaphysical law that every agent acts for a definite purpose.[2] An agent can act for a purpose either because it is made to act for this purpose by an intelligent being, or because the agent himself is an intelligent being and directs his activity to a definite end. If the cause of the unification is purely material, it cannot be an intelligent agent; therefore it acts towards a purpose merely because it is made to act in this way by an intelligent being. This intelligent being, *qua* intelligent, is extraneous to matter, for any intellect is immaterial. If, on the other hand, the agent is immaterial, it is of course extraneous to matter. Our final conclusion, therefore, is that the physical forces of inanimate matter *alone* cannot give an adequate explanation for the origin of living bodies.

180. *Emergence of Life from Matter Under the Directing Influence of God.* This position combines certain aspects of the two preceding hypotheses and discards others. It agrees with the theory of divine intervention insofar as it demands God's influence upon matter in the production of living bodies; it differs from it in that it does not require a suspension of the deterministic laws of nature (a miraculous intervention), but merely that God act through causes which are *intrinsic* to matter. It agrees with the theory that life originates from matter alone insofar as it admits that the physical forces of inanimate matter can produce life, but differs from it because it requires that these causes be directed by the Primary Cause.

[2] Cf. *Ibid.*

Does this new position offer a satisfactory explanation for the origin of living bodies?

There is no reason to suppose that God cannot exercise influence upon the forces of inanimate matter without suspending the deterministic laws of nature. All that is necessary is that God make use of the intrinsic forces of matter, which act in accordance with these laws, by directing their activity to the purpose He intends, viz., the production of the necessary conditions for the actuation of matter by a soul. The question, however, is whether God can give such a direction to the forces of matter without producing in existing matter a tendency previously nonexistent in it, for such a production would be a positive intervention in the existing order of nature. To this question, we answer that the existence of such a tendency in matter allows a double explanation—either God created it in matter which previously did not have it, or He concreated it in matter when matter itself was created. In the first case there would have been a positive intervention, and the whole explanation would be identical with the position that the divine Cause organizes matter by suspending the existing laws of nature. In the second alternative, however, this tendency would belong to the very essence of the material world, as planned and created by God. Therefore, the directing influence of this tendency would not be an intervention in the established order of nature, but merely the execution of the order of nature established by divine providence. In this theory inanimate matter from its very beginning would have possessed all the forces necessary for the emergence of life, because God Himself planned the whole course of nature in such a way that life followed of necessity when the planned combination of inanimate forces occurred.

If this position were true the human observer of nature would be faced with effects emerging "by chance" from a concurrence of causes, because he does not see that this concurrence takes place according to plan. Consequently, upon his level of explanation, he would be justified in speaking about life as emerging from a chance meeting of inanimate causes. He would be mistaken, however, if from his observations he would conclude that his explanation gives an adequate account for the origin of life.

It would seem that this theory does not violate any physical or metaphysical principles. Although it does not postulate a special intervention of God in the origin of life, it does not deny that life could originate only as a result of God's planning and providence. It certainly would be a more splendid manifestation of God's power if life were produced in this way rather than by a miraculous intervention in the established order of nature.

181. *Emergence of Life from Matter Under the Directing Influence of a Secondary Cause.* If the preceding theory offers an explanation for the emergence of life, there seems to be no reason why it should be impossible for an intelligent secondary cause to direct the forces of matter in the production of the material conditions required for actuation by a soul. Of course, such a cause would need to have a far greater knowledge of matter than is possessed by man at this time. It would not seem impossible, however, that ultimately man will succeed in acquiring this knowledge and be able to utilize it to obtain the desired effect. In that case man would be able to produce living bodies artificially. Nevertheless, it would not be a case of life being produced by the sole forces of matter, because these forces would be under the

direction of man, who is an intelligent being. Moreover, even in this case God's action would not be excluded, because man's activity does not escape the directing influence of God.[3]

A similar theory for the emergence of life from inanimate matter was offered by ancient and medieval philosophers, including St. Thomas, as an explanation of the supposedly spontaneous generation of maggots in decaying flesh. They thought that in this case the forces of inanimate matter, as acted upon by the sun or other celestial bodies under the direction of spiritual substances, made matter proximately disposed for actuation by a soul.

182. *Conclusion.* Of the seven positions formulated above with respect to the first origin of life only the third, fourth, sixth, and seventh offer reasonable possibilities. However, the third (direct creation of the whole living body) is less probable, although it cannot be called impossible. The seventh (directing influence of a secondary cause) does not apply to the first origin of living bodies, if man is supposed to be this cause. Hence the choice seems to be mainly between the fourth position (God as the sole organizing cause of matter) and the sixth (emergence of life under the influence of God acting through causes that are intrinsic to matter). Of course, it is impossible to say what actually did happen, unless there is a reliable report of a witness. But if there is such a report, its contents escape from the domain of philosophy and physical science.[4]

[3] We assume here that God's providence has been established in theodicy.

[4] God Himself "witnessed" the origin of the first living bodies and may have told us about it through revelation. Whether or not He has done so does not concern us in philosophy, but belongs to theology.

Historical Notes

183. The eternal existence of living bodies was defended by *Arrhenius* (1859–1927), *Preyer* (1831–1897), and a few others. *Keyserling* (born 1880), *Lord Kelvin* (1827–1907), and *Helmholtz* (1821–1894) held that the first germs of life on earth had come from outer space. Most authors who defend the eternal existence of living bodies combine the second position with the first.

The origin of "imperfect animals" from inanimate matter under the influence of celestial bodies, as directed by spiritual substances, was commonly admitted before the experiments of *Pasteur* (1822–1895). *Avicenna* admitted the possibility of such an origin even with respect to "perfect animals."

Direct creation of the first living bodies with respect to both body and soul was favored by *Remer,* while others (*Gredt*) were more inclined to admit divine intervention as the sole organizing cause of matter.

The possibility of life emerging from causes intrinsic to matter under God's directive influence is regarded with favor by many contemporary Thomists, such as *Sertillanges, Messenger, Brennan,* and *Klubertanz.*

The emergence of life from matter alone is the view taken by many materialistic evolutionists, such as *Haeckel* and *Huxley.*

SUMMARY

184. Regarding the origin of living bodies which were not generated from other living bodies, several theories are possible. Direct creation, however, of such bodies with respect to both body and soul does not seem consonant with divine wisdom, for it means the creation of

new matter when plenty of suitable matter is available. The organization of matter for actuation by a soul can be attributed to the sole forces of matter, to God alone, or to both. But matter alone cannot provide an adequate explanation of this organization. Rather, a complex combination of causes is required, and this combination implies either a totally extraneous cause, or at least an extraneous cause acting through forces that are intrinsic to matter. If God alone is indicated as the cause of the organization of matter, the origin of life is claimed to be the result of a direct intervention of God in the existing order of nature. If, on the other hand, the organization of matter is attributed to God as acting through forces which are intrinsic to matter, the origin of life came about as a result of God's planning and providence in the creation of inanimate matter.

It would not seem impossible that a living body can originate from inanimate matter if man's intelligence acts as the cause which unifies the forces of matter.

SUGGESTED READINGS

See at the end of Chapter 23.

CHAPTER 23

The Origin of Species

Introductory Remarks

*** 185. *Notion of Transformism.* The problem we have to consider in this chapter is concerned with the question of transformism or, as it is usually called, evolutionism. Obviously, we must limit ourselves to a philosophical study of this question and cannot consider it as a scientific theory. In other words, our study will be restricted to the possibility of transformism and does not pronounce judgment upon transformism as a scientific theory.

By *transformism in general* we mean the view which proposes, whether as a fact, a scientific theory, or a philosophical position, that the various species of living bodies have or can have originated through a progressive development from one or a few primitive types of organisms into the present more complex forms of organization. If the view is proposed as applying to all species without any restriction, it is called *universal* transformism. If any restriction is made, such as with respect to the human soul, it is called limited or *mitigated* transformism. There are many different theories of transformism, but these differences do not immediately concern us.

Transformism may be proposed as the true reconstruction of what *actually* did happen. In this sense, in which it is often described in the Sunday supplements of newspapers, it can be proposed unrestrictedly only if no other alternative is possible. In the absence of any witness' account, the assertion that all living species originated in this way implies of necessity the philosophical position that living species cannot have arisen in any other way, e.g., by creation. While the question whether or not evolution did take place does not belong to the domain of philosophy, the philosophical implication that the origin of species cannot be explained in any other way definitely belongs to philosophy.

Transformism may be proposed also as a *scientific theory* which systematically classifies the available data concerning the origin of species for research purposes, and enjoys in its different parts a greater or lesser degree of probability. In this sense philosophers cannot have any quarrel with it, because purely scientific theories do not concern them.

Finally, transformism may be proposed as a *possible* or the *only possible* explanation of the origin of the different species of living bodies. In this sense transformism is a philosophical position and therefore needs to be examined in the light of philosophical principles. If transformism is proposed as the only possible explanation of species, it is based upon the assumption of total materialism, i.e., that only matter can offer any explanation.

Those who reject transformism accept so-called *fixism* or creationism, which in general holds that there has been no transformation of species, but that all species of life took their origin from the direct intervention of God, as either directly creating them from nothing, or by special intervention producing new species from pre-existing ones. By "special intervention" is meant that the production of new species took place in such a way that it cannot be explained in accordance with the existing laws of nature.

Transformism can be applied not only to the origin of different species of living bodies, but even to *the first origin of life* itself. As applied to the first origin of life it is called "spontaneous generation" or "abiogenesis," and has been studied in the preceding chapter.

186. *Confusion Concerning the Term "Species."* Much confusion has been caused by the careless use of the term "species." Both biology and philosophy use the term, but its meaning in these two sciences is not the same. Moreover, even in philosophy itself, the term does not always have the same implications. In the strict sense of the term, a *philosophical species* is a class of individuals belonging to the same metaphysical level of being. These levels are at least four in number, viz., inanimate, vegetative, sensitive, and rational. Therefore, at least man, animal, plant, and inanimate matter may be considered to be philosophical species.

In philosophy the term "species" may be used also in a wider sense to indicate any class of bodies which are essentially different, without being metaphysically more or less perfect. For instance, many philosophers consider hydrogen, oxygen, and water to be essentially different; yet no one will claim that, say, water is metaphysically more or less perfect than oxygen. Even if one would make this claim, he would not be able to substantiate it with a proof. Perhaps he would appeal to chemical or physical science, but such an appeal is useless because these sciences are not interested in metaphysical levels of being and grades of essential perfection. In a similar way as inanimate matter may be subdivided into "species" which are supposed to be essentially different without being on metaphysically different levels, living organisms may be subdivided into species differing essentially without being metaphysically more or less perfect. For instance, one may claim that a rose and a geranium, a cat and a dog are essentially different, without attributing to these differences any consequences for their level of being. We shall give the name *"philosophical subspecies"* to those classes of beings which differ essentially without being metaphysically on a different level.[1]

In biological sciences there is question of so-called

[1] The question could be asked: Why not call such differences purely accidental? We may answer, in the first place, that as a matter of fact many philosophers assert that cats, dogs, water, hydrogen, etc., are essentially different, and we are merely indicating here the usage of the term "species." Secondly, the difference between a cat and a dog or between an elephant and a mosquito certainly is much more important than that between two varieties of butterflies. Such a difference deserves to be called "essential" if we keep in mind that the term "essential" does not always have the same value. Accustomed as we are in philosophy to see essential differences illustrated by the example of man and irrational animal, we are inclined to forget that this term is analogous, and consequently that an essential difference does not always have to be a difference as important as that between man and animal. According as we descend lower on the scale of beings, their essence is ontologically less perfect and less important, so that on the subhuman level there may be essential differences which do not amount to very much if we take our standards from the difference between man and animal. Personally, I would be quite willing to admit an essential difference even between the various states of aggregation of the same chemical substance, and in the animate world between any different biological species, precisely because on such a level the difference between essential and accidental diversity is no longer important.

systematic species. A systematic species is one of the many classifications of organisms used in these sciences (kingdom, phylum, class, order, family, genus, species, and variety). It means a collection of individuals which have distinct common characteristics and are indefinitely fertile among themselves. Some of these biological classifications may coincide with philosophical divisions; e.g., the vegetative kingdom coincides with the philosophical species of plant. Other biological classifications are, philosophically speaking, purely accidental; e.g., the thousands of varieties of cockroaches.

Possibility of Transformism

187. *Philosophical Subspecies and Lesser Differences.* When there is not even an essential difference between two classes of living bodies, transformation of one kind into another offers no philosophical difficulty, for it means merely an accidental change.

Even when there is question of philosophical subspecies transformation will be possible. The reason is that such a transformation remains on the same level of being; hence it is just another example of substantial change, against which there can be no philosophical objection. Accordingly, there would seem to be no philosophical objection against any theory which holds that even widely different kinds of animals (or plants) have originated from primitive organisms through the forces of matter inherent to these organisms and other material agents.

*The question may be asked whether inanimate, vegetative, sensitive, and rational are the only philosophical species in the strict sense of the term. Although it is not easy to give an apodictic answer to this question, we may attempt to arrive at a conclusion by taking our guidance from the principle that action follows being. If a class of animals [2] is capable of activities that are irreducible to another type of activity, and which render them more perfect as sentient organisms, they may be considered to be on a higher level of being than other animals which are not capable of this activity. Because the level of animal being is characterized by sensitivity, an additional mode of sensing may be taken to indicate a more perfect mode of being an animal, and thus give rise to a distinct philosophical species in the strict sense. If this rule is accepted, e.g., an animal which is naturally capable of sight is metaphysically on a more perfect level than another animal which naturally lacks this capacity.

Philosophical Species. Is it possible for a lower philosophical species to give rise to a higher species? In the preceding chapter we have considered this question with respect to the origin of living bodies from inanimate matter. The conclusion reached was that it is not impossible that living bodies should have originated from inanimate matter through the action of the internal forces of matter as directed by God. If life itself may have originated in this way, there seems to be no reason why the various species of living bodies cannot have taken their origin in a similar way from one or a few primitive species of organisms.

Even in *the case of man* there appears no reason why the evolution of his body from primitive organisms (and even from inanimate matter) must be considered to be philosophically impossible. Of course, as we have seen in Chapter 20, man's soul can have obtained its existence

[2] The question does not arise with respect to plants, at least if all plants have the powers of nutrition, growth, and reproduction.

only through a direct act of creation; therefore, it is impossible for the human soul to have evolved from matter. In a certain sense, even the human body must be said to be the result of an act of creation. For the human body is made specifically human by the human soul, and this soul is created; hence as a *human* body, man's body results from creation. But the question is whether the matter of his body had to be made suitable for actuation by a rational soul through God's special intervention, or if the same result could have been achieved by the forces of nature acting as directed by God. As we have seen in the preceding chapter, there seems to be no reason why the second alternative would have to be an impossibility. Of course, this does not allow us to conclude that the human body actually did evolve from matter or lower forms of life, for in the presence of several possible philosophical positions philosophy cannot give an apodictic answer.

Historical Notes

188. Historically speaking transformism is not a modern theory. It was first mentioned in the fifth century B.C. In a famous passage, worthy of a nineteenth century evolutionist, *Aristotle* cites an ancient philosopher: "Why should not nature work, not for the sake of something . . . but of necessity? . . . Why then should it not be, e.g., that our teeth come up of necessity—the front teeth sharp, fitted for tearing, the molars broad and useful for grinding down the food—since they did not arise for this end, but it was merely a coincident result; and so with all other parts in which we suppose that there is a purpose? Wherever, then, all the parts came about just as they would have been if they had come to be for an end,

such things survived, being organized spontaneously in a fitting way; whereas those which grew otherwise perished and continue to perish."[3] It sounds like a brief summary of materialistic evolution through survival of the fittest! *St. Augustine* and his theory of "seminal causes," as well as *St. Gregory of Nyssa's* "spermatic potencies," are often quoted in favor of evolution. *Cajetan* also expressed evolutionary views. However, the clear and systematic formulation of evolutionistic theories began only in the nineteenth century with *Lamarck* (1744–1829) and *Darwin.* The latter especially amassed such an imposing array of data that evolutionism became extremely popular not only among specialists but also among others.

In the nineteenth century evolution was often proposed in an atheistic way as the final triumph of materialism. God was no longer needed, and man had been reduced to a bit of slime. Small wonder that Christian writers did not look with favor upon it. Nowadays the psychological climate has somewhat changed. Many defenders of evolutionism are far more moderate in their claims and do not exclude God; theologians and apologists, on the other hand, have realized that the acceptance of an evolutionary theory does not necessarily imply the rejection of God or the lowering of man's dignity. As we have seen above, rather than being atheistic in nature evolution may mean a far greater manifestation of God's power than God's special intervention; rather than lowering man's dignity, evolution may mean that the whole world has reached its apex of perfection in man.

[3] *Physica,* bk. II, chap. 8 (198b 16 ff.). Quoted from the Ross edition of *The Works of Aristotle,* with kind permission of the publishers, Oxford University Press.

SUMMARY

189. Transformism in general may be described as the view that the various species of living bodies have or can have originated through a progressive development from one or a few primitive types of organisms. If transformism is proposed merely as a scientific theory which classifies the available data for the purpose of research, philosophy cannot have any objection, because scientific theories as such do not concern it. If transformism is proposed unrestrictedly as what actually did happen, the tacit assumption is that no other explanation is possible. However, the investigation of this assumption belongs to philosophy, as well as the possibility of transformism.

A philosophical species in the strict sense is a class of individuals belonging to the same level of being, or having the same grade of metaphysical perfection. These species are at least, inanimate, vegetative, sensitive, and rational. Philosophical subspecies are classes of beings which are essentially different without belonging to metaphysically higher or lower levels of beings; e.g., various chemical substances; animals as different as a mouse and an elephant. Biological or systematic species are classes of individuals which have distinct common characteristics, and are indefinitely fertile among themselves.

Transformation with respect to any biological classification that is below the philosophical subspecies is merely an accidental change, against the possibility of which no one can object. Transformation of one philosophical subspecies into another is merely an instance of substantial change on the same level of being; therefore, there is no reason to call it impossible. Transformation of a lower philosophical species into a higher one raises the same questions as the origin of life from inanimate matter, and therefore may be answered in the same way—namely, it does not seem impossible that the various species have developed from one or a few primitive types of organisms through the internal forces of nature as directed by God.

Regarding man, it is impossible that his soul evolved from any lower form of life, for the human soul can come into existence only through creation. His body results from creation, at least in the sense that it is made specifically human by his created soul. But the matter of his body may have been made suitable for actuation by a human soul through the forces of nature as directed by God. Whether this actually did happen or not is not for philosophy to decide.

SUGGESTED READINGS

190. Norbert Luyten, "Philosophical Implications of Evolution," *The New Scholasticism*, 1951, pp. 290 ff.

George P. Klubertanz, *The Philosophy of Human Nature*, Appendix L and N.

——— "Causality and Evolution," *The Modern Schoolman*, 1941, pp. 11 ff.

——— "Causality in the Philosophy of Nature," *ibid.*, 1942, pp. 29 ff.

E. C. Messenger, *Evolution and Theology* (New York: Macmillan, 1932).

——— *Theology and Evolution* (Westminster: 1950), chaps. 1–15. Critique and replies of Dr. Messenger.

Franz Grégoire, "Note sur la philosophie de l'organisme," *Revue philosophique de Louvain*, 1948, pp. 276 ff.

Mortimer J. Adler, *The Problem of Species* (New York: 1940).

Raymond W. Murray, *Man's Unknown Ancestors* (Milwaukee: 1948).

Edward E. Dodson, *A Textbook of Evolution* (Philadelphia: 1952).

Although it cannot be said that St. Thomas taught transformism, the following passages throw some light upon the question whether transformism, in the sense in which it has been defended above, can be reconciled with Thomistic principles.

Summa theol., Ia, q. 71, a. 1, ad 1 and 4; q. 73, a. 1, ad 3; q. 74, a. 2, ad 4; q. 91, a. 1, ad 1; q. 118, a. 2, ad 3; IIIa, q. 75, a. 6, ad 1.
Contra gentes, bk. II, chap. 89.
De potentia, q. 4, a. 2, ad 22, 23, 33, 34; ad 5 in contr.
De veritate, q. 5, a. 3 (perfectibile).
In XII Metaphysic., lect. 2, no. 2438.

SOME TRANSLATIONS OF ARISTOTLE AND THOMAS AQUINAS

Aristotle, *The Works of Aristotle Translated Into English*, ed. by W. D. Ross (Oxford University Press, 3rd impr., 1950). *De anima* is in vol. 5 of this edition. Also available in the *Basic Works of Aristotle*, ed. by R. McKeon (New York: 1941).

Thomas Aquinas, *The Summa Theologica*. Literally translated by the Fathers of the Eng. Dominican Province (London: 2nd ed., 1912–1936). Also available in American edition (New York: 1947). The first part of the *Summa*, which is quoted most in this study, may be found in the *Basic Works of St. Thomas*, ed. by A. C. Pegis (New York: 1945), vol. I.

——— *The Summa contra Gentiles*. Literally translated by the English Dominican Fathers (London: 1928 ff.). A new edition is being published by Dover Publications.

——— *On the Power of God* (*De Potentia Dei*). Translated by L. Scapcote (London: 1932 ff.) (Westminster: 1952).

——— *The Soul* (*De Anima*). Translated by J. P. Rowan (St. Louis: 1949).

——— *On Spiritual Creatures* (*De Spiritualibus Creaturis*), translated by M. C. Fitzpatrick and J. J. Wellmuth (Milwaukee: 1949).

——— *Truth* (*De Veritate*). Vol. I, translated by R. W. Mulligan (Chicago: 1952); Vol. II, translated by J. V. McGlynn (Chicago: 1953); Vol. III, translated by R. W. Smith (Chicago: 1954).

——— *Aristotle's De Anima and the Commentaries of St. Thomas Aquinas*. Translated by K. Foster and S. Humpries, (London: 1951).

Review Questions

Introduction

1. What objections could be raised against the use of the terms rational, philosophical, experimental, and scientific psychology?
2. What is the relationship between psychology, metaphysics, and the philosophy of animate nature?
3. State the material and the formal objects of the philosophy of animate nature.
4. Describe the starting point of the philosophy of animate nature.
5. What is the method of the philosophy of animate nature?
6. Define the philosophy of animate nature.
7. Name the presuppositions of the philosophy of animate nature.
8. What is the speculative and practical importance of the philosophy of animate nature?

Chapter 1—Living Bodies

1. Compare life to movement.
2. What is meant by a living body?
3. Describe the structural differences of living and nonliving bodies.
4. Name and describe the characteristic activities of living bodies.
5. What is meant by transient and immanent action?

6. What is the difference between strictly immanent and immanent in a wider sense?
*7. Distinguish three grades of immanence of action.
8. Name the various senses of the term "life."
9. Is life an analogous concept?
10. What is meant by inadequate self-movement? Is the self-movement of a finite being adequate or inadequate?
11. Prove that living bodies are essentially different from and superior to nonliving bodies.
*12. Distinguish the three grades of physical life.
13. Answer the following objections:
    a) Even so-called nonliving bodies have within themselves a principle of movement and thus can move themselves; therefore, life should not be defined as self-movement.
    b) At least some nonliving bodies, such as rubber balls, have an active principle of movement and move themselves back into their original shape; therefore, such bodies would be living.
    c) Crystals grow and multiply; therefore, these operations are not typical of living bodies.
    d) Subatomic particles move within the atom; therefore, the atom has immanent movement.
    e) No finite being moves itself to action; therefore, no finite being can be self-moving.
    f) Machines have different parts exercising different functions and move themselves by means of these functions; therefore, machines would have to be considered to be alive.
14. Distinguish between substantial and accidental unity, unity of extrinsic purpose and unity of juxtaposition.
15. How can we know what kind of unity a being has?
16. What are the possibilities of activity in a whole with respect to purpose? Which of these possibilities points to substantial unity?
17. Prove that a living body is one substance.

18. Answer the following difficulties against the substantial unity of the living body:
    a) A multicellular organism does not have any substantial unity because each individual cell functions as an individual.
    b) The living body contains a number of different chemical substances; therefore, it is not one substance.
    c) If chemical substances outside the body are also substances in the philosophical sense of the term, they must be philosophical substances in the body, because action follows being, and these substances act in the same way inside and outside the living body.
    d) Parts of a living body can be severed and kept alive; therefore, their life does not depend upon the rest of the body, so that a living body is not one substance.

Chapter 2—The Soul

1. Why must we admit the existence of a soul?
2. Answer the following objections against the existence of souls:
    a) Not even the most modern scientific equipment has shown any trace of a soul; therefore, its existence is unproved.
    b) It is useless to admit a soul, because it cannot explain any biological processes.
    c) There is no need to admit the existence of a soul, because the functioning of a living body can be explained without any directing influence of a soul, by the sole organization of the body.
    d) All efforts to assign any form of physical energy to the soul as its efficient cause have failed; therefore, its existence is unproved.
3. Show that the soul is not an accident but a substantial principle of the living body.

4. Prove that the soul is the substantial form of the living body.
5. Show that the soul is the only substantial form of the body.
6. Why is the soul called the substantial form of the body and not of matter?
7. Why are the chemical substances making up the body said to remain virtually in the living body?
8. Solve the following difficulties:
   a) When a living body dies, it remains a body; therefore, in addition to the soul which makes it living, the body has a form which makes it a body.
   b) Parts of a body can be cut off and remain alive; therefore, they have their own soul, so that there is more than one soul in a living body.
9. Why must the soul be the substantial form of the whole body?
10. In what sense is the soul wholly and entirely in each part of the body?
11. Answer the following objections:
    a) If the whole soul is in one part of the body, the whole soul cannot be in another part.
    b) If the whole soul is in the foot of a donkey, this foot itself will have to be a donkey.
12. Why are body and soul really distinct; do they enter into a real composition, and do they not need to be united by means of a common bond?
13. Is the soul extended?
14. Is the soul divisible?
15. If the soul is not divisible, how do you explain that a living body can be divided into living parts?

*16. What is the philosophical explanation for the transplantation of living parts from one body into another?

Chapter 3—Operative Potencies

1. Prove that the soul is not its own action.
2. Prove that the soul is not its own operative potency.
3. Solve the following difficulties:
   a) It would seem to be a contradiction first to deny that the soul is indivisible and then to admit that its operative potency is really distinct from it.
   *b) Operative potencies are not accidents but properties of the soul.
   c) One does not explain why vital actions occur by admitting the existence of operative potencies or faculties.
   *d) An operative potency is a perfection and as such an act. Therefore, it would always have to be acting, which is against experience.
   *e) Potency and act must belong to the same genus; therefore, the soul and its operative potency must be both either accidents or substances, which is impossible.
   *f) An operative potency which is really distinct from the soul is an accident and therefore will never be able to produce a new substance. But the reproductive power causes the new living body, which is a substance. Therefore, the operative potency is not really distinct from the soul.
4. What diversifies operative potencies?

*5. Reply to the following objection: Nothing is essentially determined by that which is posterior to it. But action is posterior to the potency from which it emanates. Therefore, action does not essentially determine potency.

6. Why are actions essentially diversified by their objects?
7. What kinds of objects diversify actions?

*8. What is the efficient cause of the operative potencies?

In what sense may the soul be said to be active with respect to its potencies?

Chapter 4—The Operative Potencies of Vegetative Life

1. Are nutrition, growth, and reproduction distinct operative potencies?
2. Do plants have any vital activity suggesting sensation or understanding?
3. Distinguish between intrinsic and extrinsic dependence upon an organ.
4. Prove that the vegetative potencies are organic.
5. What is the philosophical explanation of reproduction by cell division, gemmation, and sporogenesis?
6. Explain the process of gametic reproduction from a philosophical point of view.

Chapter 5—The Vegetative Soul

1. Why is the vegetative soul material? What is meant when the vegetative soul is said to be material?
2. Is the vegetative soul subsistent?
3. In what sense is the vegetative soul said to come to be?
4. Distinguish between direct and indirect corruption.
5. How does the vegetative soul cease to be?

Chapter 6—Cognition in General

1. Does every union with a form mean knowledge?
2. Compare the union of the knower and the object known with the union of form and subject in a material change, and the union of a plant with the substance upon which it feeds.
3. In what sense is the "to be" of the knower identical with that of the object known?

4. Is it not a contradiction that a knower who is distinct from the object known is also identical with it?
5. Show that cognition is based upon immateriality.
6. What is meant by immateriality in the preceding question?
7. Explain the statement: Cognition is the action of a being in act.
8. Why can cognition be essentially more or less perfect?
*9. Why is the cognitive union the most intimate of all unions?
10. In what sense is a cognitive potency passive?
11. Why must the knowing subject and the object to be known be proportionate to each other?
12. Does the cognitive potency need to be actuated and determined before it is fully ready to elicit its act of cognition?
13. What is meant by the impressed species of the object?
14. Why is an impressed species necessary in cognition of a finite object?
15. Indicate the double function of the impressed species.
16. Is the impressed species that which is known?
*17. Is the impressed species necessary also by reason of the object?
18. What is meant by the expressed species?
19. When is an expressed species necessary?
*20. Is the expressed species really distinct from the impressed species?
21. Define cognition and explain the definition.

Chapter 7—External Sense Cognition

1. Distinguish between external and internal senses.
2. Name the external senses and their objects.
3. Are the external senses really distinct potencies?
4. Explain the following terms: sensible, essential and accidental sensible, common and proper sensible.

5. Show that the external senses are organic.
*6. Is the brain the sole organ of sensation?
7. Explain the difference between "without matter" and "without the conditions of matter."
8. Is there any expressed species of external sensation?
*9. In what sense does external sense cognition terminate in the external object?
10. What is the difference between sensation and perception?
*11. How can motion be perceived by the senses?

Chapter 8—Internal Sense Cognition

1. Show the existence of internal sense cognition.
2. What is meant by the central sense?
3. Prove its existence as distinct from the external senses.
*4. Answer the following objection: All sensations are sensations of the same subject; therefore, there is no need for a special sense to sense the external sensations.
5. What is meant by the imagination?
6. Is the imagination really distinct from the external senses and the central sense?
*7. Indicate the causes which may cause the reproduction of phantasms.
8. Describe the estimative potency.
9. Prove its existence and distinction from the other senses.
10. What is the function of the estimative or cogitative power in man?
11. What is meant by the memorative sense?
12. Prove its existence and distinction from the other senses.
13. Do the senses have any interconnection?
14. Show the organic nature of the internal senses.
*15. Where do the internal senses obtain their impressed species?
*16. Do the internal senses produce any expressed species?

Chapter 9—Appetite in General

1. What is meant by appetite in general?
2. Is the natural appetite really distinct from the nature of its subject?
3. What is an elicited appetite?
4. Show that appetite follows cognition.
5. Is the elicited appetite really distinct from the nature of its subject?
6. Is the elicited appetite really identical with the cognitive potency from which it flows?
7. Is the elicited appetite the natural appetite of the cognitive potency?
8. Does the elicited appetite have any relationship to the cognitive potencies?

Chapter 10—Sense Appetite

1. What is meant by passions?
2. Is sense appetite an organic potency?
3. Distinguish between the concupiscible and irascible appetite. Are they really distinct appetitive potencies?
4. Name the fundamental passions.
5. What is the role of the passions in the life of animal and man?
6. Distinguish between automatic, reflex, and spontaneous muscular motions.

*7. Is the locomotive potency a distinct active potency?

8. What is meant by love, joy, desire, hatred, sadness, aversion, hope, despair, anger, courage and fear?

Chapter 11—The Nature of the Sensitive Soul

1. Are animals and plants essentially different?
2. Prove the existence of a sensitive soul.
3. Is the sensitive soul the substantial form of the body?
4. Is there a vegetative soul in an animal in addition to the sensitive soul?

5. Does the sensitive soul depend upon the body for its existence?
6. Why can the sensitive soul not continue to exist after the death of the sensitive organism?

Chapter 12—Existence and Nature of the Intellect

1. Show that the deliberate use of tools implies suprasensible knowledge.
2. Why does the invention of language imply a suprasensible power of cognition?
3. State the various senses of the term "immaterial."
4. Prove the immateriality of the intellect from its object.
5. Distinguish between proper and improper reflection.
6. Prove the immateriality of the intellect from its reflection.
*7. Reply to the following objection: Man's power to reflect upon the intellect does not prove its immateriality, for he may reflect upon the intellect by means of a special power of reflection.
8. Prove the immateriality of the intellect from its extension to all bodies.
9. Answer the following objections:
   *a) An intellect which is physically corporeal may still be intentionally in potency to the forms of other bodies.
   *b) The senses are organic; yet they can know material things. Therefore, even an organic intellect can know other bodies.
   *c) If an intellect which is corporeal cannot know bodies, *a pari* an intellect which is a being cannot know beings, which is against experience.
   d) Only that which is quantified can be measured. But the intellect can be measured. Therefore, the intellect is quantified and consequently material.
   e) Intellectual activity does not occur without body

changes. Therefore, the intellect depends upon the body.

f) Experience shows that the brain is the organ of the intellect; therefore, the intellect is organic.

10. Is intellection an act of the composite of body and soul or of the soul alone? If it is an act of the soul alone, how can we say that man understands?
11. Does each man have his own intellect?

Chapter 13—The Process of Intellection

1. Show that the actuation of the intellect comes from the phantasm.
2. Why is there a problem in the actuation of the intellect by the phantasm, and how can this problem be solved?
3. Show that the agent intellect is not God or another separate immaterial substance.
4. Describe the role of the agent intellect and the phantasm in the production of the intelligible species.
5. Are the agent and the potential intellect really distinct?
6. State the points of agreement and difference of the agent and the potential intellect.
7. Is there any expressed species of the intellect?

*8. Is the expressed species of the intellect really distinct from the impressed species, the act of intellection, and the object understood?

9. Summarize the process of understanding.
10. Name and describe the various acts by which the intellect acquires knowledge.
11. What is mean by intellectual memory? Is it a distinct cognitive potency?

*12. If the intellect retains an impressed species, why does it not have actual knowledge of the thing retained?

13. How does man know the past intellectually?

*14. Can there be any so-called imageless thought?

15. Describe the three main positions that can be taken with respect to the origin of ideas.

Chapter 14—The Object of the Intellect

1. Explain the terms material and formal object; proper and common object of the intellect.
2. Show that being is the common object of the intellect.
3. Prove that the proper object of our human intellect is the abstracted essence of sensible being.
4. How does our intellect know the singular material being?
5. How is the suprasensible known by our intellect?
6. How does our intellect know itself and its subject?

Chapter 15—Subhuman Intelligence

1. What evidence seems to point to intelligence in animals?
2. Distinguish the two senses of the term "intelligence."
3. Distinguish two senses of the term "intelligent activity."
4. What is meant by the principle of economy?
5. Does the animal capacity to learn prove its intelligence in the strict sense of the term?
6. Does animal instinctive activity prove that it has an intellect?
7. What conclusion must we draw from the absence of language among animals?
8. Could there be any true intellect, essentially inferior to that of man?
9. Indicate some of the imperfections of man's intellect.

Chapter 16—Existence and Nature of the Will

1. Prove the existence of the will as an operative potency.
2. Prove that the will is really distinct from the intellect and the sense appetite.
3. Is the will active or passive?
4. How does the will complement the intellect?
5. Is the will organic or inorganic?
6. What is the object of the will?
7. Distinguish between the elicited and the commanded act of will.

*8. What is meant by volition, intention, fruition, choice, consent, and use?

Chapter 17—The Freedom of the Will and Its Limits

1. What is meant by freedom in general, freedom from coercion, freedom from internal necessity, moral freedom, social freedom, and freedom of choice?
2. Distinguish between speculative and practical judgments.
3. Show that the will is not subject to coercion.
4. Prove that the will is endowed with freedom from internal necessity.
5. Does experience confirm the freedom of the will?
6. What is the foundation of freedom?
7. Describe the role played by intellect and will in free choice.
8. Reply to the following objections:
   a) The intellect is a cognitive power whose judgments do not depend upon the will; therefore, the act of will following these judgments is not free.
   b) If the will is determined by the ultimate practical judgment of the intellect, the will is not free. Therefor, the Thomistic explanation of choice does not safeguard freedom.
   c) The will chooses that which the intellect judges to be the greater good; therefore, the will is not free.
   d) Modern science shows that biological factors exercise influence upon the will and determine it. Therefore, the will is not free.
   e) If the will determines the intellect, and the intellect determines the will, the result is a vicious circle. Hence, the Thomistic explanation of free choice is unsatisfactory.
9. Why does the will need to be moved efficiently?
10. Why can only God move the will efficiently?
11. Does God's movement of the will destroy its freedom?

12. Can any other operative potency act efficiently upon the will?
13. What is the metaphysical reason why other operative potencies can act upon the will in the order of formal or final causality?
14. What is the metaphysical reason why the will is able to move other operative potencies to their act?
15. Distinguish among freedom of exercise, freedom of specification, and freedom of contrariety.
16. What kind of freedom does the will have with respect to the perfect good?
17. What kind of freedom has the will with respect to the unique means to a nonultimate end? And with respect to the necessary means to the ultimate end?
18. What kind of freedom does the will have with respect to all other goods?
19. Show that man's will has freedom of contrariety.
20. Does free will contradict the law of conservation of energy?
21. Does determinism contradict the freedom of commanded acts of will?
22. If the will chooses freely, why can free actions be predicted?
23. What is meant by mechanical, biological, psychological, metaphysical, and theological determinism?
24. How does the theory of liberty of equilibrium attempt to explain the freedom of the will?

Chapter 18—The Existence and Nature of the Intellectual Soul

1. Why must we admit the existence of an intellectual soul in man?
2. Show that the intellectual soul is a substance.
3. Is the intellectual soul one substance?
4. Why is the intellectual soul essentially simple?
5. Can the intellectual soul have any quantitative parts?

6. Show that the intellectual soul is spiritual.
7. Is the intellectual soul really distinct from the body?
8. Is the intellectual soul alone man?
9. Does each man have an intellectual soul?
10. Why can there be only one soul in each man?
11. What is meant by the expression: virtually vegetative and sensitive?
12. In what sense is vegetative life the foundation of intellectual life in man?

Chapter 19—The Union of Soul and Body

1. Distinguish between apparent, accidental, and substantial union of body and soul.
2. Prove that body and rational soul together form one nature.
3. Are body and rational soul together one substance? If so, how is it possible for them to form together one substance?
4. Is the rational soul the substantial form of the body?
5. Is the rational soul wholly in each part of the body?
6. How is the rational soul individuated?
7. Is so-called transmigration of souls possible?
8. Is there any need for a common bond to unite soul and body? Would such a bond explain anything?
9. Do body and soul have the same "to be"? If so, how is this possible since the soul itself has its own "to be"?

*10. Reply to this objection: If the body has the same "to be" as the soul, it must also have the same operations. But some operations of the soul are not shared by the body. Therefore, body and soul cannot have the same "to be."

11. Can souls differ in perfection? If so, how do you explain that this is possible?

*12. Is there any need to raise the question why the soul is united with a body? Could any reasonable cause for the union be given if body and soul are united accidentally?

13. Is the rational soul the only substantial form of the body? Would any additional substantial form serve any purpose?
14. Name some philosophical positions which reject the substantial union of body and soul.

Chapter 20—The Origin of the Human Soul

1. Can the human soul come from the soul of the parents?
*2. If the parents do not cause the soul, how can they be called parents in the true sense of the term?
3. Show that the human soul comes into existence through creation.
4. Can the human soul reasonably be said to pre-exist?
*5. Explain the difference between the mediate and the immediate animation theories.
*6. What is the reason why the mediate animation theory would seem to be more probable?

Chapter 21—The Duration of the Human Soul

1. Is the human body still a human body after death?
2. Is the human soul subject to direct corruption?
3. Show that the human soul cannot be indirectly corrupted.
*4. How does man's natural desire for everlasting existence confirm the immortality of the human soul?
5. Can any argument for existence after death be based upon the moral order?
6. Will the soul be annihilated by God?
7. Will the soul survive personally?
*8. Reply to this objection: To survive personally separate souls must remain distinct. But they cannot be specifically distinct, for they belong to the same species; nor numerically distinct, for numerical distinction comes from the body, which does not survive. Therefore, there is no personal survival.
*9. Can the separate soul exercise vegetative or sensitive functions?

*10. What could raise doubt concerning the separate soul's ability to understand and will?
*11. How does St. Thomas solve this difficulty?
*12. What is the position of philosophy with respect to the resurrection of the body?

Chapter 22—The Origin of Life

1. Does the theory of eternal existence of living bodies give a reasonable explanation for the existence of living bodies?
2. Is it sufficient to say that living bodies came from another planet?
3. What is the inconvenience of the position that God directly created both body and soul of the first living bodies?
4. What is the inconvenience of the position which makes God's positive intervention the sole organizing cause of matter?
5. Can matter alone provide an adequate explanation for the origin of the first living bodies?
6. What do you thing of this argument: The less perfect cannot produce the more perfect; therefore, living bodies cannot originate from nonliving matter?
7. What role can be assigned to chance in the origin of the first living bodies?
8. Does the principle of finality have any bearing upon the origin of the first living bodies?
9. In what sense does the view that life emerged from inanimate matter under the directing influence of God agree with, and differ from the theories of God's special intervention and the emergence of life from matter alone?
10. How does this view explain the origin of life?
11. Does it, philosophically speaking, seem impossible that living bodies will ever be produced "artificially"?

Chapter 23—The Origin of Species

1. What is meant by transformism?
2. Distinguish between universal and restricted transformism.
3. Distinguish between transformism as an allegedly true reconstruction of the past, as a scientific theory and as a philosophical position.
4. What is meant by fixism?
5. What is meant by a philosophical species, a systematic species and a philosophical subspecies?
6. What do you think about the possibility of transformation with respect to biological classes which are not essentially different? With respect to philosophical subspecies? With respect to true philosophical species?
7. What do you think about the possibility of man's evolution?
8. Is evolution necessarily connected with materialistic tendencies?

Index of Names

The numbers refer to the margin

Index of Subject Matter

The numbers refer to the margin